Two Town Festivals

Signs of a Theater of Power

Sidney N Hetzler Jr

Copyright 1990 ©
Split Tree Press
Sidney N Hetzler Jr
Book Publication 2012©
First Edition

All rights reserved

Imprint:
Split Tree Press
597 West Cove Road
Chickamauga, GA 30707
United States of America

ISBN-13: 978-0985334109
ISBN-10: 098533410X

Library of Congress Control Number
2012905796

Library of Congress Subject Heading:
Festival, Artists, Artistic Director,
Urban Development

DEDICATIONS

All Split Tree Participants -- 1990-2007

Albert J. Sullivan -- 1990
Boston University
College of Communication

Who taught simple writing and values,
The right to true information,
And the right to participate

§§§

Timothy J. Reiss – 2012
New York University

A teacher who held the light
Without leading the way

§§§

Sorrel Hays -- 2012
Composer of opera and symphonic music

Who always led me to believe
I could do more than I could imagine

§§§

Robert Spano -- 2012
Music Director, Atlanta Symphony Orchestra
Music Director, Aspen Music Festival

A magical artistic director who shares
His music with intellect and passion

§§§

Barack Obama -- 2012
President, United States of America

Who is perfecting America by example

CONTENTS

FOREWORD AND AUTHOR'S NOTE vii
ACKNOWLEDGEMENTS - 1990 xvi
PREFACE xviii
    Background xviii
    Subject and Scope xxi
    General Thesis xxii

CHAPTER I TIME AND PLACE OF DIFFERENCES: THE IDEA OF A FESTIVAL THEATER 1
    Stories of Origin 1
    Art Power and the Element of the Artistic Director 3
    The Element of the Empty Space.. 5
    Functions Mode of Analysis...10
    Perspectives and Semantic Framing...15
    Implications of Festivals Viewed As a "Place of the Different" 18

CHAPTER II SPOLETO FESTIVAL U.S.A.: WHERE FOOTLIGHTS CAST NO SHADOWS 21
    Menotti's New Theater..21
    Functions of a "Serious" Festival 23
    Three Basic Elements: Artistic Director, Empty Space, ... 27
    Purposes... 27
    Artistic Director: Why Menotti? 28
    The Empty City Space: Why Charleston? 37
    The Element of Purpose: Menotti's Festival Idea................... 43
    Difference and Sameness..51

CHAPTER III CHATTANOOGA'S RIVERBEND FESTIVAL: FROM A THEATER OF DIFFERENCE TO A THEATER OF SAMENESS.... 52
    The Struggle to Fill the City's Empty Festival Space 52
    Absence of an Artistic Director... 56
    The Element of Purpose: Festival Planning Seminars 59
    Functions of the Riverbend Festival: Embedded Meanings in
        Two Stories of Origin 63
    Analysis of Riverbend Objectives 66
    Riverbend: Meanings and Messages 71

CHAPTER IV TWO TOWNS, TWO FESTIVALS, MULTIPLE MEANINGS OF "FESTIVAL" 76
    An "Arts" Festival-Creature Encounters its "Heritage" Habitat 76
    Menotti's Logocracy 78
    Primary Function of a Festival: Chautauqua--Forum for Conflicting Views 79
    Comparative Categories 86
    Retrospective 91
    Restatement of Claims: Intent, Function, Effect 92
    Four Conclusions: Festivals' Shaping of "Reality," Openness, Conflict, Play 96
    Toward a Semiotic of Festival 99
GENERAL BIBLIOGRAPHY 105
APPENDIX A SPOLETO FESTIVAL U.S.A. MATERIALS 118
APPENDIX B RIVERBEND FESTIVAL CHRONOLOGY 159
AND STORIES OF ORIGIN 159
APPENDIX C DISSERTATION FRONT MATERIALS 199
NOTES 203
AFTERWORD – May 2012 228

Nothing is absolutely dead: every meaning will have its homecoming festival.

M. M. Bakhtin
"Methodology for the Human Sciences"
Speech Genres & Other Late Essays

Chautauqua is a place, an ideal, and a force.

John Heyl Vincent, Founder
Chautauqua Institution, Jamestown, NY
1880's, quoted on a postcard picturing the audience
in a traveling Chautauqua lyceum tent

Art, then, is an increase of life, a sort of
competition of surprises that stimulates our
consciousness and keeps it from becoming somnolent.

Gaston Bachelard
The Poetics of Space

FOREWORD AND AUTHOR'S NOTE

FOREWORD

Timothy J. Reiss
May 2012

That Sidney Hetzler's pathbreaking *Two Town Festivals: Signs of a Theater of Power* is finally coming into print is real cause for celebration. Still today, so many years after its completion, *TTF* remains a deeply original and fruitful analysis of the functioning of public "theatrical" spaces, of the public sphere's use of such spaces, of how towns, cities and formally-ordered social bodies more broadly forge those spaces into events and structures contestatory or confirmative of their own self-understanding. For so Hetzler starts by offering, deceptively simply (in terms signaling his time of writing but then surpassed by his writing), a division of such festivals into places of "difference" or "sameness," of "arts" or "heritage" (as towns themselves often designate them), or of "aesthetics" or "celebration," "seriousness" or "bread-and-circus" (as critics and observers may). Their space, he notes, after Peter Brook and then Ngũgĩ wa Thiong'o, *can* be anywhere performer and spectator—or better, *assistant*, the French word for the latter (one who is *present* and fulfills the event's creation of meaning [p. 8])—meet.

Even a "barren desert" can become a stage, Hetzler observes in a semi-prescient remark (p. 7) to be fulfilled by the huge success of Burning Man, in which he has participated ("semi"-prescient because in 1990 Burning Man had already, just, moved from San Francisco's Baker Beach to Nevada's Black Rock Desert, but not yet attained the status of annual "city" that it would acquire in later years). Yet an urban space provides a specific kind of "context, text and subtext": in their triple turn, the already-existing collective ambiance(s) to which are added music, dance, scenarii, song, the endlessly variable textual media, and the subtext(s) of their effects, which may or may not include political or social intention.

I use the equivocal "forge" of my second sentence deliberately: Gian Carlo Menotti forged the Spoleto festival and its Charleston offspring as multifarious urban performances characterized by heterogeneity, experimentation and collective audience participation. In the U.S. performers like John Cage and Merce Cunningham had from the 1960s sought more particularized festival sites for community performance of music, dance and art. If these were not *carnival* in the sense soon being popularized in the west by translators and disciples of Mikhail Bakhtin (and relatedly by C. L. Barber in his 1959 *Shakespeare's Festive Comedy*, out of classicists' work on especially Aristophanic comedy) of a public, *authorized*, if temporally-limited, inversion of social norms, yet they were intended and functioned as performance spaces and events open to aesthetic, political and even moral contestation: if not to the kind of legal and juridical challenges that some assert manifest in ancient or early modern western carnival. They offered, in Hetzler's terms (after Victor Turner), a "liminal space" where a gap or overlap is forged "among the network of formal institutions and social structures" that compose a town, city, campus, etc.—a gap able to be filled, if only for a time, with performance challenging those institutions and structures or, better perhaps, multiplying possibilities of "making belief."

For as Hetzler also says, in a pretty turn of phrase, what these festivals knowingly assert (like all self-conscious theater and indeed the fictive imagination in general) is that "making believe" can, does, *make belief*. In Ngũgĩ's Kenya in 1977, this was dramatically apparent. Ngũgĩ and friends had created the theatre/festival space at Kamiriithu and begun performances, for which he, Ngũgĩ wa Mĩriĩ, Micere Mugo and others wrote scenarii that townspeople fleshed with story, song, dance and presences of their place and aspirations. Jomo Kenyatta's government, above all the Vice-President, Minister for Home Affairs and soon-to-be despotic President Danial Arap Moi saw here new beliefs so desperately threatening to their authority as to warrant razing the festival space and imprisoning Ngũgĩ in Nairobi's Kamiti Maximum Security Prison till the end of 1978, when he was released as a result partly of pressure from such as Amnesty International and partly of Moi's gesture of freeing (some) political prisoners to celebrate his own accession to dictatorial power on Kenyatta's death—a living parody of Bokassa's grand gesture of political "pardons" at the end of Wole Soyinka's 1977 *Opera Wonyosi* ("Long live the Emperor!": 82). Kenyatta and Moi wanted their celebrations to forge beliefs less liberating, more *Triumph of the Will* than *I Will Marry When I Want* or *Mother, Sing for Me*. Festivals like these last, those of Kamiriithu, are clearly *not* "liminal" (any more than was that celebrated in Leni Riefenstahl's *Triumph*). They make one think their efficacity depends, precisely, on their *not* being so. Certainly, political context made them not so. But Ngũgĩ, his friends and the townspeople directed their construction and performance specifically within and at that context. So would "liminality" be a recipe for *in*efficacity? "Revolutionary" experimentation safely tucked away in the great estate's gazebo?

Exactly for that reason, such festivals can forge in a more derogatory sense. They can, that is, be made into a counterfeit of such openness and potentially fruitful challenge. That is indeed what many assert has occurred since Menotti's death at the original Spoleto festival. (See "The Festival Affair" ["Il Caso Festival"], Piero Lorenzini, June 2009, www.spoletofestival.it/ilcasofestival.en.htm). Under the guise of pursuing an ever-open and experimental tradition (itself no unequivocal idea, maybe even oxymoronic) it would have become something else: not its "opposite" (what could such a notion mean, speaking of a festival?) but, at least in this case, performance in the name of government, corporative or personal aggrandizement and self-congratulation, a PR spectacle much in Guy Debord's sense of that word. Something similar happened to Quebec's annual Saint-Jean-Baptiste festival after the *Parti Québécois* won power in 1976, when the festival (surely inevitably) slid from challenge to celebration of power. But festival does not have to be *counterfeited* into that sort of spectacle, when it may no longer qualify as *festival* at all. For when a festival *begins* as one not of difference but sameness, it can hardly be called "counterfeit." That is why I questioned the thought of an "opposite."

One of the many remarkable features of *Two Town Festivals* is that it is written not only by a profoundly informed scholar and analyst of theater and performance, of semiotics and information theory, but by a practical businessman and himself a principal participant in festival creation and community performance. It was not long after he was Public Affairs Director for the mayor of Chattanooga that Hetzler and then a group of friends developed the ideas and materials that enabled creation of Chattanooga's Riverbend Festival from 1981-2. (Later, he established among other things the hugely successful Split Tree Participatory Arts Center, whose annual Fool's Fest Dance Weekend made enough waves to be reported in *The New York Times* in 2003, despite its location well off any beaten arts path.) Hetzler and his friends, moved by Menotti's festival in Charleston, had imagined Riverbend more or less in its image. Soon after its 1982 beginnings, however, the city's "fathers" (surely the word needed here) chose to establish Riverbend not as an "arts" but a "heritage" festival. Hetzler himself, even while criticizing this turn of events, is less interested in arguing that such a festival of sameness is "worse" than Spoleto's of difference (xviii-xx), than in trying to get at the communal *meaning* such performed events involve, predominantly commercial as they may well be. These produced meanings can be as intricate as those of any festival of difference. Hence the inapplicability of "opposition"—at least in any simple terms.

If Spoleto and Charleston imply challenges to the urban institutions and social structures that are their performances' contexts and subtexts—challenges as indirect as direct, less in overt contest than in the simple heterogeneity and multiplicity of events— Riverbend and other heritage festivals would thrive more on repetition and confirmation of those institutions, structures and a history construed and presented as having built them for the best. This is why one cannot call these "forged" in any derogatory sense, far less the opposite of festivals of difference. As Hetzler shows in the detail of his analysis of Charleston's Spoleto and Chattanooga's Riverbend festivals, the semiotic weaving of aesthetic, political, symbolic, spatial and kinetic structures and events that characterize festivals of "sameness" produces effects and meanings as complex as those typifying festivals of "difference." The overall divergence of the two sorts of festival is clear, but if that of sameness generally supports structures and institutions in place, its actual performance of their constitution and representation of their meanings or everyday actuality, say in terms of a particular (hi)story of race, gender and class or of given political or military narratives, can readily be or become profoundly subversive. They can be made so not least by the nature and variety of the *assisting* members of its "audience" whom the very nature of festival always makes into performers and interpreters. And *they* of course interpret and perform out of *their* own contexts.

To be sure, the kind of festival of sameness Riverbend came to be did not, has not, in fact evolved in such direction, doubtless prevented by its resolutely private and corporate sector support, indeed patronage (88-9), its as resolutely "fun entertainment" goals and its continued "funneling" of spectators (hardly "participants") into a confined Riverfront Park space quite separate from the rest of the city. Unlike Spoleto and Charleston it never had a vision of anyone like an outside artistic director or, no less key, political freedom from local profit and publicity claim. Nor did it ever grow out of its firmly local, at best regional, frame. It depends, that is, on its *assisting* public to multiply its sense(s). Only so, it seems, are celebratory festivals of sameness *open*, open to meanings and aspirations beyond those of its authorizing place. In themselves they cannot, do not, easily make space for difference—far less perform it; whereas festivals like Spoleto *do* incorporate sameness: that openness is part of what "defines" them.

Still, and that may be *why*, a festival of difference can congeal into repetition of the same, which is what I had in mind in calling a tradition of difference an oxymoron. One has to think this the case of the contemporary Italian Spoleto (assuming its critics correct) as of Quebec's Saint-Jean-Baptiste in the years right after 1976: festival Disneylands. This last is not a festival that Hetzler sets amid his comparative cases, but from Salzburg to Edinburgh, New York's Chautauqua to Ontario's Stratford, his comparative gamut is rich. And as he argues, a festival of sameness may as readily evolve into one of difference, as occurred with Black Mountain [becoming LEAF, Lake Eden Arts Festival] or could with Riverbend, even if the chances in this instance seem altogether less than slight.

But impressive as are Hetzler's sympathetic teasing out and critical success in detailing the delicate web of context, text and subtext, of event and structure, social constraint and performative freedom, urban politics and artistic demand that patterns *any* town festival, no less justified are his own predilections, vividly portrayed still in Charleston's contemporary festival, showcasing local, national and international performance, spread through the town, so that participants mingle all the time with local, daily urban life: Spoleto is simply more critically *productive*, more politically and socially *fruitful*, more aesthetically interesting, moving and provocative, more ethically *generous*.

Timothy J. Reiss, FRSC,
Professor Emeritus &
Distinguished Scholar in Residence,
New York University;
Visiting Scholar,
University of California, Davis

AUTHOR'S NOTE

Two Town Festivals raises questions about artists and art power, artistic directors or their absence, festival ideas and forms of difference and sameness. It primarily compares the town festivals created by Charleston, SC (Spoleto) and Chattanooga, TN (Riverbend) in the late 1970's and early 1980's, and contrasts them with ideas underlying the Chautauqua Institution, Salzburg Festival and other city arts celebrations.

It examines the deep political philosophies that influenced them, their stories of origin and consequences, by offering "views," ways of seeing more than it suggests what to see, if you are standing in, experiencing and interpreting these theatrical "texts," and also other cultural representations. Its conceptual foundations offer workable ways to see shaded meanings, such as masked, even deceptive, differences and false diversity. These texts can be decoded as indicators of larger social meanings and trends. When you stand in your four-dimensional text of a festival, these views extend your thinking tools to make sense of the many signs and symbols addressed to you by festival creators, owners and sponsors.

The principle arguments are: 1) we shape our festivals; thereafter our festivals shape us; 2) most festivals provide a model for accepting differences and diversity in life, and we learn to tolerate as normal the small or large range of diversity contained within a festival's time and space; 3) in a festival's theatrical space the new and different, or traditional and sameness, are made visible, dramatizing the essential idea that "differences embrace sameness; sameness rejects difference."

These claims are derived from analysis of three key signifiers: the festival's relationship to empty spaces (its place), its purposes (its ideal), and the presence or absence of an artistic director (its force). These three elements create a festival's degree of difference or sameness. They provide the study's conceptual design and suggest, in their interdependence, several conclusions about the nature, function, and meaning of these two festivals and festival philosophy in general.

The destructive power of the opposing "sameness" philosophy, when carried to extremes, is the broad political reality reflected in Jean-Francois Lyotard's concluding admonition in *The Postmodern Condition: A Report on Knowledge*, to, in effect, "honor the differences":

> The nineteenth and twentieth centuries have given us as much terror as we can take. We have paid high enough price for the

nostalgia of the whole and the one....The answer is: Let us wage a war on totality; let us be witnesses to the unpresentable; let us activate the differences and save the honor of the name.(7)

This perplexing conclusion was the direct source of my differences/sameness thesis. Two decades of experience with life and the festival form have confirmed the main ideas proposed in 1990 and expressed since then. They will be more fully illustrated in the next work about my own Split Tree Participatory Arts Center activities that evolved during these two decades. The Afterword reflects some of the consequences of these ideas as well as a few new cultural developments in Chattanooga and at the Spoleto, Italy festival.

This work was a 1990 Emory University Graduate Institute of Liberal Arts doctoral thesis, shelved there as *"Two Town Festivals: Signs of a Theater of Power."* Its arguments are as valid today, if not more so, as then. To respect the historical context, no changes in the dissertation were made except that the formal academic front materials and chapter endnotes were moved to the end, and an Appendix B was reinstated to add expanded chronology to the Riverbend analysis. The thesis was written with both memory and documents fresh from my 1980 festival visits, from the 1980-82 Chattanooga festival creation experience and from continuing research. This adds to its value as both urban history and contemporary analysis, particularly because neither the primary festival formats nor the basic arguments have changed.

The cover image is the 1993 festival poster for both the American and Italian Spoleto festivals. It apparently was the last one selected by Gian Carlo Menotti for the Charleston, SC production due to his resignation that year. Created by Italian artist and set designer Emanuele Luzzati, it is used with permission of the Luzzati Museum in Genoa, Italy (see back page). And it is used with much appreciation because better than any other symbol it expresses the vital force and idea of the experienced and imaginative artistic director/force needed to create these unique celebrations that link past, present, future. Luzzati's works can be found at http://www.museoluzzati.it.

Why the special focus on Menotti? A Spoleto set designer since 1993, Piero Lorenzini expresses his feeling for the maestro in a June 2009 online letter, "The Festival Affair": "Maestro Menotti was truly Spoleto's magician. He could change the physiognomy of the town, transform it into a crescendo of emotions and lead its inhabitants, its life and its stones into a dream-world...for 50 years." (See link, p. viii, 249).

Menotti died in 2007, the year of his Spoleto Festival's half-century celebration under his son and former artistic director Francis Menotti, who was forced out after that year. There has been and is much debate in the small Italian town, as there was in Charleston, about whether new management can and will continue his vision and dream, but the Spoleto festivals from 1958 on remain a model for festival lovers. As Timothy Reiss concludes in his subtle and broadly ranging foreword, "...Spoleto [USA] is simply more critically *productive*, more politically and socially *fruitful*, more aesthetically interesting, moving and provocative, more ethically *generous*."

Menotti himself in 1999 gave a concise answer to why he as an opera composer made the effort to create a festival, a sort of real life opera of all art genres, in a small Italian village:

> ...It has always been hard for me to feel on the edges of society, and I felt the need to convince at least a small community like Spoleto that an artist is just as useful and necessary as a doctor, a lawyer, or an engineer. It takes patience to show your fellow-citizens that civilized man "lives" by art without even realizing it. The tune he whistles while he's shaving has been written by a composer, and his morning newspaper and evening TV comedy are prepared by writers; the beautiful material of the dress his wife is wearing was created by a designer, so were the stylish cutlery and china that grace his table. What would his office be, without the reproductions of art works that give a tone to the place? "One is craftsmanship, the other is commercial art," you might object, but without Art neither would exist. Mondrian changed the face of our homes (though not always for the better). Matisse surfaces in summer fabrics, Calder in toys, just as you can spot Stravinsky and Prokofiev in the movie sound-tracks of box-office hits aimed at a public that looks horrified if you mention classical or contemporary music.
>
> After forty-one years, I don't know how much Spoleto [Italy] has realized all this thanks to the Festival. There is no denying that the economic benefit it derives from the Festival is of the first importance; but there are many Spoletini, now, who have at last become aware of the beauty that surrounds them and make efforts to take part in it. Efforts that may seem childish at times. But it's touching to see their pride in the beauty of their town – something they were only vaguely conscious of before the advent of the Festival.
>
> To say nothing of the Spoletini who have taken to the theatre, not only as actors, but also as technicians, and whom you meet

every so often on Italian and foreign stages. That's what counts most for me; to have been useful, albeit in a small way, to the economic and cultural rebirth of a poor little town that today is neither little nor poor any longer....
  Gian Carlo Menotti, "Spoleto's No Safari," 1999,
  Festival dei Due Mondi 2010 web page,
  http://www.spoletofestival.it/safari.en.htm.

Possibly Gian Carlo Menotti may have conceived of a way to present both difference and sameness in one festival theater so that, as Bakhtin said, "...every meaning will have its homecoming festival." And we all can celebrate a togetherness festival at long last.

We always had a sense of humor during the creation of what became the Chattanooga Riverbend Festival. As noted in Appendix B, at the final 1981 seminar understanding chuckles were heard when I passed around copies of an anonymously created description of "Six Phases of a Project": 1) enthusiasm; 2) disillusionment; 3) panic; 4) search for the guilty; 5) punishment of the innocent; and 6) honors and awards for the non-participants. At the time we were at stage one, enthusiasm; all the others would follow in order, including recognition for the non-participants as memories faded and politics prevailed.

Truly, success has many mothers and fathers and I was lucky to have worked with some very public spirited friends and colleagues. I am in debt to many, many people. These are mentioned in the acknowledgements from that time in the next section, and others more recent in the April 2012 afterword. But I want to give special mention to two friends, Mary Jane and Darrell Ayers, who opened their Sarasota, FL home to me in February 2012 for concentration on this book. And I very much appreciate former professor and thesis director Timothy J. Reiss' nuanced, provocative, valuable foreword, Jody Underwood's document formatting, and Rich Bailey's copy editing and insightful 2005 article in the Afterword about what Chattanooga could learn from Charleston's Spoleto festivals.

Please let me know your opinions, responses or any corrections needed at: Split Tree Press, splittreepress@splittree.org.

Sidney N. Hetzler, Jr. Ph. D.　　　　　　May 2012
Split Tree Press
597 W Cove Road
Chickamauga, GA 30707

ACKNOWLEDGEMENTS - 1990

My curiosity about festivals started with a visit to Charleston's Spoleto Festival U.S.A. Festival in 1980, after reading a newspaper article about its effects on the city. That visit led to a visit to the 1980 Salzburg Festival. During the 1980s, I was able to return to Charleston's evolving festival and experience the power of that city's and its festival's artistic magic. Soon after I began graduate study at Emory University in January of 1985, Dr. Edna Bay, Associate Dean of Emory's Graduate Institute of Liberal Arts, suggested that in view of my experience in Chattanooga, I might consider the study of festivals. In the summer of 1985, while a student in Emory's British Studies program at University College, Oxford, I visited several British festivals and began the formal research for this study. In 1986 I visited Chicago's Ravinia Festival and other Chicago urban festivals. In 1987 I visited the festivals of Stratford, Ontario; the Chautauqua Institution at Jamestown, New York, and Artpark, at Niagara Falls, New York. I attended all but one of Chattanooga's Riverbend festivals. Without the assistance of the leaders and busy staff members of these festivals, this work could not have been written. I thank them all for giving me precious moments during their busiest time for answering questions, for admission to festival events, and for their encouragement in exploring the art of the festival.

A 1985 Emory University seminar, "Toward an Archeology of Modern European Theater," offered by Professor Timothy J. Reiss (now chair of comparative literature at New York University), provided my first exposure to various semiotic and drama theories that offered a conceptual language suitable for beginning an analysis of festivals. Professor Reiss' tolerance for my limited understanding of these vast fields of knowledge--and his endless patience with my curiosity about semiotics as a possible extension of my background in communication studies--provided the personal and scholarly leadership needed to pursue the topic of festivals to the end of the beginning that this dissertation represents. To him and the other two readers of this work, Robert Detweiler of Emory University's Graduate Institute of Liberal Arts, and Robert Segrest of the University of Florida's Department of Architecture, I wish to express my appreciation for their assistance, patience, and understanding during the slow genesis and development of these ideas. The counsel of Professor Monica Rector, a good friend and colleague in semiotics, was extremely helpful in the early formulation of the study and in suggesting an earlier title for it, "Writing Festival; Writing on

Festival," which suggests the postmodernist character of a larger work yet to be written.

I especially thank my parents, Doris and Neal Hetzler, for making it possible for me to take time away from business and farm activities for this research.

Several business associates, particularly William Krause, David N. Brooks, Jr., and Grant Tuttle of McKee Baking Company's purchasing department, were especially tolerant of those occasions when I was not present to conduct business as usual; their support generated the income without which this work would not have been written.

The editorial assistance and encouragement of Dorothy DuBose in particular as well as Tanya Augsburg and Charles Sills of Emory University's Graduate Institute of Liberal Arts in reviewing both the substance and style of drafts of this work was much needed and appreciated.

Finally, I wish to acknowledge the stimulation, help, and encouragement of professors, colleagues, festival lovers, musicians, friends, and relatives who contributed directly or indirectly to this work. They include: Edna G. Bay, Fred Berringer, Paul Bouissac, Daniel Bowles, Reneé Brachfeld, John Bugge, David Darling, Catherine Eagar, Dorinda Evans, Elizabeth Farr, John Farr, Jean-Claude Gardin, Doris (Sorrel) Hays, Joan E. Hetzler, Morris C. Hetzler, William R. Hetzler, Bernard Holland, Deanne Irvine, J. Nelson Irvine, Art Jennings, J. Kenneth Kansas, Gianni Longo, John T. Lupton, Vernon Magnuson, Gian Carlo Menotti, Linda Metcalf, Denis Mickiewicz, Carol Miles, Sharon Mills, Deaderick Montague, Will Montague, Jack Murrah, Charlotte Muse, Fred Park, W. A. Bryan Patten, Z. Cartter Patten, Robert A. Paul, David Rawle, Monica Rector, Nigel Redden, Joseph P. Riley, Jr., Arthur Rivituso, Eloise Robbins, Frank M. (Mickey) Robbins, III, Dalton Roberts, Sally Robinson, Samuel Robinson, Charles A. Rose, Thomas Sebeok, Toby Simon, Bruce Storey, Albert J. Sullivan, Allen Tullos, Charles S. Wadsworth, and Dana F. White.

Special appreciation is due to Dr. Theodore S. Stern, Spoleto Festival U.S.A.'s first board chairman, for granting permission to reproduce the transcript of his complete story of the founding of Charleston's festival, and also to him and to Mayor Joseph P. Riley, Jr., for hosting the Chattanooga Friends of the Festival group's visit to Spoleto Festival U.S.A. in 1981.

PREFACE

Background

Conflicting artistic dreams, competing images of "desirable" community social order, and opposing political and economic discourses underlie the stories of the origins of the two town festivals chosen for this analysis. One began in its American version in 1977 in Charleston, South Carolina; and the other, inspired by the Charleston model, started in 1982 in Chattanooga, Tennessee. Each festival might not have emerged from its host community. Each, with small influences, could have evolved very differently from its present form. Today, they represent greatly differing examples of the cultural practice of "town festival."

In the stories connected with their creation can be found a key to their original intended meanings, meanings that on the surface are as contradictory as the few published accounts of how they came to be.

Here is one reporter's 1984 version of the Chattanooga festival's origin:

> One of the key figures in the development of the Riverbend Festival is an urban planner from New York who conceived a precursor to the festival as "shock therapy" for Chattanooga.
>
> Gianni Longo, president of the Institute for Environmental Action in New York City, came to town about five years ago at the request of the Lyndhurst Foundation. His task was to assess the quality of life in Chattanooga and suggest ways to improve it.
>
> After discovering the city was "polarized" along economic and racial lines, Longo set as a goal "getting a lot of people together in a friendly manner."
>
> The urban expert was also interested in getting the people together downtown. "People in Chattanooga thought of downtown as a place to go to the bank, to park their car," Longo said.... "But they didn't think of it as a place to take their kids, or take a walk. They thought it was too dangerous."
>
> What was needed to change that perception was "shock therapy" of a sort, Longo said. "It had to be something of such magnitude that, despite their doubts about mingling in a crowd, people could not resist."

> The irresistible event was Five Nights in Chattanooga: five concerts by musical artists, offered free of charge, at night, in the heart of downtown.
> Thousands of people jammed the vacant lot across from Miller Park and spilled over into the streets.... "We had everything--bluegrass, blues, pop, country-western," Longo said.
> ...Five Nights proved that a strong enough attraction would draw people downtown in the evening and **led to the formation of Friends of the Festival** [emphasis mine], the primary support organization for the Riverbend Festival. (1)

Here is another reporter's 1984 version of the same festival's origin:

> Sid Hetzler, food broker by trade, music lover at heart, traveled to Charleston, S.C., in 1980 for the world-renowned Spoleto Festival. He returned to Chattanooga convinced that the city could support a festival of its own.
> Hetzler envisioned a showcase for local talent, emphasizing classical music, opera and other fine arts; a festival that would draw people downtown and introduce a broad cross-section of the public to the arts.
> Several of Hetzler's friends responded enthusiastically to his idea. A small group started meeting irregularly, **planting the seeds for what would become Friends of the Festival** [emphasis mine].
> Four years later, Friends of the Festival has mushroomed into a 30-member committee. The fruit of its labors, the Riverbend Festival, is now entering its third year. It has developed into an annual extravaganza with Formula I boat racing, big-name entertainers--such as this year's star, Crystal Gayle--and a budget of $600,000.
> Some critics of the festival--including Hetzler, who is no longer involved--claim it has grown too big too quickly, abandoning the original fine-arts spirit and endangering its own solvency.
> The festival has had its share of organizational and financial blunders. But supporters insist problems are to be expected with any fledgling project. They point to what they see as a bright future for the Riverbend. And even critics such as Hetzler and some other early Friends members concede that success for the festival is crucial to the city's positive self-image.

Jack Murrah, associate of the Lyndhurst Foundation, the festival's chief backer during its first three years, agrees. It is "very, very important (that the festival succeed), in large measure because it has become the big event it is. **It is (the city's) annual image-making set of activities that people have decided to get behind** [emphasis mine]." (2)

These are not, as may appear, stories of two separate festivals; they are manifestations of the complexity of a process that created one town's "festival theater." Both articles were printed on the same page, on the same day, in the same newspaper, although the second was featured as the primary analysis of the festival's origin.

Can both versions be "true?" Is the "meaning" of what a cultural practice is and does dependent on who is doing the "reporting?" Or is such a practice's meaning dependent on unnamed, anonymous "people" who have the power, money, and will to "get behind" and to dominate the community's "image-making set of activities," as is implied above by a foundation spokesperson. Do these stories of origin represent a festival world of "logodaedaly" in which multiple truths struggle but live happily side-by-side as a theatrical mirroring of pluralistic beliefs of "democratic" societies? Or do they signify a Darwinian theater of power in which only the "strongest" homogeneous festival forms survive by destroying threatening heterogeneous practices of festival?

Such questions and related enigmas suggested this semiotic comparison of the discursive practice of two town festivals and their "signs of power." (3) It is not an ethnography of two festivals nor a historical monograph of the founding of two urban festivals, although such studies would be valuable. This analysis is a selective semiotic construct of the written and remembered stories of two intensely creative moments in the life of these two communities, moments that resulted in two very different town arts festivals. Its purpose is to reveal repetitive key signifiers, or their absence, which point toward the more important meanings embedded in these untold stories. The initial approach, general methodology, and concluding interpretations are drawn primarily from readings in the disciplines of semiotic and drama theory. Insights from literary criticism, urban history, symbolic anthropology, and mass communication theory also are employed as appropriate.

Austria's Salzburg Festival, Menotti's Italian Spoleto Festival, Canada's Stratford Festival, Scotland's Edinburgh Festival, and New York State's Chautauqua Institution are regarded by arts critics generally as representative of the most successful contemporary examples of the town festival genre. This study will not discuss these other festivals, except for a brief concluding discussion of the alternative model of the unique Chautauqua Institution. They are cited to provide a reference for what are generally regarded as examples of the most highly developed form of the contemporary town festival. As such, these international town arts festivals function as a contextual frame for broader discussion of the signification and communication functions of these powerful cultural entities. Eventually an extension of this analysis is expected to take the form of a semiotic of festival, that is, as an interpretive construct of the relational web of signs and sign clusters designated "festival" historically and in contemporary life.

Subject and Scope

Charleston's Spoleto Festival U.S.A. and Chattanooga's Riverbend Festival are of academic interest in part because of their extreme differences. They are also useful for study because Chattanooga's festival sponsors in 1981 deliberately rejected Charleston's "arts" model of festival for a "heritage" form, a decision that led to official support for what can be termed a festival of "sameness" rather than a festival of "difference." (4) The meaning of this characterization, how and why this change of direction happened, and its general implications are the basic issues this analysis explores.

Several interpretations are derived from an analysis of three key "semiotic" (5) categories for each festival: the festival's relationship to empty town spaces (its place), the stated purposes or objectives (its ideal), the role of an artistic director (its force). Each of these three functions, which are regarded as primary elements of festivals, compress a wide variety of empirical data from each festival. They provide the conceptual design that organizes the study and suggest, in their interrelationships, several conclusions about the nature, function, and meaning of these two festivals.

Documentary materials from the oral interviews of those associated with Spoleto Festival U.S.A. are included in Appendix A, "Spoleto Materials." [The Riverbend chronology is found at Appendix B]. Collectively they, along with excerpts from documents quoted in Chapter II and the endnotes to that chapter, compose the body of materials described in Chapter I as "stories of origin."

The analysis is divided generally into four parts: analytical perspective, selective theoretical history, comparison of key signifiers, and reflection on implications of the study. Its emphasis is on interpreting the thematic organization of available materials from Chattanooga and Charleston. No complete historical treatments of these two festivals exist, and what is to be discussed here is the period of their founding and not their entire histories. (6)

Chapter I constructs the interpretive frame that explains why these two festivals were selected as examples of two basic festival forms and how they are viewed. Chapter II describes key elements in the founding of Charleston's Spoleto Festival U.S.A. in 1975-77, based on interviews from 1986 to 1989 with several individuals involved (primary source records at the festival office were not yet open to the public). Of these materials, the principal source is the transcribed oral history of Spoleto Festival U.S.A.'s first board chairman, Theodore S. Stern. Chapter III discusses the founding of Chattanooga's Riverbend Festival in 1980-82 through the story of the creation of the non-profit group, Friends of the Festival, Inc., which was established to sponsor the festival. My experience as first president of this organization provides the primary source materials for these events. Chapter IV addresses several implications generated by these two forms of town festivals, briefly discusses an alternative model (the Chautauqua Institution), and proposes several tentative views about the nature, function, and meaning of "festival."

General Thesis

The principal contention is that most "serious" festivals function as a special type of theatrical time and space where the "different" is presented intentionally and where "new" artistic and other imaginative productions often are introduced. Allowing in each case for several commercial and programming exceptions, this statement is much more descriptive of the Spoleto Festival U.S.A. in Charleston and several other festivals examined during the 1980s in North America and Europe than it is of the Riverbend Festival in Chattanooga.

Although this statement implies that a "serious" festival is "better" or more "successful" than other forms, such as a "commercial" or "heritage" festival, that would be a conclusion beyond the intentions of this argument or the evidence presented. However, that a "serious" festival (see Chapter I, Tyrone Guthrie's definition) has greater affective power seems to be the case. Such judgmental language is impossible to avoid if the aesthetic and political implications of the festival theater are carefully considered in light of its intended use as an instrument of social persuasion. The problem of differing definitions of terms, such as festival, serious, difference, sameness, and new, is addressed in its various manifestations throughout the study as a semantic concern, as well as a significant discursive reality. For this study, the terms "different" and "new" are used interchangeably in opposition to "same" and "old." The final chapter offers linguistic alternatives to such categorical oppositions, which the festival form itself tends to reject.

Questions of the social, aesthetic, political, religious, and economic desirability of the different and the new could be viewed as matters of personal taste and values. Arguing that Chattanooga's Riverbend Festival lacks "avant garde" operas, ballets, and plays, for example, and therefore offers little different or new may offend its blue grass, blues, and rock music lovers, who can point out with pride that traditional Louisiana Zydeco music apparently was heard for the first time in the city at the festival. The festival's sponsors could also rebut the charge of "sameness" by pointing out that the local symphony plays, normally with a popular entertainer, one night at each festival, and that in 1985 a composition for guitar and orchestra premiered at the festival. However, this practice was abandoned after that year. Increasingly, such Riverbend festival "differences" appear to be a tribute to the illusory theater, masking the "sameness" of biological homogeneity and artistic rigidity through an extreme commerciality that perpetuates existing political, religious, social, and economic monolithic structures.

Such issues raise far deeper philosophical concerns about the nature of the societies in which we not only survive but also enjoy and, as Faulkner suggested in accepting the Nobel prize, "endure." In sailing through such treacherous waters of subjectivity, it is my intention to be a "loving critic" rather than a "critical lover" of these two festivals, which have grown to be important local institutions as well as representative forms of contemporary festival practice and social order. That Charleston's particular expression of itself through its festival has generated international notice from the arts community suggests that such a festival of "differences" possesses important functions absent in festivals lacking such critical attention. This requires an effort to identify the key functions required for a festival to attract such critical notice from the interpretive community.

If several key elements of these two festivals are identified, and if their basic social and political functioning appears reasonably clear, then the limited aims of this dissertation will have been realized. Detailed ethnographies and full histories of both festivals and their complex relationship with their communities and larger world would be valuable in confirming, modifying, or rejecting the conclusions proposed here.

It should be admitted in this context that I do have an "ax to grind," the creation of a "sharpened instrument" of thought that pleads the political, social, aesthetic, economic, and pleasurable desirability of festivals of "difference" as opposed to those of "sameness"--"arts" as opposed to "heritage"--"serious" as opposed to "bread-and-circus." This should not be construed to mean that I regard "heritage" festivals as undesirable, but rather that these "political" theaters tend to exclude aesthetic sources of the vitality associated with the new and different ideas that drive social change and sustain the learned respect for differences that represents "civilized" behavior. This would not be a "serious" dissertation if it argued no point of view, advanced no vision, ignored the realities of personal experience, or merely represented without interpretation. And it would not be a fair document if it did not respect the differences and opinions of others equally sincere in their intentions. Yet the destructive power of the opposing "sameness" philosophy, when carried to extremes, is in actuality the general political reality reflected in Lyotard's admonition in The Postmodern Condition to, in effect, "honor the differences":

> The nineteenth and twentieth centuries have given us as much terror as we can take. We have paid high enough price for the nostalgia of the whole and the one....The answer is: Let us wage a war on totality; let us be witnesses to the unpresentable; let us activate the differences and save the honor of the name. (7)

Increasingly, during the course of the past four years of formal academic study, T. S. Eliot's observation in "The Four Quartets" that we return "to the place where we started/And know it for the first time" has been given a personal relevance that suggests caution in attempting to interpret any event in which one was personally involved. The document advocating a "celebration of togetherness," written with a friend one spring afternoon in 1981, which some have said was the first burst of energy that led directly to Chattanooga's Riverbend Festival, is a "starting point" I returned to for this study and truly began to "know for the first time." Self and non-self were not easily separated. One sense of my subjective problem in studying this particular festival, its genesis, and its intended and unintended meanings was suggested by Milan Kundera in Laughable Loves:

> Man passes through the present with his eyes blindfolded. He is permitted merely to sense and guess at what he is actually experiencing. Only later when the cloth is untied can he glance at the past and find out what he has experienced and what meaning it had. (8)

My "glance" (Chapter III) back to 1980-81, a period that led to Chattanooga's renewal of a town festival in 1982 and that also generated significant debate about the nature of festival, can be viewed as demonstrating the actual public and private participation process by which a new space was made for a festival intended to be different from any in the city's recent experience. This collective community "composition" period resembles the anthropological description of "liminal" time and space. Yet Riverbend soon departed from its original objectives, and the imaginative outpouring of local creative energy that might have been has been forgotten by many of us who were involved at the time. Most records of such "questioning" periods of civic ferment, which also apparently occurred in Charleston, can be lost to future scholars because it appears the institutions that emerge from this "in-between zone" become dominant and tend to repress knowledge of other forms that might have emerged and possibly would have threatened the present dominant entity. It is my hope that the "questioning" attitude that produced Riverbend will continue and that this study will contribute to that "festival spirit" of inquiry.

One example of such continuing curiosity about the possibility of a special festival "spirit" led to my participation in a type of festival predicted from the analysis but not experienced or noticed in the literature. I was exposed to a new kind of festival when several members of the Chattahoochee Country Dancers (New England contra dancing) group in Atlanta, after hearing of the ideas presented here, said they thought the bi-annual Black Mountain traditional music and dance festival was very different from the examples I had mentioned. This festival, located at a church camp and lake near the Black Mountain community some ten miles west of Ashville, North Carolina, was in its eleventh year in May 1989. Although some of its features are characteristic of any festival, its apparent lack of political, commercial, or religious purpose suggests there could be a festival based on the play principle as described by J. Huizinga's work on the play element in culture and J. Pieper's theory of festival. It represents a festival theater in which various types of folk group dancing and even modern couples swing dancing are its primary purpose, as opposed to civic image building, increasing tourism, or riverfront development. However, attendance is almost completely white, which suggests the hidden racist effect of traditional "heritage" festivals. More information is needed to explore this alternative festival form; however, conversations with one of Black Mountain's founders, the popular contra dance caller Fred Park, make it clear that large numbers of participants are discouraged in that the festival is no longer advertised and, to prevent overcrowded dance floors, attendance is now limited. Park is one of the festival's sources of artistic energy, probably the equivalent of Charleston's Menotti; his choreography, or "calling," is regarded as a special event, much as Menotti's directing of an opera is of unusual interest. Park's views on the festival and my participation in it strongly suggest that no purpose other than "play" or "pleasure" explains the growing popularity of this alternative to what is termed in this study a political or propagandistic festival theater.

The Black Mountain Festival of Traditional Music and Dance announced "The Black Mountain New World Festival" to follow its customary weekend program for May 1990. It advertised a celebration of "contemporary culture as influenced by global communication" with "contemporary music, all kinds of dance, new games, group art, environmentally sound technology, and surprises." The emergence of a festival of "differences" from a successful festival of "sameness" is suggested by this development, one that could also occur in similar heritage festivals such as Chattanooga's Riverbend. It should be recognized that the uncertainty of social effects in this and similar "heritage" festivals precludes simplistic conclusions about such complex cultural practices.

[Note, April 2012—This festival soon evolved into the Lake Eden Arts Festival. LEAF is a true festival of differences, produced by Jennifer Pickering each October and May on the grounds of the old Black Mountain College. Here numerous artistic breakthrough events and groundbreaking experimental educational methods were produced by American professors and European émigré faculty and adventurous students . See: http://www.theleaf.org].

CHAPTER I

TIME AND PLACE OF DIFFERENCES: THE IDEA OF A FESTIVAL THEATER

Stories of Origin

The basic desire "to festival" is not unlike the social impulse that for uncertain motives makes one ask, "What if we had a party?" Such a fragile impulse may be killed by such thoughts as: "What if nobody came?" "How do we pay for it?" "What if it rains?" "Where will they park?" Only a strong purpose can overcome such reasonable anxieties. The simple urge to overcome isolation, alienation, and simple loneliness may drive the urge to have a party, to "festival."

For example, Gian Carlo Menotti, founder of the Spoleto festivals, seems to have drawn upon his festivals as a source of renewed personal artistic energy. His actions could be interpreted as a way of justifying his own existence as an artist, as well as a political step toward proving the value of artists in general. He has said that he felt his creative life was at an end in his forties, when he turned to the work of bringing life to the village of Spoleto, Italy, using "art" to show the power of art. (9) One of Menotti's reasons for intervening in the affairs of the small Italian village was that he wanted to prove art was not only an after-dinner mint but that it could be the main meal itself, not the soup but the main course. (10) Menotti's anecdote illustrates what might be called a "creation myth" or a "story of origin" that emerges over time as a simple story told over and over in the festival programs and in the news media.

In the few complete histories of the international arts festivals, such as Gallup's recent Salzburg Festival, (11) a recurring issue is the public questioning of the original idea of the festival. Festival officials and critics frequently ask whether previous, current, and future programming is "true" to the original idea. In Salzburg's case the original idea was to stage a medieval play in front of the scenic town's beautiful cathedral. Today's musical emphasis on Mozart evolved later, although late nineteenth-century festival efforts there did include Mozart. The shape and character of that "idea" remains the core of one of the world's great art and music festivals. It suggests that such stories of origin, which in this case emphasize the town's physical beauty as a theater, can provide an access point for understanding the multiple meanings of these unique social institutions in other times and places.

Similar "creation myths" are found in stories of the origin of other festivals, whose actual founding events have been obscured by time, publicity agents, or new masters. "Who cares about the `truth?'" a cynic might ask. "Leave sleeping dogs alone," an investor in property adjacent to a festival once said privately during an interview for this study. A practical reply is that some important lesson might be learned by taking a closer look at why and how new social entities emerged from the chaotic "soup" of times past, a lesson or two that might have value when similar choices again will exist. An equally practical reply is that such stories of origin are interesting and pleasurable in themselves as an art form and need no other justification for their telling.

For a critic, the importance of the "text" of a creation myth, and its expression in the festival itself and its brochures, is that it "functions" as a steering device for continuing the festival in the direction its various shapers intended. "Why a festival in Charleston?" The actual answers vary widely. "Well, Mr. Menotti wanted a nice place to have a festival." "Menotti said our city was an art form in itself." "A friend of Menotti's persuaded him to come here." "The National Endowment said to spend tax money on artists in America, not on going to Italy." "Maestro Menotti wanted to show that artists are valuable to society and should be given better treatment." "Art should not be an after dinner mint but the main meal." (This last statement was the reason most frequently mentioned in the 1986-88 Charleston interviews). It is apparently not recorded anywhere, not even in an informal history, that one powerful local citizen did his best to keep the festival out of Charleston. (12) Possibly this incident is one reason that, after eleven years, no official Spoleto Festival U.S.A. history exists.

A deeper probe of Spoleto Festival U.S.A. reveals several complicated stories: a mayor who assumed responsibility for the festival when it appeared doomed; Menotti as a famous artist fighting inexperienced if well-meaning local control of artistic performances; Frances Edmunds, a strong architectural preservationist, who became a strong supporter of Spoleto Festival U.S.A.'s changes. It would have been more probable that some of those Charlestonians most involved, such as the mayor and a college president and a preservationist who had the most to fear from the coming of a new, "foreign," thing, would have been intimidated successfully by the powerful opposition's predictable warnings of harmful effects for the historic community.

From this perspective the presence of a Menotti, an experienced composer and festival artistic director who was and remains the principal designer of the festival, suggests a study of the festival's "story of origin" as a starting point in understanding not only what happened and why, but also what the meanings of this series of events signify. The examples of the written and recollected "stories of origin" from the Charleston and Chattanooga festivals provide the critical "textual" foundation on which to build more fully developed interpretations of these festivals and their multiple meanings.

Official "stories of origin" of a festival, and possibly those of similar social structures, can be contradictory in the written and recalled record. The participants often have differing recollections of these emotional times. The records of Charleston's and Chattanooga's festival productions suggest that several "true histories" of these mythic moments can co-exist without any reconciliation possible. The questions that emerge from this perspective have far-reaching public implications that merit careful consideration.

Of the three elements chosen for analysis, one principal concern is the use and abuse of "art power," as Charleston's mayor (see Chapter II) has termed his belief in the positive effects of art and artists.

Art Power and the Element of the Artistic Director

Why would anyone fear Menotti's festival or resist giving power to an artistic director at a festival's inception? One explanation can be found in The Illusion of Power, where Stephen Orgel describes a subtle artistic problem of audience participation in the court masque of James I of England:

> The climactic moment of the masque was nearly always the same: the fiction opened outward to include the whole court, as masquers descended from pageant car or stage and took partners from the audience. What the noble spectator watched, he ultimately became. The greatest problems in such a form are posed by protocol. Masquers are not actors; a lady or gentleman participating in a masque remains a lady or a gentleman, and is not released from the obligation of observing all the complex rules of behavior at court....But playing a part, becoming an actor or actress, constitutes an impersonation, a lie, a denial of the true self. Prynne's work on The Scourge of Players in 1633 spoke for many in viewing the woman actors as notorious whores. Now for speaking roles professionals had to be used and this meant that the form, composite by nature, was in addition divided between players and masquers, actors and dancers. (13)
>
> The masque form developed for James I and his queen rapidly separated into two sections:

The first, called the antimasque, was performed by professionals, and presented a world of disorder or vice, everything that the ideal world of the second, the courtly main masque, was to overcome and to supercede. (14)

The parallel between the festival and the "fringe" festivals that often evolved suggests the "antimasque" character of the fringe, which the main festival must dominate. Orgel also notes in this discussion of the masque that Renaissance festivals were the province of the greatest artists of the age. He points out that the age believed in the "power" emphasis of art to persuade, transform, preserve, and masques could no more be dismissed as flattery than could portraits. Shakespeare's The Tempest, he argues, illustrates the use of art to create belief, a process that appears to be a similarity between that age and the current age of carefully staged political television spectacle. The action of Prospero's masque within the play is cited to show that it is Prospero's unique vision and quality of mind that have been controlling--steering--the play:

> In an obvious way that power is the power of imagination, but only if we take all the terms of the phrase literally. Imagination here is real power: to rule, to control and order the world, to change or subdue other men, to create; and the source of the power is imagination, the ability to make images, to project the workings of the mind outward in a physical active form, to actualize ideas, to conceive actions. The mind for Prospero, then, is an active and ongoing faculty (not, that is, a contemplative one) and the relation between his art and his power is made very clear by the play. (15)

In the most literal sense, then, it is "making believe" that "makes belief," the artist "acting upon the world, not within it" in a discourse of hidden power. It is a true tribute to the idea that "making believe makes belief," that "art power" does translate into real power.

From this perspective, it seems clear why business executives in Charleston and Chattanooga and even ancient Athens (16) would fear the coming of a Prospero before their plans were fixed. That their festival's stories of origin leave out this part of the story is not surprising; what is surprising is the extraordinary fact not of critical acclaim of the Charleston festival but that it ever was born. The Chattanooga festival of, to be brief, "sameness" was predictable; the Charleston festival of, for a short label, "differences" was unexpected and unlikely in such a tradition-conscious city. One can speculate that the composer and impresario in Menotti was not unaware of the inherent tensions involved in bringing an avant garde festival to such a community. More likely it was the expectant civic leadership that was unaware of the onslaught of the "new" about to launch itself from their city. As can be seen from recollections of a leading banker's reaction after visiting the Spoleto, Italy, festival (see Chapter II), some local civic leaders apparently viewed this "new thing" more as a "beast slouching toward `Charlestontown' to be born," to paraphrase a line from Yeats' "The Second Coming," where traditional practices would "fall apart" and the "center would not hold." It was to mean the opening of new spaces where the artist would hold center stage.

The Element of the Empty Space

If the category of artistic director as a primary source of artistic imagination emerges as a basic festival function, regardless of whether such a person is in fact present or absent, then the element of the surrounding physical environmental frame that attracts artistic interest requires examination. It appears that the festival's ideological and physical space itself functions as a type of "liminal time and space," that is, a social practice existing as a "gap" or "overlap" among the network of formal institutions and social structures. (17) This has the effect of making a festival a background framing device, no more noticeable than a proscenium arch in traditional stage design, yet no less powerful in shaping the relations of elements within the frame, requiring only a "director" as Peter Brook has implied in the first word, "I," of the beginning pages of his discussion in The Empty Space:

> I can take any empty space and call it a bare stage. A man walks across this empty space whilst someone else is watching him, and this is all that is needed for an act of theatre to be engaged. (18)

The opening and closing statements of any work of art or criticism cannot be taken casually and, as a successful director, Brook should be taken literally in this observation. Brook's "empty space" term has been cited by many. A significant use of the idea, which will be explored further in the final chapter, is found in its development as a key concept by Nggi wa Thiong'o's Decolonizing the Mind:

> Drama in pre-colonial Kenya...could take place anywhere--wherever there was an `empty space,' to borrow the phrase from Peter Brook. `The empty space,' among the people, was part of

that tradition....Both the missionaries and the colonial administration used the school system to destroy the concept of the 'empty space' among the people by trying to capture and confine it in government- supervised urban community halls, schoolhalls, churchbuildings, and in actual theatre buildings with the proscenium stage. Between 1952 and 1962 the `empty space' was even confined behind barbed wire in prisons and detention camps where the political detainees and prisoners were encouraged to produce slavishly pro-colonial and anti-Mau Mau propaganda plays. (19)

That the space must first be "empty" to serve as a bare stage seems an obvious point. "Any empty space," Brook said, not "any empty theater." Therefore, we will have to admit even a barren desert as a possible stage. It need not be filled with props--rocks, trees, boxes, rubble, or even dead bodies--to do its work as a bare stage. However, it becomes a bare stage, a theater or "place for seeing" in the Greek sense, only when the "I," the "imagining, creative I," chooses to "name" the empty space a bare stage so that one person can view another on it. It follows then that the creative mind of this artistic practice, any "artistic director," requires only that a space be "unfilled" to have the potential of a theatrical space, a "bare stage" that can be filled with some "meaning."

That we as artists and spectators alike respond not only to the "stage scenery" but also to the physical and symbolic environmental context around us has been noted by no less a master of political drama than Winston Churchill, who is quoted on a poster in the office of the Spoleto U.S.A assistant director, Carmen Kovens, as saying, "We shape our buildings and thereafter they shape us." The function of "contextual empty space" will be a key issue in this effort to understand better what these two festivals are and what they do. One could paraphrase Churchill's statement for this study as: "We shape our festivals and thereafter they shape us." Just as we forget to notice our buildings, we forget to notice our festivals and similar shaping contexts, not as environments that actually determine our beliefs but as powerful theatrical arenas that unobtrusively shape our ideas about what objects are like and unlike, about what, for example, colors of persons belong together or are kept separate.

We may say provisionally that Aristotle was correct in noting that festive effects produced by the mise-en-scène put one at the mercy of the technicians, especially at an outdoor festival, but that, on the other hand, the setting design can be a highly artistic element for some directors skilled in this medium. Menotti's town festivals, from this perspective, can be regarded, in the view of the Spoleto festival general manager in 1986, as a seventeen-day performance work on the city stage, which would go far in explaining why this modern Prospero sought an American city that was "an art work in itself." The empty space was as important as its performances, all mise-en-scène with form and content inseparable.

"Festivals," then, can be classified as a form of "meaning-making" theater in bounded spaces. The emphasis is on the visual frame and the special character of the space, which apparently define the type of festival just as the shape of the stage has defined various types of theater as open air, in-the-round, proscenium arch, and thrust stage.

The Element of Purpose

The physical nature of the festival theater, although an important element in circumscribing its particular empty space, appears to be only one primary form of classification. The intentions of its creators form another classification category. From this view the theater has been labeled one of "cruelty," absurdity," "essence," "alienation," and so on, generally based on the dramatist's apparent intention. A close examination of the written record from the creative process followed by the Charleston and Chattanooga festival organizers reveals a misunderstanding, often a source of tension, about the subtle differences of goals, methods, and ends--or, in other terms, intentions, functions, and effects.

Brook's view of the "deadly, holy, rough, immediate" theater is grounded on the effect, not just on audience response but on active participation. He says near his conclusion:

> ...we can see that without an audience there is no goal, no sense. What is an audience? In the French language amongst the different terms for those who watch, for public, for spectator, one word stands out, is different in quality from the rest. `Assistance'-- I watch a play: `j' assiste à une pièce. To assist--the word is simple: it is the key. (20)

From this perspective Brook's "empty space" has not only the three primary elements of director, stage, and actor but also a fourth, an audience of "watchers," or, in his precise sense, "assisters." For the festival "without an audience there is no goal, no sense."

Festivals can be defined provisionally as an essentially theatrical genre of artistic multi-functional structures composed of context, text, and subtext--"artistic" in terms of the medium and effect if not necessarily in terms of a more "political or social" intention. Most traditional literary, semiotic, and structural analyses of artistic works have focused on these three dimensions as separate entities, with the written text receiving emphasis as the primary meaning-making code. However, less attention has been given to the problem posed by the possibility that "contexts," such as the court itself, can be the product of the artistic imagination as much as "texts," such as the actual masques, and their underlying structural subcodes, or "subtexts," such as Prospero's masque. What is most noticeable is that the festival "operates," or "functions," whether consciously intended or not by its creators and administrators, as a "container of signifiers" from which any traditional "unity of action" is often absent at the programming "textual" level but appears upon careful examination to be present at the contextual level. Within this frame, as will be described in Chapters II and III, the founders' intentions shape a signifying practice with a clear "unity of action," where the essential structural logic springs from the range of textual differences.

The logic of seemingly incompatible features can be noted in complaints about a festival. A recent history, for example, has reported two seemingly "inappropriate" elements in Austria's "elitist" Salzburg Festival, one a "carnival atmosphere" and the other an "anti-festival protest":

> In past decades many critics decried Salzburg snobbishness; now they moan about the city's carnival atmosphere brought about by the advent of mass tourism....Most of these tourists will never set foot in a concert--anywhere--but they make life uncomfortable for those who will, and destroy the intimacy and charm which are Salzburg's trump cards....
>
> In Salzburg this protest [in 1971] against the older generation took the form of the creation of an anti-Festival, Die Szene de Jugend, which as its title implies, was aimed at the youth of Salzburg who loved art and despised the bourgeoisie who paid a fortune for their tickets. The anti-Festival took to the streets, put on outdoor plays, operas, dances and poetic recitations...As time went on, the anger of the locals subsided, the Szene became more organized--and inevitably less shocking--and the city began to grant it small subsidies. Ironically, it is now advertised in the brochure of the Festival which it was created to mock. (21)

The idea of an "anti-festival," a term some Austrian sources dispute, (22) emerging within this "elitist" summer music festival and then becoming advertised in the main festival's brochure makes less aesthetic sense when the festival is seen as a collection of discrete performances than when a larger contextual aesthetic logic is assumed in which the contextual "trump cards" of "charm and intimacy" are juxtaposed within a "carnivalesque" atmosphere.

The possibility of isolating three levels of context, text, and subtext can lead to a new "textual" interpretation of the many meanings created by emerging, conflicting "voices" within encrusted performance categories and traditions. The extent of the presence or absence of these voices of "difference" appears to be the key code determining when a social practice becomes a "festival."

Even the word "festival" itself has powerful meaning. This is seen in its many commercial appropriations for shopping malls, newspaper advertising sections, a used car lot's "festival of values," and even by extremist "festivals of racial, ethnic, and religious heritage." Of deeper interest for this study are the specific elements of the festival theatrical practice that possess such "borrowing" power. Commercial users may not appreciate the significance of the idea of encouragement of "differences" that provides the foundation of their commercial exploitation of the practice.

As with any powerful technology, we can wish at times that its nature were a better kept secret; the evidence is clear that Nazi propagandists understood the belief-making power of art and festive spectacle as a form of political theater--a frightenly effective modern "theater of power" when its purpose is revealed:

> Without in any way restricting the artistic concept, we may refer to stage and screen as effective instruments of nationalist education. In so doing, we transcend the colorless concept of the "moral institution," which permits extremely free interpretations of esthetics and substance, and depend entirely on the objective to be achieved [emphasis mine], because the concepts and principles of ethics are open to argument as long as these ethics are concealed within the folds of a meaningless creation of such concepts. The problem is clearly defined, however, as soon as we designate as good everything which serves the interest of the nation and as harmful everything that is detrimental to that interest [emphasis mine].
>
> Dramatic art within its various forms grew out of political needs as in the Greek City State (Polis) or out of devotional needs as in the case of the Greek tragedy, and finally it developed through the desire of the masses for entertainment (comedy). Today, the devotional need of the masses is no longer satisfied by the theater but finds expression in the great devotional mass demonstrations of revolutionary National-Socialism which dominates the picture of our day....

It is certain that under present conditions the theater will continue to depend on financial support and government subsidies. This fact alone opens the way for complete control and planned direction, thereby eliminating the need for actual censorship....

Such achievements place the artist above the politician....He is endowed with the power of awakening, quickening, and actually forming those profound forces which constitute the nation's soul, whereas the calculating politician is merely left to act as guide and leader. (23)

Images from actual footage of Nazi "devotional mass demonstrations" in Triumph of the Will reach most persons at some deep "emotional" level. Only by questioning the "purpose" of such "demonstrations of unity and sameness" can their true functioning be revealed for critical inquiry. It is of more than passing interest to note that the word "festival" does not appear in this early Nazi document. It was not until the late 1930s that the Nazis appropriated the Salzburg Festival and paraded its "openness" before the world, a dramatic story told in the Sound of Music film and in Gallup's A History of the Salzburg Festival.

Functions Mode of Analysis

What is a festival? One method of defining a complex cultural practice such as festival is to search for equivalent terms that describe its purpose and effects, which is a method of classification by the external qualities of a signifying practice. Standard dictionary and encyclopedia definitions of the word "festival" and related terms include both descriptive and active elements. Used as an adjective, "festival" means joyous, mirthful, gay. Used as a noun, "festival" signifies celebration, entertainment, or series of performances of a certain kind, often held periodically, such as a "Bach" festival. The related term "festivity" includes those same qualities as well as merriment or things done in celebration. A "celebration" is an action to praise, extol, commemorate, glorify, or honor. It is also an action to observe a holiday or an anniversary with festivities or to have a convivial good time. The sense of deliberately constructed meaning signified by celebration is not the same as the more diverse set of phenomena signified by festival.

"Carnival" is a term closely associated with "festival" in the sense of a revelry or time of revelry, festivity, merry-making, or an entertainment with side shows, rides, or games; it can be an activity usually operated as a commercial enterprise by social or charitable organizations. The Latin term, "carnem levare," means "to remove meat," which is associated with the period of feasting and fasting just before the beginning of the Lenten season, of which Mardi Gras is the last day.

Another related activity, "fair," is a gathering of people held at regular intervals for barter and sale of goods. A fair also can be a festival or carnival where there is entertainment and things are sold, such as a bazaar for charity. A fair can be an exhibition, often competitive, of manufactured products with various amusement facilities and educational displays.

"Exposition" normally describes a large public fair or show, often international in scope; its related meaning in literature and music suggests information or meaning brought out that was not previously present. A simplifying commonality is not easily perceived. "People closely gathered together for a brief time in a small space with a specific goal of new experience" is a working definition that comes near to abstracting all but one element of these various standard definitions of such social practices. The exception is a purpose that seemingly is no purpose at all: play--joy, mirth, revelry, merry-making, entertainment. However, is this "purpose" possibly a hidden "effect" masked by the language of acceptable intentions? A broader defining mode is required to address such a semiotic problem in which knowledge of what is knowable is grounded in the limitation of language itself.

The question remains, therefore, how does one define a festival (and similar signifying practices) in addition to labeling its apparent aims or effects? Is there a definition process less dependent on subjective views and desires? To ask, "What is a festival?" generates as many responses as there are festivals themselves. Neither fair nor carnival, neither jamboree nor jubilee, the diversity of "festival" defies easy classification and definition by the tools of familiar language. One is tempted to reply that we cannot know what any thing "is" through our existing, subjective linguistic filters. However, "functional" linguistic filters suitable for a particular object and signifying practice can be derived from a sampling of thoughts from those closest to the practice. This is an approach derived from Vladimir Propp's advice in Morphology of the Folktale to extract classification from the material itself. (24)

Following this method, Vincent's late nineteenth-century "functions" characterization of the influential Chautauqua Institution, one of the oldest American summer arts festivals, provides an initial interpretive classification. Through this "template," festivals can be viewed as unique places waiting for a set of ideals expressed through the force of the artists and participants. (25) A sense of the thought represented by these three "functions" categories--place, ideal, force--and their interrelationships can be gleaned from a few samples of the written and recorded words of a few visionaries involved in the creation and evolution of Charleston's Spoleto Festival U.S.A. As an always incomplete archaeology of past civilizations can be constructed from pot fragments, so a partial archaeology of festivals can be constructed from bits and pieces of fragmentary evidence we find in various statements made about this festival:

"...an example and inspiration." "...breeding ground for undesirables." "...reflects the culture of the times." "...$350 million dollars to this area." "...a long drawn-out Robert Wilson piece--a twenty-four-hour, seventeen-day piece." "...joy and pleasure." "...musicians and actors...feed off each other's inspirations." "...convince hardnosed businessmen that there is some financial benefit." "...for the joy of it." "...a social and political message." "...not very sympathetic to [bringing] art to the people." (From Spoleto Festival U.S.A. interviews, 1986).

Economic and aesthetic purposes and effects, underlying social and political functions--all are mixed in this sampling of comments made from 1958 to 1988 in interviews and written statements about Gian Carlo Menotti's Italian, American, and Australian Spoleto festivals. This selection of seemingly contradictory statements suggests that it is futile to search for a unity, or single overall theme, in the inherently plural textual structures of festivals. Even the idea of a textual "unitary theme" seems problematic. Unlike a carnival's historic relationship to the Catholic church's Lenten season, festivals often lack a defining "opposition" such as is found in Bakhtin's "official/unofficial" carnival dichotomy. However, one key to defining a festival by its social functions is found in Bakhtin's view of a festival's "absence of footlights:"

The absence of clearly established footlights is characteristic of all popular-festive forms. The utopian truth is enacted in life itself. For a short time this truth becomes to a certain extent a real existing force. (26)

This suggests the possibility of a theater veiled with multiple scrims that can be drawn to reveal the puppeteer at work. A study of the world of Menotti, as one of the more successful festival "puppeteers," offers the potential for valuable insight into the backstage arena of one of these city operas where footlights cast no shadows.

A "functions" mode of revealing a festival's "nature" and possible "meanings" can be derived from the social, political, economic, and religious signification and communication functions performed. In addition to key phrases from festival creators and managers, a broader sense of "festival" compiled from standard reference works can suggest functional categories. One function is that of a ritual celebration, or reenactment during certain periods or times that anticipate events or seasons (agricultural, religious, or socio-cultural), that give meaning and cohesiveness to an individual within a community. These days or periods generally originated in religious celebrations, and there are ritual commemorations that usually include sacred community meals.

In this sense, the festival can be understood as a social device functioning to make certain meanings "sacred," therefore "untouchable," or "magical." The time-space in which the festival is situated is "bounded" in this sense and temporarily placed off-limits from more secular purposes. Admission into this marked space is governed by various devices, and a wide range of social behavior is temporarily allowed. A festival's potential range of "functions" becomes determined by the particularities of its space, and the purposes and power of the individuals who control the uses of the marked space.

For example, following the original objectives, the Chattanooga Riverbend Festival has made its site, the Ross's Landing public park at the riverfront where the city began, a "special" place. It has been "consecrated" by several hundred thousand "festivallers" for seven years. Now that Chattanooga's commercial developers have claimed the festival's surrounding riverpark area for a privately operated complex with a hotel, offices, and an aquarium, its public availability for the festival is uncertain. This economic development became the primary goal of the festival's financial backers, a driving impulse that lay in part behind the economic exploitation of the original Riverbend Festival idea.

Several conflicting views of this use of the "art" of the festival can be defended. One could argue that this one festival was successful and that it reached its goal of making its location more meaningful to purchasers and thereby more valuable to its private investors. Or one could argue that selfish entrepreneurs captured a valuable public property and "deconsecrated" the people's park. Other interpretations can be advanced and defended. However, neither stated objectives nor arguable effects adequately probe the depths of the festival's multiple dimensions. For example, the deliberate intention of tying the festival to development of the water frontage (27) could have had a significance--a "textual" implication--much deeper than mere reward to private investors.

Overarching any specific "function" is the contextual "logic" of any complex signifying practice such as a festival. Logic in this sense is the system of principles underlying any art or science, rather than the more precise meaning of a science of correct reasoning. In this sense, the kindred entities of festival, carnival, and fair are a "logos," in the Greek sense of a combined form of word, speech, and discourse. The festival logos, then, provides "logodaedaly," a playing with "signs"--symbols or objects in close spatial and temporal proximity--functioning as a theater to transform meanings. This provides the festival forms's contextual logic of diversity, difference, chaos, disorder, inversion, nonsense. In all this the space exists for free play, for randomness, for unexpected outcomes. The festival provides a model of logic for accepting the arbitrariness of life; we learn to tolerate as normal the great range of diversity contained within its time and space.

"Function," then, is meant to signify that specific and particular action observed in an activity that connects it to its physical and imaginative environment. The special logical context of an action's function defines the activity, enabling identification not only by its purposes or effects alone. For instance, a tractor's steering wheel has the function of controlling the direction of the machine; within this mechanical structure's contextual logic, the steering wheel must be connected to at least one wheel. The machine's logic requires this "function" if any change in direction is possible.

Similarly, a festival's artistic director, general manager, or board chairperson controls its direction. This person (or persons) must be connected to those performance activities that point the festival in its particular direction. The evidence from the festivals examined is that the artistic director provides "precision" steering. The absence of either precise function, steering wheel or artistic director--both customarily present according to the current practice and logic of both structures--would invite attention to what, if any, alternative devices for direction setting are functioning. Awareness and naming of the "functioning" level of such features within a structure's logic makes possible a representation of the broader contextual logic in which various key devices or elements operate.

A deeper understanding of a festival's meaning and meaning-making process, then, comes from a semiotic representation of three interdependent qualities: intent, function, and effect. This critique of Chattanooga's Riverbend Festival and Charleston's Spoleto Festival U.S.A. applies this idea and its practical application. It is this idea of examining unnoticed functions that enables the observer to peer beyond idealistic or misleading intentions as well as accidental, random effect and to draw tentative conclusions about the signifying discourse of festivals.

This approach gives rise, for example, to the possibility mentioned above that festivals act as powerful integrating or segregating media, or as media that perform both these and other functions. Yet festival designers may have had no such idea in mind, and may even deny that festivals integrate or segregate disparate elements of a community, that festivals portray the desirability of social differences, or that they reinforce ethnic samenesses. As communication media, it may be that certain festivals speed up a surfacing of "new art," that is, "representations of new ways of seeing," even when planners are convinced the event is nothing more than a giant urban block party, as one Riverbend president claimed. (28)

A decoding of these patterns of functions can portray a "reality" formerly "out of sight" in which both the modern as well as the Renaissance festival can be seen, in British historian Roy Strong's metaphor, as a "theater of power." (29) Although the similarity of functions of fifteenth- and twentieth century forms of festival practice is uncertain, Strong's analysis points to a theater that combines various practices of power (economic, political, artistic, special interest). This possible parallel suggests it is especially important to question the nature of the interpretive "template" or "grid" or "contextual logic" through which this theater imposes its power. The "functions template" is one such grid that directs one's attention to "offstage" forces, activities, and aims.

Perspectives and Semantic Framing

Various semiotic and structural analysis constructs provide the primary perspectives for development of a critical inquiry of festival practice. Eco, in particular, has offered a workable explanation of the mechanism of context as one of the multiple structural levels of festivals in terms of "overcoding, undercoding, and extracoding" operations:

> Overcoded...entities float--so to speak--among the codes, on the threshold between convention and innovation. It is by a slow and prudent process that a society admits them to the ranks of the rules upon which it bases its own very raison d'être. Frequently a society does not recognize overcoded rules that in fact allow the social exchange of signs. A typical example is provided by the

narrative rules, as outlined by Propp...the plot laws introduced by Propp were an abductive proposal that brought to light the existence of an overcoded language. These laws are now universally accepted as the items of a recognized narrative subcode. (30)

If festivals can be viewed as overcoded entities on the threshold between convention and innovation, an unrecognized rule-making operation simultaneously indexical, iconic, and symbolic that allows the social exchange of signs, then it is reasonable to ask whether potential "laws" of an accepted, recognized narrative subcode for festivals can be identified. As Eco has argued above, "Frequently a society does not recognize overcoded rules that in fact allow the social exchange of signs." Eco could have been speaking of festivals as "overcoded rules," "entities [that] float--so to speak--among the codes, on the threshold between convention and innovation. It is by a slow and prudent process that a society admits them to the ranks of the rules upon which it bases its own very raison d'être." This would lend support for a form of "Brechtian" theater that functions:

> as a political and social act whose goal seems both to place in question--or to counteract--the other form of theater [the Artaudian "metaphysical" theater], and to oppose and change actual social reality. From being an analysis of codes of action, indeed, it becomes an effort to produce real social praxis, and within a history for which the human individual as an authentic participant in the social collectivity will itself be responsible. (31)

The Nazi view of art and theater can be viewed in light of this perspective on the importance of "goals" and "purposes." The question, it seems, is not "whether" art forms have a purpose but rather "what" that purpose is. In a final note to his chapter on the theory of codes, Eco also points to what is a basic contention regarding festivals as meaning-making artistic contexts, or "circumstances":

> But there is one aspect which is more interesting from the semiotic point of view, according to which the circumstance can become an intentional element of communication. If the circumstance helps one to single out the subcodes by means of which the messages are disambiguated this means that, rather than change messages or control their production, one can change their content by acting on the circumstances in which the message will be received. This is a `revolutionary' aspect of a semiotic

endeavor. In an era in which mass communication often appears as the manifestation of a domination which makes sure of social control by planning the sending of messages, it remains possible (as in an ideal semiotic `guerilla warfare') to change the circumstances in the light of which the addressees will choose their own ways of interpretation. In opposition to a strategy of coding, which strives to render messages redundant in order to secure interpretation according to pre-established plans, one can trace a tactic of decoding where the message as expression form does not change but the addressee rediscovers his freedom of decoding. (32)

In summary, the festival theater can be seen as a deliberate framing device in which not only context, or "circumstance," but also texts and subtexts are in artistic free play, where participating spectators are "addressees" in potential opposition to "senders" (sponsors and performers) in a dramatic "semiotic guerilla war" in the time and space of the festival. A view of "homo ludens," "humans at play," as yet has no place in this general construction of what appears to be little more than a Darwinian "theater of power." However, a space must be reserved in the concluding remarks for evidence that a festival's "multi-functionality" also can be a time and space for no other purpose but play, pleasure, romance, "jouissance."

For no other reason than the several millions of dollars that have been spent on the Charleston and Chattanooga festivals since their beginning, this issue could be regarded as worthy of careful study. Also, the shape, form, and evolution of the "empty" urban theater deserves thoughtful attention as, in Menotti's phrase, an "art form in itself." However, beyond the economic and physical environment is the interplay of the force of one or several individuals' festival vision with the forces of resistance and reaction. This process, in Charleston and Chattanooga at least, was a behind-the-scenes, winner-take-all struggle for dominance.

In such an extreme set of oppositions lies the interest and value of comparing Charleston's and Chattanooga's tale of two festivals. Possibly the narrative reflects a larger "tale of two cities" and how other forgotten or repressed festival stories were still-born or aborted. That story, however, would require social science and economic methodology not yet developed, and would need not only an enormous budget but also a nonexistent, yet emerging conviction, that the "festival" is important enough to justify significant public and private analysis.

Implications of Festivals Viewed As a "Place of the Different"

In light of this introductory framing of the subject and several approaches to it, Strong's view of the "mirroring" function of a Renaissance festival takes on new significance:

> Revamped medieval romance, the imagery of Sacred Empire, of Christianity and classical myth and history provided the absolutist monarch with an encyclopedia of universally understood symbols with which to promote his rule. (33)

"Promoting his rule" is a much more interventionist function of a festival theater than merely presenting "allegories" of the times. So also do contemporary festivals provide state, corporation, university, and church with an "encyclopedia of universally understood symbols" that compose the contemporary American city festival's "mise-en-scéne" and that actively "promote" the wishes and desires of civic "rulers." What the overall consequences of such an encyclopedia of symbolic signs, if it exists at all, might be is a matter that would require significant research resources and new methodology for the numerous festival materials and studies available for review. The power of the new technological "theaters" of public media in contemporary society is such that the potential new insights into the imagistic nature of human communication processes may justify the costs.

The well-documented history of forms of theater from Aristotle to Shakespeare to Artaud to Brecht to Tyrone Guthrie is evidence of the importance of the physical element in the dramatic meaning-making process. Salzburg opened in 1920 with an outdoor performance of Hofmannsthal's Everyman morality play on a temporary stage in front of the main cathedral. Like Menotti, the director saw the town as potential theater.

If a society believes that such "make believe" literally makes belief, then a theoretical door is ajar through which can be glimpsed the possibility of new insights into the nature and function of the creative and communication processes by which the "social exchange of signs" occurs in festivals and related genres. If no sign exists out of context, then attention must be focused on the actual mechanisms of the sign-context relationship and the possibility of a shift from a one-way, ethnocentric sender/receiver communication model to a helical, multi-dimensional, contextual reception model. Attempts at construction of a "semiotic of festival," an "overall picture" of festivals, as Strong suggested, should produce syntheses that will increase understanding of basic aspects of the "stupendous development" of festivals and of their resurgence in shaping as well as in mirroring their eras as truly unusually powerful "signs of the times." Or, as one drama scholar has worded the issue of the "nature and function" of a "festival theater" so precisely:

> The [Brechtian theater]...goes toward a social realism and a socio-political practice. It proceeds from an analysis of social (and other) "codes" as found in positivism and capitalism, toward their setting into crisis. This eventually leads to a theatre as a political and social act whose goal seems both to place into question--or to counteract--the other form of theatre, and to oppose and change actual social reality. (34)

The evidence that follows suggests that the modern arts festival, exemplified by Spoleto Festival U.S.A., has evolved into just such a Brechtian theater with political, social, environmental, economic, and theological implications so powerful that Eco's term of an emerging "guerilla semiotic warfare" is no understatement. The written and recollected intentions of the founders of the two festivals in Charleston and Chattanooga leave little doubt that both festivals were a "socio-political...effort to oppose and change actual social reality." In the Riverbend case, however, the initial emergence of a Brechtian theater was suppressed by the use of a more dominant form of the very same ideological practice that its founders intended to "place into question." If these views appear paradoxical, they represent the actual events described in the following two chapters. They suggest that a broader semiotic perspective is required for extended analysis of their meanings and implications.

This new but very old social theater could be called "Menottian," the reasons for which should be clear in the following chapter. Maestro Gian Carlo Menotti's festivals appear to be a new genre of theatrical practice incorporating the Aristotelian "illusory" stage, the Artaudian "metaphysical, imagistic" dramatic event, and the Brechtian arena of "political and social action." That this metaphor has the plurality of a three-ring circus is understandable in view of the differences contained within the festival theater. It is possible that festival is the general historical class of which theater is a sub-genre; however, little festival theory exists to support this claim and thus drama theory must suffice for this initial study. The possibility that the festival is a primary class of social practice is suggested by noting that in my newspaper clipping files on festivals there is a Festival of Circuses, but to date no circus of festivals has come to my attention.

The Spoleto Festival U.S.A. had a small circus during 1986 and 1988, a circus enjoyed by children and at the same time by attentive adults. It was a delightful parody of the nineteenth-century "political" circuses that told immigrants how lucky they were to be Americans. In 1986 everyone laughed with the children when four horses balked at coming through the tent door all at once and lost their riders; only later did the audience learn that this was not part of the script. Planned or random, it worked, an expression of what Charles Wadsworth termed "art as organized surprise," where even the mishaps appear to be part of the "play."

Too much in too small a space, or the inverse, often is a source of the tension that provokes laughter. I suspect Maestro Menotti has not attempted to articulate fully and publicly in his Italian, American, and Australian festival communities his vision of a new festival theater form of civic opera, in which all these small "worlds" are a living theater that has so much artistic diversity in so many small spaces, or so much commercial sameness in one relatively small space, as evolved in Chattanooga.

As the next chapter on Menotti's festival in Charleston with its forerunner in Spoleto, Italy, describes, Menotti and his brilliant associates have left some signs along the trail for others to decode in learning how his festivals create so much pleasure for those who prepare and make the "pilgrimage" Tyrone Guthrie recommended in 1953 for those coming to the Stratford Shakespeare Festival. (35)

CHAPTER II

SPOLETO FESTIVAL U.S.A.:
WHERE FOOTLIGHTS CAST NO SHADOWS

Menotti's New Theater

The development of Menotti's three festivals in Italy, America, and Australia is a cultural story of major importance. (36) Menotti's plan to create a festival different from Salzburg and Edinburgh evolved from his strategy of viewing "art as the main course." (All quoted comments on Spoleto Festival U.S.A. in this and other chapters are from the 1986 and 1988 interviews unless otherwise indicated. (37)

That art was not merely an "after-dinner mint" for entertainment and escape from the day's chores was the "new" idea Menotti brought to America from its 1958 beginning in a small Italian village of the same name. "Differences" are not received with eagerness by entrenched interests in many communities; "differences" with the emotional intensity of the performing arts, particularly when challenging the supremacy of capitalist values, can generate equally intense responses from love to hate. It appears from the record in both Charleston and Chattanooga and from the histories of Salzburg and Stratford that when a major festival is proposed, powerful political and economic forces quickly rise in reaction to fears of restructuring the very identity of the community.

This happened in both Charleston and Chattanooga with dramatically different consequences. In Chattanooga, the "powerful private citizen" character in the drama probably won because there was no "powerful public figure" or "college president with resources" to come to "rescue the stranger's new and different idea." Many communities have successfully driven off the "stranger" and "bearer of new ideas," as Menotti could be portrayed. This view suggests the special, albeit improbable, nature of "traditional" Charleston, its visionary mayor, college president, and "preservationist," and its strong municipal governmental political structure as being more willing and able to provide an "empty space" than was Chattanooga.

Charleston presented a hospitable, receptive theatrical stage for Menotti to present a seventeen-day, real-life opera where the "city itself is an art form," as the maestro was quoted on numerous occasions (Appendix A) in explaining why he picked Charleston from a list of Southern cities proposed by his staff and the National Endowment for the Arts. This aesthetic marriage of Menotti and

Charleston, artist and town theater, resulted in an unusual performance event, according to general manager Nigel Redden in a l986 interview:

> I feel that the Spoleto Festival is not like other festivals. It is not like the American Dance Festival, which I worked for, or the Jacob's Pillow Dance Festival. I have put on some festivals myself--one called New Music America and another called New Dance USA. I think this is more like a long drawn-out Robert Wilson piece--a twenty-four-hour, seventeen-day piece.

Wilson's work has been termed a "theater of visions," (38) part opera and part architecture, sometimes lasting a day or more, such as his epic, as yet unproduced in its totality, twelve-hour the CIVIL warS: a tree is best measured when it is down. In other words, Redden envisioned a Menotti operatic production enacted throughout much of the city itself. If this is a "Menottian" theater, it is one with few if any contemporary parallels in its intended multiplicity of directors, bare stages, actors, and audiences. Menotti's response to the city as an art form is so self-conscious, so deliberate, it is surprising that there is no evidence of a Robert Wilson work in the Spoleto festivals to date. (39) Possibly, however, a Wilsonian idea is present in Menotti's town theater. That such a complex idea could not be readily transferred elsewhere without such a creative director, no matter how spectacular the site or wealthy the patron, seems an obvious conclusion.

Looking at the design and boundaries of the "emptiness," one gains a perspective similar to that of seeing "negative space" in the visual arts field. As was suggested in the preceding discussion, both an ideological and physical time and space apparently must exist or be created, as a precondition, before other elements of the festival theater emerge. This pattern appears in the genesis and evolution of Chattanooga's Riverbend Festival. It also emerges in the 1986 and 1988 Charleston interviews. For example, the manager of the Melbourne Spoleto festival, Colin Sturm, noted that both Spoleto, Italy, and Charleston were stagnant, "empty" spaces that Menotti's artists brought to "life." Charleston Mayor Riley has termed this "art power." (40)

Yet the power of art has its limitations when the framing is inappropriate. Menotti said at a press conference at Spoleto 1988 that he felt the Melbourne festival was a failure and he did not feel needed there. Mayor Riley quickly responded to this comment by assuring Menotti and the assembled press corps the maestro was very much needed in Charleston, a sign of public support signifying "public receptiveness" more than courteous display of official hospitality. If the Australian festival (the first was in 1986) did not go well for Menotti, it may be that the sheer size of Melbourne prohibited opening up the space for his type of festival. From the perspective of the importance of a festival's physical setting, assuming the necessity for an "empty space" in the host community offers practical reasons for exploring the success or failure of some festivals. The lack of ideological "empty space" offers another strategy for examining the deficiencies of flawed festivals.

Functions of a "Serious" Festival

The festival's general triadic framework has been presented: a place, an ideal, a force. Yet a festival is difficult to represent, as noted earlier, by its visible features. A specific central idea, a vivid framing device, is needed that places a festival's complexity in a new perspective, a frame that provides insight into the basic nature, function, and meanings of practices such as Menotti's Spoleto festivals.

One such dominant image is available from Stratford's first artistic director, Tyrone Guthrie. To what did he attribute the festival's success? His reflections about the first 1953 Stratford, Ontario, festival came soon after directing the internationally acclaimed productions of Richard III and All's Well That Ends Well under the new tent with its unusual thrust stage. This was "a new kind of theatre...built for the new manner of production which was practised there...," Robertson Davies wrote in the preface to Renown at Stratford. (41) Guthrie addressed the issue of the value of a festival itself:

> In conclusion I want to urge the advantage of the Theatre Festival over just having a theatre which works week in, week out, year after year....
> This is where the Festival comes in. It makes attendance at the play something of a Pilgrimage. The wise Pilgrim will not be in too much of a hurry. Masterpieces demand respect. One must give to them at least the same attention as to a serious business conference. One must be prepared to do some homework beforehand, some meditation afterwards.
> A Festival should offer, as Salzburg, Edinburgh, and Stratford, England, do, opportunities to absorb great works of art in an appropriate atmosphere, with other people of similar taste bent on the same errand. For this reason small, countrified towns, where life is comparatively calm, make the best Festival Cities. (42)

The festival itself can become a community's "powerful, dominating imagistic template" for an entire year, much like Bakhtin's argument that in a festival form "the utopian truth is enacted in life itself" and "for a short time this truth becomes to a certain extent a real existing force." (43)

A "serious" festival functions as much more than a device for the development of increased tourism, new business, or civic image enhancement (although often these are its mixed blessings). Guthrie's idea of a festival "functioning"--whether intended or unintended--to make attendance at an arts event a "serious" experience akin to a "pilgrimage" with "some homework beforehand, some meditation afterwards" points toward a deeper significance of the potential nature and function of the festival theater, one with theological overtones of belief-making power. And his sensitivity to the value of a suitable festival city as a sort of great cathedral, one where a festival could be the "peak of the year," explains Menotti's strong preference for Charleston's eighteenth-century shell over other Southeastern American cities. Here the "urban" space was less filled, more open for the "new," yet "comparatively calm."

In considering why Menotti's festival found a home in Charleston, the importance of the "empty" urban "contextual" frame cannot be overemphasized. In the essay, "Center-City, Empty Center," in Empire of Signs, Roland Barthes saw Tokyo as offering the opposite of the typical Western city:

> ...in accord with the very movement of Western metaphysics, for which every center is the site of truth, the center of our cities is always full: a marked site, it is here that the values of civilization are gathered and condensed: spirituality (churches), power (offices), money (banks), merchandise (department stores), language (agoras: cafés and promenades) [emphasis mine]: to go downtown or to the center-city is to encounter the social "truth," to participate in the proud plentitude of "reality." (44)

Guthrie and Barthes agree with the notion of the essential character of the physical city. Guthrie's "too busy" is Barthes' "always full," a city of presences, not absences where there is "room" for the new and different to co-exist with the old and the same.

Meaning in the Western city, functioning as an ideogram, is condensed at the center, where, predictably, there is little space for the new, for renewed meaning. Yet festival "pilgrims" seek the sacred "festival space," a place and time for "some homework beforehand, some meditation afterwards." Significantly, Barthes groups language with "agoras," from the Athenian chief marketplace or public square, and "cafés and promenades." That one downtown center site holds the "social truth" became the central idea of Chattanooga's festival, entirely the opposite of the ideogram of Charleston's multiple "realities" and "truths" that emerge from its many indoor and outdoor "empty spaces." One may ask, then, where and how are, in Barthes' words, "the values of Western civilization gathered and condensed?" Some possible answers to this significant matter are found in the stories of the creation of the Chattanooga and Charleston festivals (a third ideogram is found in the example of the Chautauqua Institution, discussed in Chapter IV).

It is from this perspective of the festival as "ideogram," a "writing" that directly represents a set of ideas and relationships, that Christopher Hunt's provocative suggestion of an arts festival functioning as a "disguised" religious festival urging us to "artistic devotion" strikes close to the heart of the nature and function of any "serious" festival. Like Northrop Frye's sense of the Christian Bible in The Great Code, (45) these festivals can function as a community's imagistic "great code," even as an international "great code," similar to what Roy Strong described as a Renaissance "encyclopedia of universally understood symbols." (46) Like the great religious documents, to which festivals are related historically as a visible expression of beliefs, the best are few in number and exist in very special places. These festivals are "special" as much for their place as for their programming, as Christopher Hunt has pointed out in his programming notes:

> It is no accident that the great arts festivals of the world-- Salzburg, Edinburgh, Aix-en-Provence, Dubrovnik, Prague--all happen in cities with historic charm, a kind of architectonic intimacy that creates a context in which the `willing suspension of disbelief' can most easily happen.

An initial concept of the Spoleto Festival U.S.A. "ideogram" is needed, one evolving from the general premises described previously, but one more directly focused on one primary function of a successful festival theater such as Spoleto Festival U.S.A. It is this: "Menotti's festival theater can be viewed as a cathedral for the making of belief, a "church" in itself where various "fringe" festivals spring up as carnival opposition." This idea of a festival "church" was offered by an experienced festival artistic director and arts critic, Christopher Hunt, in introductory comments for the 1981 Spoleto Festival U.S.A. Official Souvenir Program:

Spoleto U.S.A. is rather different. The variety and range of these programs reflect not just one art form but a spectrum of artistic experience. It also happens in a place peculiarly suited to the creation of a special atmosphere, a place to which visitors come for days or a week at a time and not just for the evening; a place where the residents feel a certain pride in the occasion....Charleston is such a place, and it is in the combination of environment, identity of audience purpose, and varied programming that its special claim to distinction lies.

...it is the context that needs remarking--and the significant fact that the selection of programs is unified, and not the polyglot recipe of many impresarios....Not that everyone wants or needs feel obliged to have their horizons expanded: a truly festive atmosphere allows one to choose between the simplest level of pleasurable response to any event, and the most profound. Art need not only be about Ultimate Truths, nor should we be too earnestly devoted to it. The religious origin of festivals--whether the Dionysian feasts of ancient Greece or the medieval church festivals of Europe--does sometimes seem to have made a disguised come-back in those who urge us to artistic devotion. (47)

Is Spoleto Charleston the "context" for a "disguised" religious festival urging us to "artistic devotion"? A tentative answer would have to be, "yes, but more...." The significance of context was noted in a recent collection of essays on the festival:

> Folklorists and anthropologists have been increasingly aware of the importance of context in the events they investigate, both the immediate performative context, and the abstract context of the worldview, with its set of norms and values that ultimately affect all social phenomena in a culture. (48)

This broader contextual perspective depends on gaining a clear understanding of a festival's beginning, its "story of origin," even if the memories and a few documents of its founders and opponents and later key leaders are the only presently reliable available sources of what happened and why.

Three Basic Elements:
Artistic Director, Empty Space,
   Purposes

An initial set of categories devised for Spoleto Festival U.S.A. constructs a basis for contrast with the Chattanooga festival. The following table briefly summarizes several key features of the 1980 Festival, which were described in the May 1980 Chattanooga Times newspaper article in which Spoleto U.S.A. first came to the author's attention.

NAME: Spoleto Festival U.S.A. (1980)
TYPE: annual multi-arts festival with parallel city-sponsored Piccolo Festival
MODEL: Spoleto Festival, Spoleto, Italy
PURPOSE: avant garde showcase of new art, principally performance works
RESULTS: city turned into cultural mecca, setting for premier works, worldwide acclaim, $25 million into economy, model of town arts festival, expanded local cultural horizons, turned city into art form itself, tell the world about Charleston's beauty and ambience
PROGRAMMING: debut of an Arthur Miller play The American Clock, Bellini's opera Sonnambula, film, dance, choral, jazz, country, jazz, chamber music, folk music, art exhibitions, crafts
LOCATION AND THEATERS: Galliard city auditorium, 17th century Dock St. Theater, many other downtown locations, some outside at College of Charleston, Middleton Place plantation
BUDGET: $1.6 million in 1980
INCOME SOURCES: ticket admissions, public and private donations
DURATION: seventeen days
TIME: late May through early June
SPONSOR: National Endowment for the Arts, City of Charleston, Festival of Two Worlds Foundation in New York City, foundations, corporations, individual donors
MANAGEMENT: local board headed by College of Charleston president
ARTISTIC DIRECTOR: Gian Carlo Menotti
WORKERS: paid staff, volunteers
AUDIENCE: 100,000 visitors
AUDIENCE ACCESS: traditional ticketed events; free public activities
RELATED EVENTS: finale at Middleton Plantation
FOOD: restaurants, booths at plantation
REACTION: worldwide critical acclaim
PROFIT: none, guarantors covered substantial deficit (49)

Following Propp's approach, the selection of three of these categories--the human force of the artistic director, the empty space of the place, and the purpose of the idea--was derived largely from their repetitive appearance in the transcribed interviews. These "stories" are beginning points for selective exploration of these two festivals. In their briefest form, these categories can be posed as simple questions:
Why Menotti?
Why Charleston?
Why a festival?

Artistic Director: Why Menotti?

The value of Menotti's contribution as artistic director of the Spoleto Festival U.S.A. was emphasized in all interviews in 1986 and 1988. As artistic director, Maestro Gian Carlo Menotti generated and commissioned original performing and visual art works. Yet it was his often repeated conception of "seeing the city as an art form in itself" and literally using empty city structures for the birth of new art that proved most innovative. During the 1988 Spoleto festival, for example, a parking garage near the Dock Street Theater was emptied during the festival to become an art gallery; an empty real estate office became a nightspot; a vacant store became a restaurant.

At the very beginning in 1958 in Italy, Menotti first planned his chamber music concerts in a very old church in Spoleto, a small village in the Umbrian Province near where Hannibal crossed the Alps, one largely left out of the process and effects of industrialization. Charles Wadsworth, chamber music host and pianist since 1959 for the Italian festival, and since 1977 for the Charleston festival, pointed out:

> Menotti said in 1958 there might not be a very large audience, but that the attendance was not as important as providing an environment in which the musicians enjoyed playing and felt as free as possible to perform and to create the best possible music that was in them. These chamber music concerts proved to be one of the most delightful parts of the entire concept of Spoleto in Italy and Charleston. Now the chamber events sell out quickest of all the festival activities and remain an integral part of the unique Menotti vision. Menotti also made it clear that the emphasis was to be on young, new, unknown artists who would be given the opportunity to perform before a critical audience and that it was important that these talented musicians feel the festival was as much for them as for the audience. (50)

This continuing emphasis on the value of the artist and the festival as an educational and enjoyable experience for young and unknown performers is one key to the critical success of Charleston's festival. In this educational role, a qualified, effective artistic director was the primary source of energy and vision in the Charleston and Salzburg festivals, which, like other serious town arts festivals, are as much summer schools for artists as summer diversions for audiences. These had evolved out of the imagination of successful artists like Menotti and Reinhardt. Chattanooga was not allowed to have someone in such a position at the outset of its creative process for reasons that will be made clear in the next chapter. It seems, therefore, that the absence or presence of an artistic director is a key to gaining entrance into a broader consideration of what a festival is and does in its home community and in the wider environment.

Understanding the functions and individual views of the artistic director (or directors) is the primary key to understanding the nature and function of a festival. Asked what he would advise someone starting a festival, Theodore S. Stern, the first board chairman, cited Menotti's special role:

> I have been asked about starting a festival many, many times. It comes down to this. You need a Menotti, who's so unusual. He's the only person I know who knows all the arts....He knows music. Menotti directs, he's a director, producer--he's a genius, and that's why we have a problem in trying to decide what happens after Menotti....Menotti--every orchestra knows him, the theater people know him, the dance people, the opera people, the music people.
>
> What makes the festival so successful? In three words, Gian Carlo Menotti. His ability, number one, to direct, his knowledge of all of the arts--he always gets the visual artists to do the poster....The only poster ever done by Henry Moore, the sculptor in England, was made for Spoleto U.S.A., because of his friendship with Menotti. (51)

Charles Wadsworth, who began with Menotti in 1959 in Italy, recalled Menotti's early contribution in bringing the force of "art power" to the small village of Spoleto:

> Menotti, as he set out to present a festival, and for me what made it the most exciting festival that I know about, set out to produce a festival which he was very well aware would not be a sure fire hit. He said if I'm going to be like Edinburgh or Salzburg where all I do is bring in great guest artists, well known orchestras presenting repertoires that they know are

going to be successful, this is not something I'm at all interested in. I feel that the festival must be a creative festival, that it must be willing to take chances, it must be willing to accept the fact of failure, and out of this kind of experimentation you're going to get things which are much more exciting in the long run....

Gian Carlo from the very beginning was taking chances on artists who were unknown....But there was an overall artistic view of what was necessary to give a special profile to the festival. That came from Gian Carlo and his imagination, his faith in brilliant young people, and in the creative arts. The Spoleto Festival as we know it would not have been what we know unless there had been specifically Gian Carlo.

The "overall" artistic view bringing a "special profile" was that of extreme diversity of programming that would bring thousands of appreciative arts lovers to the small village. An obvious question was whether arts festival, or any "serious" festival, could be produced without an artistic director. "Not successfully," said Wadsworth:

It could be carried off maybe as a financially successful venture by a businessman but to me the festival should be much more than that. It should have some very strong artistic point of view that you're trying to get across. I think you need a creative mind to do that....I would have no interest whatsoever in taking part in a festival which was run by a businessman with just a slight speaking acquaintance with the arts. Those people are the kind we want on the board of directors, who can say, "You're the artist....We have to raise the money....We will tell you how much we can raise and how much you have to spend. You can dream and tell us how much you'd like." Then you meet somewhere in the middle.

Finding the "middle" ground, he suggested, was the heart of the problem. (52)

Gian Carlo throughout the years has been a tough one for business managers to deal with because he has dreamed very big at times with budgets that go way, way out of range....It depends on what your aims are....Art is organized surprises....There's a young man named Joshua Bell...he came here last year at 17, and he's going to set the world on fire. He'll be playing today [at the Dock Street Theater] a huge piece, which is a very unusual work by Chausonne, a concerto for violin, piano, and string quartet; he's never played it [publicly] until this morning....Now that sort of electricity communicates itself. So, that's what the festival means to me.

...I took a part about four or five summers ago in Miami in the International Contemporary Arts Festival. It was run by a man who has a great head for business and a wonderful man in the world of opera....But it was a struggle. The prices were too high for people in Miami to pay. There wasn't the basis for cultural interest. So it was a matter of the wrong place at the wrong time and with the wrong people.

The new, the different, the risky, the experimental, the failure, the creative, the unsafe, the chancy, the unknown, the special, the unordinary, the young, the big dream, the surprises, the electricity--all of Wadsworth's key words point to his experience with a successful festival that is, to paraphrase him, "a matter of the right place at the right time with the right people."

If, as Wadsworth suggested, art is "organized surprise," the administrative director who does much of the "organizing" could be expected to have a special insight into the practical workings of Menotti's "seventeen-day performance work." Although not involved directly in Spoleto Festival U.S.A. until early 1986, General Manger Nigel Redden viewed the role of the artistic director as providing an "aesthetic" focus that makes the arts function "as a means rather than an end":

> The real strength of this festival is for better or worse people have agreed that Gian Carlo Menotti is the artistic director, that it has an artistic focus, and that he should be in charge of this thing....He makes compromises, he does things that he doesn't want to do, but he's enough of a realist and enough of an artist to keep the whole thing going.

Redden focused on the reliance on a "single mind," a potentially dangerous political pattern if participatory processes are valued. Modern consensus management methods and jazz or chamber music follow a mode in which the "steering" function is less visible and more broadly shared.

> It is the coherence question, that the artistic director, that is, a single mind, can give the festival a coherence that it might not have otherwise....Not necessarily that an artistic director has to be involved in every aspect of what's going on....I think that a festival, in order to be significant, has to have some idea. Usually the

easiest way to embody that idea is through the artistic director. And it should be an artistic idea, not an extraneous idea....

I think a festival that has an artistic sense has an opportunity to be better than the other because it's serving. I mean there's a kind of integrity that comes with that which can't come with something that has nonartistic motives but nonetheless achieves them through the arts. I mean the arts become a means rather than an end.

One inevitable issue of the "single mind" leadership model was the dilemma of the festival's direction after Gian Carlo Menotti is no longer connected with it. Redden predicted:

...I think we'll be a very different festival. Because I think that this is more malleable than most organizations. It really can be very different from one year to the next. There are few things that are fixed about it, except that we've going to stay in Charleston. We're going to be a summer festival. We're probably not going to be over seventeen days long. We're going to be high arts, whatever that means, and that can mean jazz or circuses or a lot of other things. But it means the arts.

I don't know what it would be like after Gian Carlo. I think Gian Carlo sees festivals as a...I think he's an impresario, that's what he feels his role in life is...I think he's an extraordinary impresario. He's been an extraordinarily successful composer, but I think he could have been a...lot more so if he hadn't done these festivals.

Redden's suggestion that Menotti could have been an even more successful composer "if he hadn't done these festivals" is offset by the possibility that the festivals have become major aesthetic compositions, Wilsonian performance works that are new dramas in renewed "town" theaters. Redden's emphasis on the value of a "single mind" in producing artistic coherence suggests the uniqueness of the Spoleto festivals in that they are not primarily the work of the volunteer, untrained civic committees that shape so many commercial town festivals. That is not to say that the volunteer spirit is not vital to such events but rather to emphasize that its spirit receives a powerful impetus from the vision of an artist such as Menotti.

General manager Colin Sturm, anticipating the opening of his first Spoleto festival in Melbourne in September 1986, emphasized the special economic value of an artistic director who is skilled in the art of entertainment:

> You've got two types of festivals. One which is a carnival, summer festival out in the open, marching girls, sports, swimming, stores selling things in the street...That can be done reasonably cheaply.
> But when you start about a festival that means the use of venues, halls, theaters, bringing people in from out-of-state, entertainments, and so on, you're then getting into the entertainment business. The entertainment business is a very expensive and very specialized, and, if it's going to work well, almost needing a genius at business. You were saying that you hadn't had an artistic director [at Riverbend]. The whole point of having an artistic director is to have somebody who is essentially uninterested in the financial end of things, who is looking purely at what is going to work in a general entertainment sense. And you then have...someone who is a business manager. Now without the combination of the two I think you run a risk.
> ...Because unless you can sell the tickets, you are not going to have a festival that will last very long. So you have to look at your market place.

As a "market place," an "agora," the buying and selling of ideas is a basic function of a festival, where all sorts of "ideograms" can compete for attention and customers. Overlapping programming, reworked masterpieces, new labels, unknown products --all are part of the festival as a marketplace of the new as well as a storehouse of the old. Although this "marketplace" aspect is not a primary emphasis of this study, it cannot be ignored if the basic, multiple functions of a festival are to be revealed.

The special power of the artistic director to shape the festival's aesthetic form and institutionalize its pattern drew the attention of public relations director David Rawle, the long-time "salesperson" for Menotti's Charleston "venue":

> I think Spoleto would continue to thrive without Menotti because part of his genius is that he has been able to institutionalize Spoleto. It is now larger than any individual by his own admission. I think it is a great tribute to him that he has been able to create that kind of institution.

Whether Menotti has been able to institutionalize his festivals is one of the more important questions that his vision of festival leaves unanswered. The maestro said at a 1988 press conference that he was satisfied with the present mixture of art forms, particularly with the avant garde programming, which he felt had become better accepted by audiences in recent years.

Rawle suggested that Menotti's festival ideal of primary emphasis on an "art" of juxtaposed programming and venues created a unique urban environment:

> I think that he felt that art was, in his words, considered too often as an after dinner mint and that it ought to be the main meal, the main course. One way of making it be so was to create a festival in which an entire community could be immersed. It is difficult during the festival to pick up a newspaper, talk to an individual, visit a shop, or watch television or listen to radio without having a sense of Spoleto's presence. This is a joyous celebration of the arts and the festival form provides it.

Menotti's special function as artistic director is seen in the image Rawle evoked of bringing an entire community to an "arts feast" for a "joyous celebration of the arts" as an ultimate end. The festival's forms itself provide a complete "immersion," a term suggesting the religious overtones of a serious festival noted by Tyrone Guthrie and Christopher Hunt. As a "market place," an "agora for artists and audiences," what is the "festival form" but a "theater of differences" with, as Bakhtin said, "an absence of clearly established footlights"? The multi-colored lights of the Christmas tree are "festive," someone observed. (53) If all the lights were one color, red perhaps, the response would be possibly "interesting" or "pretty" but probably not "festive." The "fest" most often appears as the root word of social, religious, or pleasurable activities that mark a time and space of differences from the routine of ordinary life.

Tension springs from Menotti's idea of differences, contrasts, oppositions, inversions, pluralities, diversities, assortments, miscellanies, varieties, medleys, divergences, variances. Unlike the effect of modes of analysis that compress meaning and relationships to fewer and fewer symbols, the effect of what is "festive" and alive is the expansion to multiplicity, even to seemingly meaningless diversity. It is this illusion of uniqueness that endows any festival with its appearance of endless variety of forms and content. Yet the tension of unlike entities in proximity, as in musical dissonance, creates interest and gives pain mixed with pleasure to the eye and ear. It is the function of an artistic director to mingle and blend the elements at hand without fearing or rejecting contradiction, inconsistencies, the comfort of sameness, the familiar, and the nonthreatening.

In summary, the comments from Spoleto Festival U.S.A. officials quoted above and in other materials suggest the crucial contribution of an artistic director in shaping a festival.

open or closed to the new;
what the city as an art form said to Menotti;
creation of free environment for players;
play for each other as well as even small audiences;
young, new, unknown artists performing before a critical audience;
artistic director has a message;
menotti knows all arts and all artists in all fields;
high failure risk events;
artistic director gives overall artistic view to give special profile to festival, also faith in brilliant young people and in creative arts;
artistic director should have strong artistic point of view that he is trying to get across;
need creative mind more than businessman mind;
art is organized surprise;
agreement to have an artistic director is a strength;
an artistic director provides focus and serves as a common court of last resort;
single mind of artistic director gives festival coherence because the festival idea is embodied in one person's mind;
artistic festival has integrity because it is serving, doesn't have non-artistic motives but achieves them anyway through the arts; keeping arts end rather than means;
Menotti is impresario and composer; people like having an artistic vision even if they disagree;
a festival can be summer carnival or theatrical entertainment;
an artistic director looks at what works purely in entertainment sense and puts personal stamp on festival;
artistic director selects artistic package;
Menotti wanted to make art the main course rather than after dinner mint;
created a festival that immersed entire community;
festival form provides joyous celebration of the arts that none can avoid during festival time.

"Menotti," and his "message" and "vision," is mentioned frequently; the value of the individual contribution cannot be diminished. The artistic director is performing the essential function of the "I" in Brooks' study of the theatrically created "empty space." Regardless of the particular goals, it is the existence of this function that endows the festival with its potential "integrity" as an end in itself, something other than a summer carnival alone, valuable though this may be for certain community needs. Paradoxically, the artistic "integrity" mentioned by Redden may produce significant economic benefits that greatly exceed productions of a more commercial, narrow aim.

That this is not the normal businessman's view of the ends and means of art is noted by Constance Hardinge in "The Artistic Director" from the National Association of Regional Ballet handbook for new ballet board members:

> Basically our boards should be responsible for all legal and organizational activities, for fund raising, ticket sales and public relations. We [artistic directors] are responsible for everything else....Opinion and advice should always be sought from those who are knowledgeable, but the final word must always be the artistic director's. In this area there is often a lack of clarity and problems arise [emphasis mine]....In the constant daily crises we face it isn't easy to remember our real purpose. We are the link that holds illusion and reality together for future generations .

Artists and their "artistic directors," as "links holding illusion and reality together for future generations," apparently provide a function (analogous to a form of cultural DNA) not often experienced by the ordinary arts patron or board member. That influential Charlestonians, after an intense struggle, welcomed the contributions of Menotti, that they shared their civic power to such an extent with him, is in retrospect an extraordinary historical event.

If Charleston's festival can be considered the American prototype of a new "Menottian" theater, one in which all the spatially proximate visible world is literally a stage with all the "men and women merely players," then Shakespeare's modest use of the term "merely" can be placed in a more ironic context. These dramatic productions, born out of a sensitive artist's response to an "empty space," evolve into powerful meaning-making devices that none can avoid during their run nor completely escape before and after. Like Christmas and the Fourth of July, and other great cultural festive rituals, the reach of their symbolism cannot be blocked from awareness without deliberate social isolation. It is in the interplay of the "I" as artistic director, the "bare stage" of the empty urban form, and serious, purposeful ideas that these festive "theaters of power" are shaped into a "place for aesthetic play."

The Empty City Space: Why Charleston?

If the discussion of the function of the artistic director could be expressed at its simplest form as a question of "Why Menotti?," then the category of the function of the festival's theatrical space could be framed at its most elemental level as "Why Charleston?" Some uncertainty about who did what when, where, why, and how exists about the answers to this question. However, underlying these disputed facts is the unquestioned dramatic reality that this traditional South Carolina city and its improbable avant garde arts festival have been engaged in a special, intricate relationship since Menotti first saw it in 1976 and decided to look no further on the list prepared for him of other Southern cities. Redden suggested one important difference in Menotti's festivals by focusing on the central "artistic" idea behind the festival:

> I think what distinguishes this festival from other festivals, or rather from some other festivals that were started by cities, is that it started with an artistic idea rather than a cultural development idea or even with a place idea. It was very much about artists and it happened to be Charleston rather than, "Let's take Charleston and try to figure out what we can do to make something exciting happen in Charleston."

It is clear enough that Charlestonians did not decide to have a festival and find an artistic director and staff to produce it. What is less clear from the record is the weight given to the three types of festivals--artistic, cultural development, and place--mentioned by Redden. Menotti had constructed a utopian community in Spoleto, Italy, where the artist ruled for a few summer weeks, an inversion in this larger sense with aspects of a Bakhtinian carnival reversal of official/unofficial. Menotti needed a special city for an American production of his artistic utopia. From his statements in the various Spoleto brochures and the recollections of those involved in the American festival, the signs point toward a more complex relationship than that "it happened to be Charleston." The city's particular character was very important, as Redden explained:

> I think one of the other very key things about the city is that it happens to be architecturally beautiful; that is, that this is a place that is an appropriate setting for a festival that celebrates those areas of human imagination that are concerned with beauty and with some of the intangibles of the human spirit. That is why it was started here [emphasis mine].

Charleston was a city of American cultural firsts: first opera, first ballet, first play performed. (54) It was an old world city in the new world. It was a narrow peninsula on the Atlantic seacoast. Like Spoleto, Italy, it had been left out of much of the South's industrialization. Its downtown had been preserved in a state resembling the original eighteenth-century seaport town. Destroyed as a viable urban center by the Civil War, it no longer was a city of firsts of any kind nationally or regionally. Its civic leaders admitted its economy was stagnant, dominated by the huge U.S. Navy base.

It was, in short, an urban "empty space" waiting for a Menotti to call it a "bare stage," to fill it with performers, and to invite an audience to observe--much as he had done as a child growing up in Italy. (55) Other Southern festival possibilities, such as Winston-Salem, had some of the qualities he sought for his festival music-theater. Yet none except Charleston had the look and feel of the old European town in the "uncivilized" American South, the juxtaposition of old world and new world architecture. Even a Chattanooga, if it had made the initial list, would have had more pure dramatic scenery with its "mountains looking at each other" at the river's entrance from the Tennessee River canyon. But it lacked the dramatic, contrasting of the "old": Charleston's European town houses, empty theaters, narrow streets, and setting on a small ocean point.

Charleston worked perfectly as a large-scale thrust stage, for want of a more precise term. It captured its creator, actors, and audiences for a magical seventeen days in late spring--"cruise ship magic," as Redden remembered from his youth at the Spoleto Festival in Italy. From the discussion of Menotti's purposes that follow in the next section, it becomes evident that the festival idea depended on the nature of a place as much as it depended on what Redden termed an "artistic idea." It seems that, in Redden's sense, Menotti's Charleston festival originated as an intricate, intertwined artistic idea, place idea, and cultural development idea. The complexity of this interplay is illustrated by comments of Mayor Joseph P. Riley, Jr. in the opening of his official welcoming statement to the 1978 second festival program:

> In 1941, Charleston's noted artist and author, Elizabeth O'Neill Verner, wrote, in Mellowed by Time, that Charleston "is the one colonial city in America with a living record which tells us, more vividly than all the books and all the old prints in museums can ever tell, what the New World inherited from the civilization of the ages. We started again, not to destroy the old law, but to fulfill it. Here the land is speaking--put your ear to the ground and listen.

Here, more so than any other colonial city, we live amidst a living record of the New World's inheritance from the old world. Our architecture, our townscape, our art, which form the setting and backdrop of the Spoleto Festival, are themselves a "festival of two worlds." (56)

Riley's and Verner's aesthetic response to a "theatrical" location was not a new idea invented by Charleston's publicity agents. Salzburg evoked a similar reaction. "Every square, every street here seems to have been expressly created as the setting for a play," wrote the festival's founder and artistic director, Max Reinhardt. (57) The theatrical city spaces described by Reinhardt apparently were strongly felt by Menotti when he saw Charleston. There is little disagreement that Charleston, to Menotti the impresario, had the theatrical form of a Salzburg and appeared one of those special works of urban art.

The 1986 and 1988 interviews brought out the importance of Charleston's beckoning theatrical space. An excerpt from Stern's recollections in 1988 particularly demonstrates a pre-existing desire to have any proposed festival match the city's beauty:

> I think the fact that Charleston itself is so unique, that I wanted to see a festival here to match it, not just another festival. And this could contribute to the well-being of our community....I think it can be an educational and a cultural center....To make this thing an artistic success, a social success, and a financial success, certain elements were essential. And Charleston fitted in beautifully.... Charleston was the cultural center of colonial times. And we are just returning it to its former peak condition.

It was the Charlestonians' pride of "place," repeatedly expressed both from those dedicated to bringing in Menotti's festival and those equally dedicated to preventing it, that arouses more than superficial interest in the physical environment that excited Menotti and the many contributors to his dream of a chimerical summer village for artists and art lovers. Could his Italian creation take root in an American location? One answer to the question of "Why Charleston?" is found in Stern's understanding of Menotti's reasons for selecting the isolated Italian village of Spoleto, which followed the maestro's idea of finding a place suitable for presenting young American artists to European audiences:

> From that point on [before 1958] he had to find a place to have this festival. It wasn't the cities, because, he says, and he said this is true of Charleston as well, that the city must be an art form in

itself, that people should walk around the city as well as enjoy the festival and they tie in together; they're in concert and in harmony [emphasis mine]. He chose a small town in Umbrian Province, Spoleto, which historians tell us was where Hannibal crossed the Alps and the big battle was at Spoleto. Here is an old, old town that was bypassed by the twentieth century. It has its original Etruscan walls, original forum, theaters, opera houses. It was the seat of culture of the Umbrian Province. It was destitute, economically completely depressed; people were leaving; there was no industry. The culture which could be presented was nonexistent. So he selected this really depressed area, yes [replying to a question], like a theater that had been empty for many years.

After nearly 20 years of artistic success with the town arts festival in Spoleto, which became a prospering village, Menotti and American cultural leaders decided that a similar effort should be attempted in this country. Although the official story of federal sponsorship of Spoleto Festival U.S.A. is undocumented, the basic reasons given by Stern focus on the need for an appropriate "home" for the festival:

>   The United States National Endowment of the Arts in Washington approached Menotti...and suggested that he establish a Spoleto Festival in the United States...Menotti was placed in charge of trying to develop a plan to present the festival in the United States. The general feeling of the bureaucracy in Washington was that no festival existed in the Southeastern United States, and that this festival should be in the Southeastern part of the United States. Menotti was asked to select a city where this festival could find a home.
>   He decided to come to Charleston first, and I remember that visit extremely well. It was before the Italian festival in 1975, because Frances [Edmunds] knew they were going to come here when she went over there. And I think first of all Menotti said, "I fell in love with it at first sight." He said, "Charleston is an artistic form in itself, and that is what I would like." But he was further impressed with, number one, the College [of Charleston] because if we could have the festival prior to the Italian festival we would need dormitory space for over 600 artists and technicians....
>   Without the College, there would have been no festival, because of the housing situation and the logistic support. Menotti loved the idea of the College, he thought the festival should be near an educational institution, he loved the idea of the historic part of

Charleston, and he loved the idea that the Mayor was so enthusiastic and the community for which he spoke....

Then, Mrs. Rufus Barkley, I'll call her Nella for short, became extremely interested and she headed up a committee to encourage people like the National Endowment, Priscilla Morgan, and Christopher Keene to select Charleston as a place for the festival. She had various committees, of which I was chairman of what you might call a logistics committee. She had a fundraising committee and because of his great influence and political power as well as economic power, Hugh Lane was elected chairman of this committee to try and get the festival here.

It is in the context of "finding a home" place that the full transcript of Stern's "story of origin," which reflects his privileged perspective on Menotti's choice of Charleston and on the events of the festival's origin, becomes the central narrative connecting the three primary categories of this analysis, where the combining of the three elements of place, idea, and force find their material expression in the city's physical reality.

It is a story more complex than Redden's view of what might have been the origin of a festival of "place": "Let's take Charleston and try to figure out what we can do to make something exciting happen in Charleston." It is an account of the combining of the three elements, where no one causal factor, such as "place," can be isolated from others. The story as told by Stern has all the public drama of his wife's description of waiting for the black or white smoke to signal the election of a new Pope. His narration of how he and Charleston's new mayor overcame one influential town leader's sincere effort to stop the festival, following a visit to the Italian production, is the key to understanding the necessity for an ideological "empty space" to combine with physical "empty spaces":

In 1976, Hugh Lane, Nella Barkley, and Mr. and Mrs. Tom Stevenson went to Spoleto to see really what it was all about. A matter of record is that when Hugh Lane returned to Charleston, he said he would have nothing more to do with it. He did not want to expose the citizens of Charleston to people dancing without clothes and felt that the people who would come to Charleston would be depraved, queers--I think he used those words--and he offered to return all the money that people had donated to this effort. And he did. I think he returned something like a hundred thousand dollars to people because he had misled them.

In addition, Hugh Lane said that the festival was not economically feasible and would never be a success. This is part of a letter that he put in writing, which he subsequently has regretted but not denied. He was chairman of the board of the C&S bank. But he was the head of everything here, head of the United Way. You know, he was number one citizen, and he went all over the state to generate these contributions. He does speak to me now, but he'll never admit the festival has done any good.

Mayor Joseph Riley and Stern combined their personal influence and the resources of municipal government and the College of Charleston to overcome powerful private resistance that ordinarily would have stopped at once any such major civic initiative:

> It was at this time [late summer 1976] that Nella Barkley and Hugh Lane went to a Festival Foundation board meeting in New York, which Frances Edmunds attended. I can only give hearsay information, but I do know that prior to the meeting Mrs. Barkley wrote a letter to the board saying that she would assume the responsibilities of general manager for $20,000 a year, but she wanted full authority, full responsibility for the operation of the festival. That letter was copied to the chairman of the Festival Foundation, who at that time was Ernest Hillman, and Menotti. Frances Edmunds advised me that she had never been more embarrassed at a meeting because they just raked Nella over the coals and showed no respect for Hugh Lane. Menotti was particularly obnoxious, and said that he was not going to give up any authority, that she wasn't worth the $20,000 she was asking. They left, bitter--this was in August 1976....
>
> Nella and Hugh Lane returned to Charleston. Nella wrote a letter resigning and Hugh Lane reiterated his position that he was not going to subject Charlestonians to be a breeding place for undesirables. Now this withdrawal by Nella and Hugh Lane would have been catastrophic had not the Mayor called Menotti and other members of the board of the Festival Foundation and asked them to meet in Charleston...[emphasis mine].
>
> I recall the meeting extremely well because it was held in the President's house at the College of Charleston in September of 1976. The Mayor had asked if it could be held in the President's house at the College. At that meeting, which was a very vitriolic meeting, in which Mr. Lane walked out with Mrs. Barkley, the Mayor stated that he was convinced that the Spoleto Festival would do a great deal for Charleston, that he disagreed but appreciated the views of the dissidents. He turned to me and he said, "Will you take over?" I said I would never say no to him and I've never turned down a challenge....

...My wife was sitting outside the dinning room where we had our meeting. She looked out of the window and saw all these TV cameras and reporters outside the house; she stuck her head out and said, "Are you waiting for white smoke or black smoke?" But it was all over the press. They caught Hugh Lane and Nella Barkley leaving and naturally they were waiting to see what was going to happen. The Mayor came out and said that I had agreed to be the chairman and to take over and there was going to be a Spoleto.

The basic question was, "Will there be a festival in Charleston?" And I must say, it was the unanimous view of both the members of the Festival Foundation board and the few Charlestonians who were there that we should have it, and that we should have it next year in 1977. That gave us nine months to prepare for it....

I don't know what the records will show. If you ask me, and I leave myself out of it, the responsibility for initially setting up Spoleto fell on the Mayor and the College, on both of our willingnesses to never say never and it couldn't be done.

Repeatedly, the powerful "gravitational field" of the physical city itself surfaced in this, in other interviews, in program statements, and in press reports. The determination of Mayor Riley to bring the world of "high" performing arts to his town against the explicit wishes of a powerful business leader, the combination of city and college resources, the ambience available to Menotti at the city's coastal resorts, the fact of the college's availability at the right time with a generous president willing to do far more than his share, wealthy donors who shared the dream with Menotti, the international Spoleto festival board's willingness to come to Charleston for dialogue with festival supporters, the facilitating role of the National Endowment for the Arts, and Walter Anderson's personal encouragement--all reflect an extraordinary response to "absence." It is a response much like Brook's view of the seductive "empty space" that he has only to call a "bare stage" to begin the making of "theater." That all these elements, not any one of them, happened to combine at the same time was the key that unlocked the magical space and produced Menotti's new theater in America.

The Element of Purpose: Menotti's Festival Idea

If Charleston's dreamers started with an image of a festival as no more than a civic fundraiser, they soon found out, as Stern made clear, that Menotti had something else in mind that would introduce more diversity to their city than anyone could have imagined in their wildest civic dreaming. The unusual nature of this particular festival idea was noted by Stern:

> Previously "festival" to me meant just trying to fundraise. When you talk Spoleto, they say you know that's a different kind of festival. Number one, it's an international festival; number two, we are not rushing to get Pavarotti, Domingo, or other luminaries--but Menotti has had the ability to select young people who are going to be the Pavarotti's and the Domingo's. People know that they can expect something unusual, different....
>
> ...And it's different; they don't know what opera is going to be shown but they know it's going to be different. He's very careful about who directs them, produces them, the designer. Dance, no one knows what's going to be there but they know it's going to be different. And that they most probably will never see it again.

The power of the festival imagined by Menotti demonstrated its gravitational field over arts critics, corporate executives, and performers. Charles Wadsworth, immersed in both festivals from their beginnings, focused on Menotti's original idea from the 1958 beginning in Italy:

> When he invited me in 1959 to start a series of chamber music concerts in this delicious little seventeenth century theater, which seats about 300 to 350--same as this theater [Dock Street Theater, Charleston]--he said, "I want these concerts to be different. I want you to be sure that you only bring brilliant, gifted young talents to play here. And I want you to be sure to find some way that the concerts are informal in nature." He said to me, "Perhaps there won't be anybody there but myself and a few of the artists working for the festival, but I want to do it anyway. It'll be something in the middle of the day, one hour."
>
> And it was true the first few days....The third summer we were already getting extraordinary acclaim from everyone and we were fighting them off....Along the way I developed what I think has been an important factor in my end of things in chamber concerts, which made them very different from concerts that went on anywhere else in the world. I communicated with the people verbally to try to get them into an even more relaxed mood than they might be ordinarily. You have a very important factor in summer festivals particularly in that people are free from work pressures, daily pressures. They're obviously somewhere to have a good time.

> I wanted to add to that further by getting the people so relaxed that they could open themselves to the performers and to the music and that in turn would create a special feeling among the performers, that they would be able to give in a very free way and enjoy the act of performing.

Wadsworth's humorous hosting for the noonday concerts is part of the legend of the Spoletos, a radical contrast from the normal framing expected for chamber music. He was proud of this contribution to bringing "music" to festival audiences:

> I don't care whether it's avant garde or early Baroque or the obvious romantics, I think music and the arts must communicate to people on a gut level. It is not an intellectual pursuit, the enjoyment of chamber music, which is considered by many an elitist form. If the people are uninhibited in their listening, then they are going to be able to take the message that the composer intended. The composer is not really interested in how appreciative people are of the devices they have used in getting their feelings down on paper. So this created a special atmosphere in a festival situation, which already gives you one hand up.
>
> For me, it was an incredible opportunity to find artists who I thought were great and then I started combining things into very unusual ways with instruments, voice, percussion, and all sorts of things that would create stimulation in the listener.

Wadsworth explained the special purpose Menotti had in mind, which led directly to the "combining" function of the Spoleto festivals, bringing to mind Brook's earlier quoted remark about the role of the audience as "artists" assisting in the performance, in the "birth" of meaning:

> The festival is unique and different from almost all other festivals because from the very beginning Gian Carlo wanted all of the arts to be represented so that the musicians and the actors could all feed off each other's inspirations and it would bring a certain excitement to my work. One summer [in Spoleto] he had an extraordinary series of poetry readings, so you had Ferlingetti from the West Coast there, and Kerouac, and Ezra Pound on the same afternoon reading from his works. For me to have Ezra Pound coming in my concert--it can't help but create electricity, or to see Visconte there in the box. We all found we were exciting each other by what we did.

Wadsworth focused on the sameness/difference issue in pointing out the success of the tradition of single discipline festivals, suggesting the aesthetic backdrop against which the Spoleto festivals differentiate themselves:

> The ones in this country which are the most successful are the ones which usually lean towards one discipline, rather than all the disciplines, as the Marlborough Festival is only chamber music....Tanglewood is a great festival but it's all orchestral stuff and it is repertoire they have been playing in the regular year; but it's a beautiful place to sit on the lawn and listen to the music. The place is terribly important in terms of summer festivals [emphasis mine].
>
> In this country there are not other festivals like Spoleto, which really sets it apart....the Edinburgh Festival or some of the Salzburg Festival [is] more the kind of festival we are doing here. At Salzburg you have Karajan, who is an extraordinarily strong personality who has been guiding that one for a number of years. That is usually the case.

As a "place, an ideal, and a force," Spoleto Festival U.S.A. unquestionably is an exceptional success as a town festival, possibly a new form of festival that evolved in its habitat to meet the changing needs of a new era. Wadsworth stressed the high risk of failure associated with Menotti's idea of festival:

> The idea of Gian Carlo to have an orchestra made up of young students or people who have just graduated--these hundred people have been called from student bodies all over the country, that to me is one of the exciting things about this festival. There is not that kind of chance taking in other places.

Colin Sturm's managerial perspective balanced the necessity of blending the aesthetic and economic ingredients involved in producing Menotti's unique vision of an artist's utopia. Sturm stressed knowing the "purpose" of a festival:

> To start from the beginning you've got to make an assessment of the purposes of a festival. A festival has two important foundation stones. They're part of the total structure. Without them both being effective you haven't got a festival that will work. The first part of a festival structure is whether the community wants it. If it's not bubbling up from the community, it's going to

automatically fail. You cannot impose something of this sort onto a community from above.

Spoleto was started by an idea from Gian Carlo Menotti, which came from his friend, the American composer Sam Barber, who said, when they were both young men, that art should not be just the froth on the top of the main soup, that it should have a concrete, measurable effect in a community. To test that as a premise, they both looked for a town in Italy and in the States-- they were looking in both places, but they found quickest a town in Italy which was absolutely on its beam ends.

Its population consisted of very elderly and very young people. All the young, middle age groups had to leave because there was no work, no money. Unemployment was something like 60 percent. So they thought that if they were going to prove their premise, then the festival would have to do things that in a commercial sense were good.

So when they suggested this to the city fathers, they grabbed at the chance to try anything. Therefore, my first point was that the community wanted it, what community that was there. The end result is that Spoleto is a thriving little city as a direct input of the festival. It brings lots of tourism into the place. There's been a great deal of building and regeneration of the medieval buildings has been carried out with public money from taxes that the money has generated. So there has been a measurable effect. The improvement in beneficial life style through the arts is enormous.

[The other approach] is the sort of festival which is an area grouping of people who are going to put their hands into their own pockets, do a great deal of voluntary work themselves, and probably have a ball. But it'll stay at that particular level. In Australia, we think of this as the Scout All complex, you know. The Boy Scouts are a nice worthwhile community activity; the parents of the kids get together once a month or whatever--you've got an activity which brings the community together for that particular purpose.

The critical role of the local governmental structure, and its particular leadership, was, Sturm felt, much more important in creating the political environment in which a festival could flourish. Although Charleston Mayor Riley's key political role has not been stressed in this analysis, it seems the only indispensable factor that explains why Menotti was given the power to shape a festival. Without Riley, Charleston would not have had a festival, or at least, as Stern's story makes clear, probably not with someone like Menotti in charge of the "imagination department." (58)

Finally, what is the basic purpose of Spoleto U.S.A. as seen by current management? Nigel Redden called attention to the basic "artistic" aim, where the "mix" was important; "differences" suffice for the idea that Menotti transported from Italy to America.

> The thing that I think is crucial about the history of this festival is that it started from an artistic idea, which was basically to give Italian audiences a sense of what American artists were doing....He also wanted to create a kind of sort of artist's colony, that it very much was about artists, artists working together and artists seeing each other's work--that was very much an aspect of the festival. I think it left from that pretty quickly, that is, it became much more a festival about performances, a festival about doing specific events but always the mix was important....
>
> There are advantages to the festival in Italy. Spoleto is a more compact town; it's also got a center, which this town doesn't have. There isn't a place as a tourist that you would go to; in Italy there definitely is......There's magic in Spoleto--the cruise ship magic--that I think festivals bring [emphasis mine]. All these people descend on a place that is beautiful for a specific period of time and they all have these wonderful magical experiences together. And, they fall in love and they have affairs and they have fights and they meet people who become bosom buddies for two weeks and who they never see again. On a human level that's very important; it's extracting you from your daily life.... Artists [are] the key to the whole thing.

Redden saw a complex relationship between economic development and arts, between the confusion of the ends and means of art. (59)

> This is an arts festival and the arts come first in this festival. Not Charleston, not economic development, not even paying the bills, although obviously you have to pay the bills to keep going. But if the only reason we are keeping going is to pay the bills, then frankly we would all quit. There would be nothing here. All these things are very fragile; I mean this exists only in the mind. I mean this is a conceptual piece....in a way it's a performance art work....So our integrity in terms of artists has to be the founding supposition. Without that precondition, there's no point in talking about the other things.

He noted, as Tyrone Guthrie had pointed out, that a big city and a "serious" arts festival are incompatible, leading to a "cultural tourism" activity in which "art" is used to entice the tourists and generate money-making events:

> The LA Olympic Arts Festival was very influential in the way people are thinking of festivals in this country. It's not our way of thinking of festivals; it is a big city way and I think it's the antithesis of what this festival is....Cultural tourism is a big issue right now and obviously cultural tourism is something that's gone on in Europe forever. People, Americans, have gone to Europe for cultural reasons and people have visited America for geographic reasons.

Spoleto Festival U.S.A.'s prime constituency, Redden said, is the larger arts community of critics and audiences, the argument being that if this "higher" goal is reached then the Charleston community will be pleased. Yet Redden intended to protect the festival's contextual "intimacy" from mass media demands:

> I think it's extremely important that we do things that have a kind of intimacy and scale that is human; because I don't think two million has anything to do with the human scale at all. And I don't think it's a question of being elite or exclusive. I think its a question of doing something that is worthwhile. The kind of things we're doing are not things that should be looked at in five minute doses in between flipping channels, having dinner, having telephone calls. That's not what we should be doing because these are serious things that do need to be given serious attention that you can give when you are in the theater [emphasis mine].

In Redden's portrayal of the idea and purposes of Spoleto Festival U.S.A. and the Italian festival is found the heart of Menotti's theater festival of differences. It adds to the city's cultural treasures, to its citizens' knowledge and storehouse of images, to its place as a primary destination for critic and tourist alike, to a home for a "serious" encounter with the creations of artistic professionals in many fields.

Stern saw the main idea of the festival he helped create with the prevailing Aristotelian view of the theater as a "mirror of the times":

> A festival reflects the culture of the times, particularly a comprehensive festival such as Spoleto. It reflects all of the different art forms in existence at that time. We have modern dance, classical dance, opera, chamber music, theater, mime--all the existing art forms.

Behind these forms are purposive, forceful individuals such as Menotti, Mayor Riley, and Stern himself. Stern quickly accepted the idea of a festival of "diversity," as he put it, combined with a city that was an "art form in itself"--an empty space ready to be called a bare stage--and the show opened in May 1977. Stern recalled that extraordinary event:

> The first festival was one of the most successful festivals. We had the Zulu Dancers, which had appeared at Spoleto, Italy, before, and they were a tremendous hit. We had a dance gala, which featured Alicia Alonzo and Gudenov. The Zulu dancers and the finale at Middleton Gardens, with fireworks, stand out in my mind as most memorable. At the finale we had the orchestra at the finger lakes. We had the 1812 Overture, and we had the Citadel cadets re-enact the final shelling of Moscow actually firing their cannon, which was followed by a magnificent fireworks display....
>
> We had at the opening ceremonies a major speaker with the governor and the mayor always attending and some extraordinary event, surprising the audience. One of these was the Flying Wallenders, a circus tightrope group, and we had them go from City Hall over a tightrope to the Federal Building. We always have puppets, brass quintets, and also singing stars like Esther Hines singing the Star Spangled Banner.
>
> We didn't know what would happen. We had the leading citizen of Charleston say it could never succeed. But Mayor Riley was just elected to his fourth term. His opposition ran against its costs from the local area.

The interplay of "place, ideal, and force" created an unusual combination of effects, said David Rawle, who stressed the idea of diversity and differences in the festival's presentations:

> The special economic significance of Spoleto to Charleston is it has in its nine years contributed about $350 million dollars spending directly and indirectly to this area. Secondly, it has attracted companies that wanted to move here because of the quality of life that Spoleto has helped catalyze. Thirdly, it has helped boost the economic vitality of the other arts organizations. Politically, it has opened up people's minds to a wide variety of ideas and cultural influences because it is so international in its presentation. Aesthetically, it is the perfect complement to Charleston because Charleston itself is an art form.

Whether these effects were planned from Spoleto U.S.A.'s inception or merely random but probable consequences from small changes is not knowable. Few Charlestonians would disagree that Menotti's avant garde festival of all the arts and the city's parallel Piccolo Festival have boosted the economy and the arts. That the festival has opened minds to broader ideas is an issue that would produce more debate within the community, judging from Mayor Riley's 1987 political opposition and its use of the festival as a major campaign issue.

Difference and Sameness

Spoleto Festival U.S.A. is a very complex idea. Its multiple mirroring function of Menotti the person, Charleston the place, and Spoleto the idea was touched upon by David Rawle in explaining why this particular festival was different from others:

> It is a reflection of the artistic direction of its founder and it is a reflection of the Charleston community. And it is celebrating the beauty of its own historic city while also reaching out into new directions....The greatest challenge is to stand up from others and to differentiate yourself. That requires a focus and a discipline to hold that focus.

Menotti, Riley, Stern, and many Charlestonians triumphed and successfully met that challenge. They did and do in fact allow Charleston to become for a few weeks each year a "breeding ground" for diversity, difference, and the succession from the old to the new. The sexual metaphor seems especially suitable for the festival as a "birth place of the new," and for thinking about festivals lacking such "breeding grounds" of diversity.

CHAPTER III

CHATTANOOGA'S RIVERBEND FESTIVAL: FROM A THEATER OF DIFFERENCE TO A THEATER OF SAMENESS

Chattanooga's Riverbend Festival (60) was created out of the interplay of the same three elements as Charleston's Spoleto Festival U.S.A.: an empty space, specific purposes, and an artistic force. Early in the beginning stages, however, the artistic director was removed from the organizing group's agenda. The aesthetic and ideological consequence of the lack of the force of an artistic director, such as Gian Carlo Menotti, is the focus of this analysis of the Riverbend Festival's origin.

The Struggle to Fill the City's Empty Festival Space

It is doubtful anyone can present a "story of origin" agreeable to all parties involved in the founding of events such as Charleston's or Chattanooga's town festivals. Various persons in Chattanooga were struggling to fill the city's "empty" urban spaces with a festival in the early 1980s. (61) Several concerned citizens observed that something was missing in the city; others sensed the empty space and were working at their own versions of what to put in this felt absence, or "bare stage." Just as Charleston and Spoleto, Italy, were economically depressed and had been apparently "empty" or little used in relation to past periods, so this ideological, political, aesthetic, social, and even physical space in Chattanooga was unfilled, analogous to an empty file folder with nothing in it but a heading whose "reality" was at that period no more than the "category" itself. (62)

Several community groups responded to the absence of a town festival. (63) One effort was a 1978 Allied Arts Fund document, indicating the prevailing "fund-raising" festival idea, although the project was never realized. Another was the Riverbend organizing group's response in 1980 to information brought from Spoleto Festival U.S.A. and the Salzburg Festival, which indicated a growing curiosity about the general effects of town festivals. A third was the Lyndhurst Foundation's interest in community development strategies, such as a City Fair, and the foundation's 1981 "Five Nights in Chattanooga" summer concerts. Finally, a reaction of the business community to some missing ingredient in civic life was the Chamber of Commerce's 1981 renewal of a small downtown arts festival. (64)

Eventually, the collective group process of bounding the empty space was a formal plan submitted in November 1981 to the Lyndhurst Foundation for administrative funding. For most who were involved in the festival's founding events, this was the key document that synthesized and defined the "empty space" of the "festival theater." (65) With the new festival group's proposed staffing and volunteer plan, budget, and action timetable, the first phase of the process of creating, or defining and bounding, the empty festival space, the "unfilled" theatrical space, was completed. These first documents were in effect a series of scripts and revisions for the social drama that would become the Riverbend Festival.

As one musician, Doris Hays, had suggested in her proposal, "A festival is a creature which needs to fit its habitat." The new "festival creature" responded to its habitat, its "empty space," strongly enough to be repeated; and it has become community ritual. If it had not been repeated, if it had become an occasional pageant, it would have been no more than a one-time theatrical production, such as "Five Nights in Chattanooga," which some believe, as noted in the Preface, was the first Riverbend festival.

That the festival became ritual suggests it met a continuing need to "infuse" a temporary "empty" civic space with its energy. Yet what became the Riverbend Festival seems to have been a "masked" theatrical structure, a "masque" with social intent, one resembling the popular festive-form "absent clearly established footlights," in Bakhtin's sense. Apparently if the intent is to have a repetitive, nonpermanent temporal and spatial structure, often it is called a "festival," possibly because of a message those in control desire to be transmitted or reinforced. This interpretation, using most of the key sources from that period (excepting the foundation documents, which were not requested for this exploratory analysis), reinforces the interdependence of place, ideal, and force in creating the nature, functions, and meaning of a festival. These three crucial elements in the Charleston festival's analysis appeared to be as fundamental as the red, yellow, and blue that are the primary colors of the visible spectrum. They were:

Purpose: avant garde showcase of new art, principally performance works
Theaters/stages: Galliard city auditorium, seventeenth- century Dock St. Theater, many other downtown locations, some out-of-doors at the College of Charleston, concluding at nearby Middleton Plantation

Artistic director: composer Gian Carlo Menotti

The difference from Chattanooga in purpose, in locations, in the perceived value of an artistic director--all suggest that the initial presence or absence of these particular elements carry the encoded potential for the social construction that could evolve if those energies remained joined to enable the essential imaginative free play associated with "festival." The first Chattanooga festival proposal on May 5, 1981, included statements about the city as well as ideas for a festival. It expressed the basic "empty space" of the community. It is the central (but repressed) document that probably would have led to a "festival of differences" had it not been for the foundation's intervention in pursuit of its private agenda for community change. The following excerpts from the complete document (author's Riverbend materials) illustrate the relationship of the three elements that even at that time seemed central to the emergence of any significant festival:

[Empty Space]: One of Chattanooga's principal problems is its sociality. Unlike the citizens of many other picturesque cities, Chattanoogans begin a mass exodus from downtown at 3:30 every afternoon. By 6 p.m. the center of the city is virtually deserted. Why? Because very little is happening of interest. The resulting loss of retail and tax dollars is considerable. But beyond the loss in dollars is a loss in community spirit and pride and the loss of a cohesive urban life style and shared interest. By one definition a city is a focus of shared interests and common concerns. A deserted city center is a tangible sign of a citizenry alienated from its city. In short, the potential inherent in Chattanooga's new physical improvements may never take hold if the city remains a social desert. Some have described the Chattanooga community as divided, dispirited, and lacking in broadbased social vitality. We think there is some truth to this view. A key missing ingredient is a set of community activities which physically pull people of different stations in life together....

[Purposes]: Learning from the precedents set by Charleston, South Carolina's Spoleto Festival, and Austria's Salzburg music festival, we see no reason not to create Chattanooga's own "celebration of togetherness with diversity" through a quality of first-rate artistic expression that pulls the community together and attracts substantial regional and possibly national interest. In addition to this idea, the celebration could bring together, both traditional and innovative, opera, symphony, dance, theater, film, visual exhibits, regional arts (such as story telling, gospel singing, bluegrass music, etc.).... We prefer "celebration" rather than "festival" because the former term suggests a specific theme while the latter is more general. A "celebration of togetherness" focuses directly on our main goal, which is to create widespread community participation and to bring diverse ethnic, social, religious, and economic groups together.

[Artistic Director]: Much will depend on the personality and vision of the artistic director. The selection of this individual is the key factor in achieving artistic and financial success. We suggest someone equal in stature to Gian Carlo Menotti, artistic director of Spoleto Festival in Charleston....Rather than attempting to do the work of the artistic director, which involves balancing appropriate programming, availability of guest artists and groups, and budgetary realities, we are attaching a copy of the Spoleto calendar as an example of what is working well now in Charleston and with modification could work here.

This proposal represents many of the ideas reflected in Charleston's festival that were attempted in Chattanooga's first 1982 festival. It caught the idea of "difference," of juxtaposition of genres, of contrasting styles, of the role of the arts as an energy source--not only as an "after dinner mint."

However, there is no substitute for professional competence in the arts as in any field; pop singer Roberta Flack was "juxtaposed" to sing with the Chattanooga Symphony in 1982 but, it was explained later, the festival's business staff did not know or forgot to schedule joint rehearsals. Singer and symphony performed in sequence rather than together. This tragi-comic miscue now seems a symbol of that year's preceding and continuing ideological struggle between the "serious" performing arts and the "good time" entertainment arts, a dichotomy that some argued then and now should never have been necessary if the effort had qualified artistic direction from the beginning.

The May 5 proposal met with favorable reaction from the foundation. The organizing group, now four in number, met with the executive director and the foundation's consultant. It was decided to submit a planning grant proposal for approximately $25,000. This would include retaining the consultant to research a variety of arts festivals, to provide travel funds for local officials to visit Charleston's upcoming Spoleto Festival U.S.A., to prepare an audiovisual presentation to communicate the festival idea (which was not accomplished), and to provide funds for other consultants and expenses to generate broadbased community understanding and support for a major arts festival. (66)

After this was resolved, it was agreed to organize a nonprofit corporation, Friends of the Festival, Inc. Although a small legal expense for incorporating was set aside in the planning grant, four individuals then took it upon themselves as volunteers to shepherd this fledgling idea through its early and tentative steps. The rapidly expanding group represented a mixture of liberal and conservative views, artists and non-artists, politicians and businessmen, blacks and whites, old and new families, city and country, etc. Over the following months, these intentional individual differences were reflected in the debates, and the basic aesthetic philosophy of the initial festivals. (67)

From the theoretical perspective of an empty theatrical space, it appears in the May 5 proposal and in the planning grant proposal that the organizers confused the political function, which was necessary to open up a new space, with a more artistic function of filling a defined theatrical space. Yet the entire Chattanooga "mise-en-scéne" itself was a powerful framing device. In this proposal and others as well, the Charleston and Salzburg view of the "city as a stage"--albeit a "bare stage"--became a dominant frame, suggesting the actual "emptiness" of the physical Chattanooga city was itself deeply felt by the festival "dreamers" and others.

What appears in retrospect to have been intended as a participatory process of responding to an "empty space" was, not surprisingly to any but naive "dreamers" and "believers," a political process that soon discovered that the conceptual space was not a "bare stage." The May 5 proposal was written and edited by the group with a reasonable degree of awareness of what the foundation's goals were and of what its executive director had suggested be included. None of us had any illusions about the power of this newly active foundation, or of its intention to change the status quo in the city. (68)

Absence of an Artistic Director

A thematic, selective analysis that focuses attention on one or a few repeated concerns reflected in private documents, the available public record, and personal experience is valuable in illustrating the opening of ideological and physical space for such a new, different meaning and practice of "festival." From a chronological outline of recorded proposals and meetings leading up to the Riverbend Festival, and following it, one repetitive issue insists upon attention: the presence or absence of Guthrie's type of serious art and artists within a festival. This was a major issue in both the Charleston and Chattanooga productions. This is not a history and much must be left out of the study; however, the explanatory comments in the endnotes provide in part the context essential for understanding why certain steps were taken in 1980-81.

As noted previously, the need for an artistic director was included in the first document that outlined the philosophy and approach to a festival on May 5, 1981, when a $1,000,000 "Celebration of Togetherness" festival was proposed to a local foundation. (69) The ideological struggle between "art for a few" and "art for the many" began at this point. Some of the authors of this proposal argued that a few artists could put together a first class festival while others argued that input from many people was needed if Chattanooga were to have a successful town arts festival. This crucial issue was not resolved as late as 1988, when a comprehensive evaluation of the Riverbend Festival was conducted.

On June 30, the idea of **beginning** with an artistic director --a key symbol of aesthetic purposes--was actively resisted by the executive director of the foundation (by far the dominant foundation in the city, with assets of approximately one hundred million dollars at that time). The director specified in a letter to the initial four-person board of directors that "the hiring of an artistic director at this time would be a serious mistake." The letter said in part:

> As Sidney's list indicated, the desire to hire an artistic director is a priority for Friends of the Festival. Yet the actual discussion on that point centered around the Foundation's willingness or encouragement in having you approach other foundations to secure funds to hire that individual; that seems like a good step to take at the proper time. What I failed to address yesterday is my very strong opinion that the hiring of an artistic director at this time would be a serious mistake. I believe that two things, at least, must precede such a move. First, the planning and feasibility study must be completed and its recommendations and implications must be studied thoroughly. Second, but occurring simultaneously, it is imperative that the Board of Friends of the Festival be expanded, broadened and rather dramatically diversified.
>
> While it would appear that actions must begin now in order to ensure that a festival take place in 1982, we greatly prefer that your actions proceed on a logical and orderly basis which will ensure that a festival, once created, exists on an annual basis for a number of years. To touch all of the necessary bases properly might--or might not--take quite a while. (70)

The original idea of creating an artistic festival with a qualified artistic director, which was approved formally in November by seminar participants and consultants, had hit a solid barrier to its evolving "artistic" nature. To some in the group, "later" meant "too late." There seemed no alternative except to drop the search for an artistic director until funds as well as support were assured. It was as if the curtain fell before the play began. It seems logical that members of the group should have advised the foundation that the project was impossible without an artistic director's input at the very beginning of the creative process. But this was not done; it was a significant omission and error of judgment. (71)

Today the Riverbend Festival remains without an artistic director, except for the "blues" programing guidance of University of Tennessee at Chattanooga professor Russell Lindeman. It is under the management of the same business person, Bruce Storey, who produced the Lyndhurst "amenities" project in the summer of 1981, "Five Nights in Chattanooga." It now appears, even without taking into account private aspects of various individual actions, that what seemed to be at the time an inviting "bare stage" had a director, script, partial cast and scenery, and was more in need of an audience than creative participation.

Yet an actual civic "empty space" beckoned; enthusiasm was building; many agreed the city needed some celebration of itself. Almost any sound was better than the felt silence, almost any activity better than the obvious empty streets. The group accepted the constraints but continued the open process. The strength of this process and evidence of continued broad support for an artistic director is seen in the November 23, 1981 proposal's concluding paragraph:

> An artistic advisor will be selected immediately upon approval of the grant request. The exact role of the artistic director will depend, in part, upon the individual selected, but the artistic advisor will be involved in all artistic decisions for the festival.

However, when the formal grant contract with a $60,000 check was awarded on December 2 for a "Chattanooga Festival," the foundation made doubly certain of its intentions regarding artistic direction:

> [Description]: This grant is to be applied to the administrative costs of planning, organizing, and managing a Chattanooga Festival in 1982.
> [Special Conditions]: This grant is conditioned upon the hiring of an experienced promoter whose track record in local concert promotions is approved by the Foundation.

The cover letter also stipulated:

> Additionally, this grant is conditioned upon Friends of the Festival's employment as Project Director an individual whose experience, reputation and track record as a promoter of public events in Chattanooga is acceptable to the Foundation. (72)

The sponsoring foundation was determined not to fund an artistic position, which it "preferred" to be left to another foundation. It would fund only administrative costs of $60,000.

The aesthetic issue became critical after the full board was created. The festival's attorney, J. Nelson Irvine, advised the new president and executive committee in a memorandum on March 11, 1982, of the threat to the new organization's tax status if its artistic "context" was modified by excessively commercial objectives:

> I note reference to the statement by Sid Hetzler that the main thrust of the festival should be artistic rather than commercial. I think it is important for the members of the executive committee to understand that the tax exempt status of the organization is an organization to promote the arts. Thus, the purpose of the organization's activities is artistic. The commercial involvement is only incidental insofar as the accomplishment of promoting the arts in the community is concerned. I think this is something that has been understood all along, and I don't think it needs further discussion but I wanted to remind the members of the committee of this and the context in which this organization is operating.

No record of a reply to this legal advice was found.

The absence of an artistic director left the festival without its "force," driven only by its "empty space" and the power of its "idea"--two legs of a three-legged stool, more than a little wobbly without the presence of an imaginative artist. This absence led in curious directions; because arts knowledge was an essential festival ingredient, many experts had to be consulted to help educate interested local supporters about the idea.

The Element of Purpose: Festival Planning Seminars

Probably the festival founding process's most innovative activity were the July-August seminars arranged for the new festival board and prospective board members, persons who, regardless of their particular job titles, wealth, or beliefs, were thought by the four organizers to be receptive generally to new ideas. (73) Four seminars for the new Friends of the Festival group were held for approximately thirty interested persons. Festival experts from Baltimore, Boston, and New York spoke, and the process concluded with a goal-setting workshop and party. The seminars were open, and the group was encouraged when the county executive, the mayor, and several influential commissioners participated at the beginning and ending of the seminars.

All the seminar speakers stressed the importance of clarifying a festival's purposes. At the final session the group voted not to choose between a high arts and a popular festival, which was to prove a false opposition in theory and practice. The consultant's report, "The Making of the Festival," concluded that in America there were two types of festivals, "arts" and "urban":

> 1. Arts Festivals, a majority of which are strictly focused on music and created with the purpose of presenting unusual high-quality programs in an informal setting. They are usually designed to attract a broad local, national, and sometimes international audience;
>
> 2. Urban Festivals, which are created with broad grass-roots support and aimed at celebrating the ethnic,cultural and artistic heritage of the city.
>
> **These two forms are analyzed separately** [emphasis mine].

Here was one source of the warring ideologies of "arts" and "heritage" distinctions. By forcing the issue into "separate" category status, the fundamental flaw in the emerging creative process developed into a "this or that" series of choices. That is to say, the group was being asked to choose a category that was the "same" in either respect, a practice that did not embrace the possibility of "different" and even contrasting programming in the same festival. Although this was not the original idea proposed on May 5, in our uncertainty it seemed logical at the time to be asked to select a festival that was "all of one kind" aimed at either special musical offerings or local heritage. Eventually the seminar participants voted that there was no need to exclude and to be one exclusive type of festival. They decided the festival should be both popular and elitist, at times expressing dislike for the terms themselves and their connotations.(74)

The consultant's report on festivals in America was not as extensive as the organizers had hoped, but it did outline much that was not available to us in any other source. Its most significant feature was the classification of the purposes of an "arts" as opposed to an "urban" festival. This language reflected, among other matters, the foundation director's attitude that inhibited our search for an artistic director:

> At the onset of forming a new festival, the issue of an artistic director should be secondary to managerial and promotional aspects, unless one is readily available to the area. **The artistic director can come later to the scene, once the festival has established itself** [emphasis mine]. In the meantime, artistic decisions can be made by individuals drawn from the local community. (75)

This report confused most of the group, some of whom noted that it contradicted itself in several places, especially in its recommendations on artistic leadership, where the greatest need for direction and guidance was experienced. In the second section describing an "urban fair," which was the consultant's original idea, the report recommended:

> There are three seats of power in the management of festivals, the artistic director, the chairman and board directors, and the executive director.
> The artistic director of the music festival should be a natural choice, an individual with ties into the community and with the expertise to cover such a position. In the absence of a natural choice artistic advisors can be used. Selected from the community and/or outside, the artistic advisors will help in the formulation of the program and in the selection of the artists. **The advisors should be invited in the early stages of planning and should be selected to conform with the thematic requirements of the festival** [emphasis mine].

On the other hand, for an urban fair the report advised:

> Artistic direction is not a requirement for the urban festival. The sponsors may, however, want to keep a distance from the process of selecting performers and artists to avoid recriminations. This is normally done through the creation of a number of art committees each devoted to a specific art form. Selection of

programs can then be done through auditions and competitions.(76)

The impending emphasis on riverfront economic development, a natural evolution from this particular "empty space" that soon became nearly an exclusive focus (even the specific river-related name later adopted was suggested), was described in the study's emphasis on location as a theme:

> A theme should be derived from the objective of the Urban Festival and should reflect the natural attributes, personality and reputation of the city itself. Geographical features could play a great role in Chattanooga. The Riverbend Festival could be a celebration of the history of the community through the role played by the river and could focus on the existing unexploited potential of the river, and its recreational value. (77)

Spoleto Festival U.S.A. was selected as "the best example of this new generation of [arts] festivals." In the arts section, under the "purpose" category, the report explained:

> Economic and community considerations are today the two most important objectives set forth in the creation of new festivals.
> In the past, music festivals have been implemented for the fulfillment of the aesthetic and musical needs of small groups of musicians determined to look for new musical challenges and the enlargement of their professional boundaries. **It did not take long, however, for the people involved to discover their cultural and economic potential and the beneficial impact that festivals were having on the cities hosting them** [emphasis mine].
> Today, new festivals are designed and promoted to fully realize the economic potential and impact on the community. **The Spoleto Festival is probably the best example of this new generation of festivals** [emphasis mine]. Spoleto is strongly supported by the city leadership because of its boost to the tourism industry. Tourism is today Charleston's fastest growing industry....
> Gian Carlo Menotti and the other festival founders recognized from the beginning the essential importance of involving the tourism industry in the planning and promotion of the festival. Articles about Spoleto talk as much about Charleston as the festival.

Applying the intent, function, and effect concepts discussed in Chapter I, one can see in this report's premises about "art" the relationship of the difference in intent and effect, and a sense of how quickly the creations of artists can be exploited and appropriated. Yet Menotti created a festival for the joy of it, as a brief utopia for artists, as a haven for old and new world differences--not as a commercial Disneyworld of the arts. That Spoleto was cited by the foundation's own consultant as the best example of an American festival is a powerful comment on what should have evolved in Chattanooga but was inhibited.

But did it make any difference whether Menotti created a festival for the joy of it or solely to attract tourists? As Redden explained, in Charleston the original integrity of the artistic idea was preserved and all else was a consequence of a "serious" town arts festival, which can be an economic bonanza but as a by-product and not as a main goal.

Functions of the Riverbend Festival:
Embedded Meanings in Two Stories of Origin

The idea of embedded meanings suggests the "hidden functions" of festivals, which can be illustrated with two stories of Riverbend's several "true" stories of origin. One such meaning can be seen in an analysis of the downtown entertainment event, "Five Nights in Chattanooga," mentioned at the beginning of the Preface. Another is shown in an analysis of a alternative festival proposal from Doris Hays, a musician and composer who grew up in Chattanooga and now lives in New York City but who has not lost interest in the welfare of her Southern hometown.

During the mid-1981 planning and research for a festival, the Lyndhurst Foundation directly sponsored through the city an event called "Five Nights in Chattanooga." This was a series of free downtown concerts sponsored by the city and funded by the foundation, apparently at Longo's suggestion as an "urban animation" project he had developed for other cities. The $100,000 "musical gift to the city" drew an estimated several hundred thousand persons to the city's heart, a vacant parking lot, in the late afternoon and early evening over a period of five weeks. One stated purpose, according to the consultant's assistant, was to attract different types of people to each show and to persuade a diverse group to remain in or return to downtown to have a good time. Performers included blues singer B.B. King, Sarah Vaughn, Hank Williams Jr., a well-known bluegrass performer, and a rock group.

The public agenda of the concerts was to learn whether anyone would come in to the city at the end of the work day, when normally the central city is emptied by 6 p.m. The hidden agenda of "Five Nights in Chattanooga" was to see whether members of both "races"(78) could coexist in the same space and to what extent audiences would differ as the entertainers differed. Predictably, the "races" coexisted; predictably, too, audiences differed. In view of the city's past history, there was fear of racial violence. Also there was a desire to show other city leaders that this type activity was a positive model for festivals. No one knew what might happen when Chattanoogans of all categories of skin color, income groups, and ethnic and religious origin came together and were free to interact on a mass scale. In fact, the only fight reported or that I noticed was between two "black leather jacket" white men arguing about a woman accompanying one of them.

Five Nights was not presented as "carnival," but it had overtones of carnival in the popular sense, especially its "bread-and-circus" rationale. Its purpose, however, was completely that of the "power structure's" agenda for community change. The paranoia of certain leaders was not justified; this model of "festivalling" proved valuable in reducing fears of the "crowd." Yet it failed to show the extent and range of what the town arts festival can be and could accomplish. And it may have reinforced the arts "patron" system oriented to the donor's needs rather than to the desires of audiences and performers.

This "segregation by musical taste" approach continues in the Riverbend; each night is "sold" to a local corporation, which receives the advertising benefits from that evening and is named in the program. Five Nights had some positive effects in placing emphasis on the performing arts, and on the "music" form of "art" power to attract very large audiences and to create more community interaction in unused downtown space.

Yet this model may collapse of its own commercial weight as an advertising medium when the festival public park is converted into real estate projects, developments described in the August 1988 comprehensive study as having great impact on the festival's site. These real estate plans have become the primary goal of the festival. One local businessman, Jack McDonald, told me in 1986 he expected to make at least a million dollars from his investments in the riverfront area. With such an incentive he has been from the early years a strong supporter of the festival in organizing sales to employers of the inexpensive admission "pins." It "takes all kinds" to make a festival; however, it is doubtful the festival would have continued if McDonald had not developed our original idea of one pass for all events into the successful revenue source it has become.

The second story reveals the repression of an innovative artist's response to Chattanooga's empty but scenic spaces. At our request, the former Chattanoogan and internationally known musician Doris [Sorrel] Hays (79) offered her idea for a particularly imaginative type of arts festival, "Southern Voices."

Hays' provocative, but to some frightening, proposal briefly opened another kind of empty space where "differences" not only coexist but thrive. Her October proposal, had it been followed, would have led to a very different festival theater in which the work of artists would have been celebrated. Copies of this proposal were read by several in the group, but her ideas generally evoked fear of something foreign to community experience. Some urged support for her approach as a part of a festival, but without success. Also, no one knew how to produce "Southern Voices" without passing some degree of control to the artist; all knew by then the foundation's opposition to that direction.

The proposal's poetic quality evoked powerful images of originality seen in Charleston and Salzburg, images now part of the forgotten meanings of the "Southern Voices Festival." Key excerpts from the proposal (author's Riverbend files) indicate the power of the physical environment and the idea evoked:

> ...A Festival is a creature which needs to fit its habitat. And, since it is a creature we make, I think of what kind of creature will be nurtured by the locals--be supported by citizens and in return, full grown, give pleasure to those who make and support it. My creature Festival then, is one which has characteristics of the local scene. It sings. And how! This Festival, then, should always have a chance to sing! Hymn sings, sacred harp sings, blues sings, country music sings, gospel sings, massed chorus sings, special avant garde performance events sings (my kind of singing), orchestra-chorus sings. One of the first and strongest reasons to call this festival "Southern Voices."
>
> ...This festival-creature goes to all parts of the city as I see it-- to insurance companies and factories, to the courthouse lawn, to the river bridge, to the mountain parks, to the university campus, to the senior citizen center, and sings, too, with the people where they are. The creature not only sings, of course, it dances and rhymes and paints pretty pictures and makes marvelous, outlandish sculptures and reads outrageously wonderful poems. This festival is of the city and of the region, not laid on it from the outside. It has the accent of many voices of the region. It's not an adopted creature, but one born of the existing cultural institutions: a fifty-year-old orchestra, a vital opera company, and tons of

singers, lots of fiddlers, and more composers, writers, performers of all kinds than the majority of the population would know except for the festival celebrating their existence.

...Star performers come and go. They are naturally a part of this festival but the underpinning for that which is already there needs spotlight, aid, support, and moral uplift. Past and present, the existing, and that new to be added to it, all are part of this creature. The past in the form of a living mountain tradition, such as sacred harp and fiddling. The present in the form of commissioned art works.

...I see an armada of pleasure boats floating down from Lake Chickamauga, down the Tennessee River to congregate around a steam boat at the wharf by the bridge....

The Chattanooga "habitat" was not ready for this meaning, and its local poet, if not her prophetic vision of an armada of pleasure boats at the downtown bridges, was rejected. The ideological nature of the empty space already had been fixed, one in which artists were to be hired to move the city toward social and economic goals at its riverfront. A comparison between this and the original May 5 proposal shows how the work of the artist can be perceived as its own end, not as a means to an end external to the art work. (80)

Analysis of Riverbend Objectives

The information from consultants, trips, speakers, and other documents was summarized by a volunteer seminar member. (81) The most important elements in that report are its list of objectives, which can be seen in contrast to the purposes stated and implied by the Charleston and Salzburg models. Those original objectives, which were heatedly debated during the seminars and evaluation session, included the following:

1. show how arts projects can be self-supporting and add significant new arts events with minimum drain on existing business and charitable resources;
2. provide a varied series of high quality arts performances and activities in a festival setting;
3. serve as a cohesive force;
4. promote artistic activity and aesthetically pleasing events;
5. act to catalyze downtown and riverfront revitalization;

6. enhance benefits from tourism from the 1982 Knoxville World's Fair;

7. provide opportunities for various elements of the community to interact;

8. gain national publicity for the city and its fine arts support;

9. improve community self-image and help residents feel good about the city;

10. provide opportunities for central city business economic development;

11. showcase local fine arts performers and groups.

The foundation consultant's extensive report had urged the group to select between two choices, an urban fair or a music festival. The group rejected this binary proposal and voted to combine these types into one festival. The following analysis of these objectives suggests that the "arts" were gradually moved off the city stage while leaders pretended otherwise.

These written aims provide a beginning point in searching for a dominant meaning expressed by a festival and in creating a semiotic of festival. Written objectives, if they exist, are one valuable source of intended, if not received, meanings. These formal words define the intended nature of the "empty space" of a festival theater within the chronological sequence of actions by which a festival space is defined ideologically and physically.

The meanings of Chattanooga's new festival theatrical space were bounded by these statements that were a result of cooperative group action. These "texts" are productive for study because they reflect not an individual but a group vision of an imagined destination, a desired future state, a fantasy not yet reality, a dream of images to come, a wish to be fulfilled, hopes, values, purpose, expectations, intended results; in short, "future." They "reflect" the collective intentions of the particular social group, often thought of as the founders of the original festival idea.

Simultaneously, goal statements are "refracting" powerful institutional and individual ideologies, sources of funding, public and private interests. Taken as a whole, they represent highly compressed meaning symbols of the entire community of interests, not only the thoughts of those few who actually drafted the text but also of the image of the intended audience of financial and political supporters. Goal texts can be traced in their evolution over a period of years or they can be arranged through various schematic categories to bring out underlying functions that generate critical insight.

In 1984 or 1985, the above goals were "re-coded" under three headings: (1) to draw the community together (3,7,9); (2) to present the arts (11,2,4); and (3) to promote economic development (1, 5, 10, 8, 6). Only goal six, related to the Knoxville World's Fair was changed, although the central idea was retained, to read "To enhance tourism in Chattanooga." Using only key words, the new classification was:

> Draw the community together
>   Serve as cohesive force
>   Increase community interaction
>   Improve self-image; feel good about city
> Present the arts
>   Showcase local fine arts performers
>   Provide high quality arts performance in festival setting
>   Promote artistic activity
> Promote economic development
>   Demonstrate self-supporting arts projects
>   Avoid draining local business and charitable
>   resources
>   Catalyze downtown and riverfront revitalization
>   Promote central city business development
>   Gain national publicity for city and its fine arts
>   Enhance tourism

In the comprehensive 1988 evaluation of Riverbend, these three primary categories were unchanged. An appendix briefly summarized the objectives as used by the study team:

> To draw the community together by serving as a cohesive force for the Chattanooga community, by providing opportunities for the various elements of the community to interact, and by improving the city's self-image and helping residents to feel good about the city;
> To present the arts by providing a showcase for local fine arts performers and groups, by providing a varied series of high quality arts performances and activities in a Festival setting, and by promoting artistic activity and offering aesthetically pleasing events; and finally,
> To promote economic development by demonstrating ways in which arts projects can be self-supporting through innovative entrepreneurial efforts. And, as a result, to add significant new arts events for Chattanooga with a minimum drain on existing business and charitable resources; by acting as a catalyst for downtown and riverfront revitalization; by providing opportunities for economic development, particularly central city businesses; by achieving noteworthy national publicity for the city

and its activities in support of the fine arts; and by enhancing tourism in Chattanooga.

These objectives have remained largely unchanged in their actual wording since they were taken from the 1981 "Making of the Festival" study and incorporated into the final proposal for the Lyndhurst Foundation.

However, the 1988 evaluation recommended several additions that would "fine tune" these objectives: increase minority participation (lack of black involvement has been a major problem from the first days of the festival seminars), recognize the volunteer role, provide new opportunities for local performing artists and institutions at the festival, program the renovated Tivoli Theater and the proposed Bessie Smith Hall, work with the RiverCity development company and program events on the river before, during, and after developments are completed, help RiverCity educate and excite residents about specific projects such as the Tennessee Aquarium, assist RiverCity in marketing Chattanooga, package the Bessie Smith Jazz Strut for national television, balance attendance levels during the ten days of the festival, improve the comfort level of crowds by improving the site appearance, and by becoming actively involved in the process of planning the new Riverpark.

These additions, in light of the views advanced in this study, reflect the structural flaws of what is essentially the "heritage" festival dominated by the RiverCity Company and Lyndhurst Foundation. No mention is made of finding qualified artistic leadership at any point in the study. Only in contrast to a Spoleto Festival U.S.A. does the lack of such leadership become noticeable.

The festival's modified, three-part classification scheme resembles the first cut of a structural coding not unlike Propp's grid of functions in folktales. As with his folk tales, it is possible to arrange the categories so that elements in them illustrate other patterns, such as function, intent, and effect. Near the end of his analysis, Propp observed:

> The constancy of functions endures, permitting us to also introduce into our system those elements which become grouped around the functions. How does one create this system? The best method is to make up tables. (82)

Propp's "table of functions" are the actions of a tale, separated from who acts. The table resembles the Riverbend Festival's unintended but apparently necessary "reductionism" from eleven categories to three. These three objectives further abstracted and classified the "purpose," or "intentions," of the festival and defined the ideological boundaries of the imagined festival space.

Although the words were unchanged, this 1984 or 1985 realignment, upon closer scrutiny, reveals significant differences. For example, references to "art" and "artists" appear just as often, five times. But the original text refers to these terms in the first two, and in three of the first four, objectives. The first list ended by eventually mentioning fine arts "performers."

In the second version "social" functions come first, arts second, and the economy last. Two of the arts projects now fall under "economic development" rather than "presenting the arts." It can be concluded that the arts have a lowered priority in the second goal statement. This repetitive "element"--role of arts and artists -- "signifies" a changed view of the artist in the Riverbend Festival. Evidently that original "dream" was modified and the semiotic relationships of elements within the festival shifted positions. When the analysis moves from text to the context created by the objectives, several reasons for the changed function of the artist are suggested.

By 1988 it appears to have been recognized that local performing artists (no mention of visual artists) and institutions should be provided new opportunities at the festival. But there is no mention of the vital element--an artistic director or directors--that virtually every significant festival that respects the serious arts, which the Riverbend Festival objectives purport to do, includes.

The second list of objectives re-codes the "art" element, which was nearly one-half of the original eleven objectives. A defensible conclusion is that the festival's intended meaning has changed in this one aspect, the value of art and artists--not in simplistic terms of "art for art's sake" but in terms of the larger issue of the actual work of the artist in this community.

The separation of terms of purpose, function, and effect is one method of clarifying this re-coding of objectives and shifting of priorities. Language of purpose appears to be the concrete intellectual act that defines the particular character of any new empty space, a process observable within Chattanooga's well-documented making of its festival. Purposive terms describe the direction of a journey and not the mode of traveling or description of the expected destination. The following key terms were selected from both the original and revised list of objectives. Re-coded in the categorical grouping below, the terms reveal some underlying distinctions about the nature of this festival theater:

    Intent (purpose)
        draw together

present arts
  economic growth

Function (how)
  cohesive force
  elements interact
  performances
  festival setting
  catalyst

Effect (result)
  improve self-image
  feel good
  showcase artists
  artistic activity
  self-supporting arts
  revive downtown
  revive riverfront
  central city publicity
  enhance tourism

One conclusion from the positioning of the revised three categories is that a higher level of abstraction is needed to express the "purpose," or why the festival is desired, suggesting the possibility of unconscious drives not easily articulated. Second, the re-coded context modifies the original meanings, contradicting festival officials' recurring statements that the objectives were not changed, only the sequence. Third, most objectives reflect results, not process; to specify only effects is to risk unacceptable methods of achieving them. Fourth, the functions describe the "theatrical space" in which the journey is made without reference to intent or effect. Fifth, a chronological view of these unfolding events reveals the festival's shifting dominant purposes through repeated presence or absence of signifiers. Finally, if, as Bakhtin said, "every meaning will have its homecoming festival," which is a highly visual expression of the forms of meanings, then it is possible to ask: To what kind of home have the meanings of this festival come? Were they welcomed? Were they rejected? Why?

Riverbend: Meanings and Messages

For this study, the remainder of the story is anti-climatic. The officers and new board members assumed office in February and planning proceeded. The festival was held in August 1982. It was preceded by in-home chamber music fundraising events and by three concerts at the local baseball stadium. These included three expensive entertainment groups--the Beachboys, the Commodores, and Rick Springfield--and festival officials expected adequate profits to finance the actual festival at the riverfront. Springfield alone cost $65,000. Even with the efforts of professional promoters, the Riverbend went into its first actual festival with a $100,000 deficit. But the deficit bought an enthusiastic and excited community; the festival had been born and had taken its first step.

One indication of the general reaction to the Riverbend (and simultaneous Miller Park and Fort Wood festivals), even with its various difficulties and problems, came from an editorial by Pat Wilcox in the Chattanooga Times:

> After a week of music and fun, the Riverbend Festival is over, and Chattanooga can luxuriate in the afterglow of success. Sponsoring foundations and corporations, particularly the Krystal Co., took a bet on Chattanooga--and won. But the volunteers who spent countless hours planning and organizing the festival often worked against the odds of disbelief. Surveying the crowds of festival-goers, one such organizer recalled many requests for help turned down simply because "they didn't think this thing would ever happen." But happen it did--and in a big way. Over the weekend the Downtown Arts Festival and the Fort Wood neighborhood celebration added to the festive fair. Together, the crowds they drew brought all downtown to life. Congratulations are in order for the believers. They've made believers of a lot more folks--and that bodes well for next year.

"Next year" meant the festival would become ritual, repeating its magical time and space--and making more "believers"-- but believers in what ideas? The three festivals did not coincide again; such a "celebration of togetherness" was not desired by the various groups involved.

Like Gargantua, after its birth the Riverbend Festival grew, and grew, and grew, and appeared likely to outgrow its cradle. In 1987 nearly 100,000 persons gathered "down by the riverside" to hear the "Chicago" jazz group perform, where most of the huge crowd could enjoy the performance only from giant loudspeakers and videoscreens. The few dozen who gathered to hear three visiting chamber musicians at the new Miller Park open-air pavilion at noon and sunset strained to hear over the traffic noise. Riverbend officials could not put the musicians in any one of several nearby acoustic space because of "politics," the chamber music committee had been told at its first and only meeting several months before.

By 1986, the Riverbend Festival was shifting almost exclusively toward support of riverfront development tasks, as the 1988 evaluation confirmed--away from the original objectives. A rigidity had settled on the programming. There were no more premier works, such as a 1985 commissioned work for fiddle and orchestra by New England composer Marie Rhines, played on the river barge. The physical nature of the empty space is a critical element in the art of the festival. Sarah Vaughn had noted in a 1981 newspaper interview during "Five Nights" that "music is not an outdoor sport," suggesting that a proper acoustic space like the Tivoli Theater would have been far more appropriate for such a subtle combination of fiddle and orchestra. A year earlier, Rhines had been sponsored by the Lyndhurst Foundation as an artist-in-residence at Baylor School, a private college preparatory high school in Chattanooga. Rhines' work expressed her scholarly interest in fiddling and in Apalachian folk tunes pased down from the area's British musical heritage. After the Riverbend premier, apparently neither Rhines nor any other composer was invited to prepare new compositions. Later that year, another composer from Chattanooga asked the foundation for production support of a new work that possibly could have premiered at the Riverbend Festival. The Lyndhurst Foundation representative responded that it no longer funded such grants to artists (it does have a program of individual artist grants, "Lyndhurst Fellows," but applications are not accepted).

This added to the signs that the Riverbend and its primary sponsor finally had turned away from any attempt to follow Spoleto Festival U.S.A.'s "serious" programming that introduces the new, different, and unknown to the community. It was a complete reversal from the limited multi-arts efforts of the 1982 through 1985 programs. It could be written in May 1986:

> The community has not welcomed nor encouraged new ideas and ways of expressing them by its artists, whose existence seemingly serves to promote economic growth and attract new business. Our leaders talk of arts, not artists. The campaign slogan is a pitch for jobs, not joy. The pledge is for more of the same, not the new, the different, the stimulating. The "new" is not well received in Chattanooga, and it may be that the absence of community leaders, with a few exceptions, at these artistic events speaks eloquently....
>
> It is Sunday's announcement of the Riverbend Festival schedule that makes this "fear of the new" so clear--the

commercial artists, the motor boat races, the events that are fun and that sell pins but that say "more of the same" and "why bother" to some known or unknown artistic talent with a new, untested message or medium. Why does the Riverbend not merit a listing in the New York Times summer music festival section? What is nearly a million dollars buying for our town? It is an expensive summer "block party," to use one festival president's term. If a Rick Montague had the power six years ago to specify a "promoter" rather than an "artistic director" to shape the Riverbend Festival, then he also has the power to help foster a climate of innovation and support for the "new" sources of artistic energy without which communities stagnate and decline....(83)

The extreme range of favorable and unfavorable responses to these thoughts indicated that "negative" interpretations of a town festival can generate highly emotional reactions to what a Lyndhurst foundation official viewed as the city's "annual image-making set of activities" (see Preface, Slack article).

The 1988 comprehensive Riverbend evaluation, funded by the Lyndhurst Foundation, is outside the period of this study. From the perspective of an essential "empty space," the report noted that the economic development of the Riverfront Park where the festival is located would displace Riverbend for several years. Such self-destructive evolution of this commercial festival would be predictable, based on an idea of empty space that becomes filled and no longer functions as a theatrical empty space where the "new" can emerge, where the "different" has its first breath of life, where even conflicting "voices" can "sing" their songs and "play" their works. The $100,000 study reinforced the idea that concluded the discussion of Spoleto Festival U.S.A. and that is this work's thesis: difference embraces sameness but sameness rejects difference.

In summary, a broader context appropriate for a larger study would show the kind of urban "home" into which the evolving meanings of "festival" were invited in 1981, and would show specifically how the various civic forces underlying the festival bounded a newly constructed "empty space" in the organizers' collective thinking. A 1981 Allied Arts fund raising study contains detailed documentation of the thinking behind the move toward centralized control of the museum, symphony, opera, and other member organizations, an environment that opposed the idea of a festival at that time. The written corpus of material accessible for this study--that is, the contextual, ideological boundaries in which most debate and argument occurred--points toward the strong possibility that these meanings of "Riverbend" are a microcosm of meanings of the larger community and regional and national society. Although two different ideas of a festival had surfaced, one called fine arts or elitist and one called popular or social, in the final actual grant proposal the group had attempted to retain both elements. It is the Hays document that most vividly illustrates the difference in intended festival meanings, ranging from a social objective of "celebrating togetherness" to aesthetic aims of "celebrating the existence of local artists."

A broader conceptual framework is required to address these and similar issues. It rests on a Bakhtinian communication philosophy that fosters more multiple interpretations throughout the social communication process, where an idea of "differences" could "someday have its homecoming festival."

CHAPTER IV

TWO TOWNS, TWO FESTIVALS, MULTIPLE MEANINGS OF "FESTIVAL"

An "Arts" Festival-Creature Encounters its "Heritage" Habitat

Two contrasting ideas of festival frame the issues raised by the Charleston and Chattanooga festivals. These are found in the "difference" and "sameness" opposition, the "arts" and "heritage" purpose, the "open" and "closed" festival form. They can be seen in the following viewpoints generated by Chattanooga's experience with its festival:

> **Foundation President**: Cities and towns are holding heritage festivals--taking a new look, establishing community pride. The towns which "sell out" and follow a foreign culture without struggling to incorporate and assimilate that culture as a subset of its historical authenticity will become fractured, schitzophanic [sic]--rootless. (84)
>
> **Composer**: A Festival is a creature which needs to fit its habitat....My creature Festival then, is one which has characteristics of the local scene....The creature not only sings, of course; it dances and rhymes and paints pretty pictures and makes marvelous, outlandish sculptures and reads outrageously wonderful poems....It has the accent of many voices of the region.(85)

These views seemingly agree on the importance of the local nature of a festival, but they diverge on the degree of diversity tolerated within its "habitat." "Subcultures" quickly can become ethnic, religious, or class minority groups erased from a city's "authentic" dominant history. "Outrageously wonderful poems," which could become outrageous "full frontal nudity" in Martha Clarke's Miracle of Love in one of Charleston's public theaters during the 1986 Spoleto U.S.A., could in a Chattanooga become a censored production, which has been a recurring practice in the community's publicly-owned theaters. Charleston easily could be the town apparently charged by the foundation director quoted above with "selling out" and "following a foreign culture." The central point is that it is not the particular city or even "foreign culture" that is in question but any cultural practice "different" from the prevailing preferences of those individuals who control a community's resources and direction of change. The effect is that the community remains on the "same" course until "new" information from a more powerful source alters its direction and perceptions.

If Menotti and the NEA served as such a change agent for Charleston, then Charleston's festival provided this "new" information to Chattanooga individuals and town officials. The record shows that Charleston's Spoleto Festival U.S.A. set both a strong positive and negative example for the founders and organizers of Chattanooga's Riverbend Festival. Whether Charleston, as would be implied by the first view above, "sold out" to a "foreign culture" or successfully "assimilated" the Italian Spoleto festival is impossible to prove, if, in fact, that is the example the speaker had in mind. There is no evidence to indicate that Charleston has shown signs of becoming "fractured, schitzophrenic--rootless." However, if that actually is what happened, it seems a path associated with world fame and increasing urban wealth. If the term "schizophrenic" means "a state characterized by the coexistence of contradictory or incompatible elements" (Random House Dictionary, 2nd edition), then the view proposed earlier of the multi-functional dimensions of a festival of "diversity" as opposed to a single dimensional festival of "unity" is cast in bold relief.

In the foreword to Lyotard's *Postmodern Condition*, Frederic Jameson points out Gilles Deleuze's "influential celebration of schizophrenia" (in books like the *Anti-Oedipus*)." Later he also notes: "Lyotard's affiliations here would seem to be with the *Anti-Oedipus* of Gilles Deleuze and Félix Guattari, who also warned us, at the end of that work, that the schizophrenic ethic they proposed was not at all a revolutionary one, but a way of surviving under capitalism, producing fresh desires within the structural limits of the capitalist mode of production as such." (86)

There should be little doubt that festivals, like world's fairs, function as "desire machines," as Robert Segrest has written about the Chicago world's fair. (87) From this perspective, Montague's attack on the schizophrenic is predictable in that the "fractured" state of things would threaten "totality" and monological "historical authenticity." Such an environment obviously would reject Menotti's festival theater of differences and the avant garde. The result literally is monologue conquering dialogue, the great theme of diversity that concerned Bakhtin in all his works. That Charleston went against its "historical authenticity" makes its Spoleto Festival U.S.A. all the more improbable. The Riverbend example suggests "assimilation" of "subcultures" quickly becomes unintended "erasure of differences."

It is the issue of "sameness" versus "differences." To be specific, a claim is made for the positive value of the so-called "schizophrenic," coexisting, contradictory, incompatible elements in Hays' proposal. This idea was not tolerated by the ideological dominance of "historical authenticity" in the Chattanooga experience described. Neither idea should be carried to its logical extreme; it is the blend and balance that represents the artistry of both personal sanity and social progress, and in serious festivals where all these dynamics often are staged.

There are conflicting views about the influences behind Chattanooga's Riverbend Festival, but the available record indicates that when the city's leaders had the opportunity to benefit from the example of the National Endowment for the Arts' "gift" of an arts festival to the Southeast, and possibly to request similar support, an official of the Chattanooga-based Lyndhurst Foundation, however well-intentioned, deliberately used his foundation's enormous power to block the appointment of an urgently needed artistic director at the outset of the creative process.

It is definite that what became the Riverbend Festival "celebrated" few local artists and cultural organizations (a continuing criticism supported by the foundation's extensive 1988 analysis (88) of the festival). It appears the ideological divergences of the philosophies inherent in a "heritage" or "arts" festival, to use the simplest oppositions, proved substantial, leading in the first case to a festival of "sameness" and in the second case to a festival of "differences." Although there are important exceptions to such a stark opposition, the tale that is reflected in the Chattanooga story of "unity" stands in great contrast to the stories of Charleston's diversity as told by Stern, Wadsworth, Sturm, Redden, and Rawle. Their narratives reveal the considerably broader range of imaginative expressions of a festival's "place, ideal, and force."

Menotti's Logocracy

"Logodaedaly" gives a more precise sense of the idea for the complex cultural practice of "festival" contrasted in the examples of "difference" in Charleston and "sameness" in Chattanooga. The kindred entities of festival, carnival, and fair are a "logos," in the Greek sense of a combining form of discourse. The distinctive festival logos is "logodaedaly," a playing not only with words but also with other artificial and natural "signs." These can be any symbol or object, all "signs" in the Peircian sense, in close spatial and temporal proximity in which a public "festival" theater functions contextually to transform meanings. "Logodaedaly" expresses the festival's contextual logic of diversity, difference, juxtaposition, inversion, and opposition.

In the *Oxford English Dictionary* sense, a "logodaedalist" is an "inventor of words," or "signs," in the extended sense. From this view, Gian Carlo Menotti functions as a "logodaedalist" in the Spoleto festival productions. At festival time, he is head of a temporary state of "logocracy," or a "community or system of government in which words [signs] are the ruling powers" (OED). In Menotti's "logocracy" the space exists for free play, for randomness, for unexpected outcomes, from personal risk of exposure to the never-before-seen. Menotti's festival theater provides a model of "logodaedaly" where cultural and other differences are presented as "normal" within the wide range of diversity contained within the festival's time and space.

However, one other festival model provides a more fully developed expression of the practice of "logodaedaly" than has been observed in Menotti's Spoleto festivals. This is the Chautauqua Institution, founded in 1874 near Jamestown, New York.

Primary Function of a Festival: Chautauqua--Forum for Conflicting Views

One primary function of a festival of differences is to provide a forum for expression of conflicting social practices and opinions. After its first festival, during which a local politician set up a booth in the festival river park area, the Riverbend board voted against this practice. Yet at Charleston the opening ceremonies of Spoleto are an important occasion for political speeches from national, state, and local officials. This deliberate staging creates the festival's political "work" function, which is illustrated by one aspect of the Chautauqua Institution's programming policies.

The philosophy of Chautauqua provides a well-known example of a festival that encodes the idea of "logodaedaly." Any medium of communication has at least five basic functions: entertainment, information, persuasion, education, and profit-making. The balance and dominance of any one or several of these determines the particular nature of the medium and the characteristics of the channel, which influences the type of information flowing through it. Chautauqua stands alone in examples of the festival genre in representing a mixture of all these elements from its earliest days in the 1870s, when education dominated, to modern times, when entertainment dominates. It is its mixture of purposes that makes it unique among festival spaces. Chautauqua's 1987 conference week on the American Constitution invited persons of widely varying political persuasions to lecture and participate in debates and discussions; another week was devoted to American and Soviet issues with Soviet citizens participating.

Chautauqua's history and programming focus attention on this festival's philosophy of persuasion and entertainment. Was it designed to persuade participants to hold specific beliefs? Was and is that a deliberate purpose, as it was in the case of Riverbend? The original reasons for the institution's central purpose emerging at Chautauqua in 1874 becomes an important marker of its continuing "spirit." Lewis Miller, who had the original idea as early as 1871, explained the basic purpose in his 1888 opening night address:

> We are all one on these Grounds! No matter to what denomination you belong; no matter what creed, no matter to what political party of the country. You are welcome here, whether high or low. You can have a right to go anywhere you can get. And it is something like the sample-rooms, but not in a vulgar way. You know they go to this place, and they sample this and sample that a little, and then they take whatever they like, go home, and use what they want. And so here you are welcome to go about examining the various organizations and the various things introduced to you, taking such things as you want. **Believe just what you want to, what you please about them and take them with you or leave them here as you like** [emphasis mine]. And you are entirely welcome to all our good things at Chautauqua. (89)

"Believe just what you want to..."; this is not the spirit of a Riverbend, which offers such a narrow "sample" to its citizens. Chautauqua is closer to Spoleto in its ecumenical nature, but even Spoleto lacks such a deliberate, all-embracing dialogue.

The religious philosophy of Chautauqua is the key to decoding its meaning. On another occasion Miller explained the purposes and functions of the new activity:

> The original scheme was a Christian education resort which should change...from an evangelism idea to Christian development, when all phases of modern civilization should be made to give recognition to true Bible development, that modern civilization was Christian civilization. That pleasure, science, and all friends of true culture should go side by side with true religion. To develop such a scheme and give it the strength to gain a place

in the thoughts of the various phases of society, it requires the cooperation of the different denominations and educational interests. (90)

This was not an excluding fundamentalist doctrine but an embracing, accepting Christianity, "side by side" with pleasure, science, and culture. The shift in emphasis from "evangelism" to "development" meant acceptance and even encouragement of differences, of plurality of belief as opposed to adherence to a single "official" truth. Yet the Chautauqua "Experience," as many who visit there say, does not exclude rhetorical, persuasive religious doctrines that seek converts to their beliefs. The intent to persuade an audience not to believe in any one doctrine but to accept multiple "truths" is encoded in the idea of a festival of differences--"logodaedaly," a form of political tolerance beyond traditional liberal and conservative views. "Multilogue" suggests the sense of this idea.

The story of the six blind men touching and describing the elephant illustrates this point. The difference festival is an "elephant" in which some of the blind see a religious message, others see a political message, or others see nothing at all and simply enjoy the feel of the "creature." This theme of plurality, explored in Lyotard's *The Postmodern Condition*, is a central meaning of festivals that combine many diverse art forms and many opposing statements. This message contrasts with festivals that have a single theme, a single purpose, such as a "heritage" expression of a native culture.

Vincent's characterization of a Chautauqua lyceum as "a place, an ideal, a force" on a post card, which shows a large tent with open sides and a crowd of women in gowns and men in shirtsleeves, illustrates the many levels of interrelationships behind this particular festival's philosophy. These three concepts are interconnected in a multi-dimensional bond with the other triadic relationships discussed previously.

Vincent first viewed Chautauqua as a place, a necessary first category. Every festival has its place. As Bakhtin said, "Every meaning will someday have its homecoming festival." A festival requires its homecoming "place," a specific and material location or physical address that is a major part of the visible expression of the festival idea. (91)

Vincent's second quality was an "ideal." In what ways does a festival, particularly such a mature institution as Chautauqua, represent an ideal, or set of ideals? The ideal is expressed in the unattainable dream-vision. The purposes, goals, or intentions of the original dreamers always fall short of the visible reality. The ideal, then, is that which the festival expresses in its choices of artistic directors, programming, audience, place, and other physical devices. One such device, very similar in function if not in intent to the Riverbend Festival's practice, was present from Chautauqua's beginning:

> The gate ticket, one of the unique aspects of Chautauqua, originated at the very first Assembly in 1874 when it was decided to charge an entry fee rather than take frequent collections at lectures, classes or services. This fee was referred to as a form of tuition, representing each person's share of the expense which is necessary in maintaining an educational program.
> The gate ticket entitles the holder to hear concerts, lectures, other performances and services in the Amphitheater, numerous other religious services, recitals, arts exhibits and programs; to enjoy beach facilities, library privileges and agreeable fellowship with people of congenial tastes.
> It is true that operas and theatre productions... require extra payment for which reserved seating is required...people from outside the gates who have purchased opera or play tickets and intend to come for these performances only, are not required to pay the usual evening gate fee....
> The atmosphere of quiet enjoyment on the Grounds, one of its other unique characteristics, is almost completely the result of the gate-fence arrangement.
> For the most part, the people one sees on the Grounds are those who have chosen to come for the specific enjoyment of the place, school or program. It is assumed that anyone with a gate ticket automatically becomes in his own way that special type of person known as a Chautauquan. Among these people the Chautauqua experiences strike up a strong bond winter or summer.
> **If there is any one characteristic that these Chautauquans have in common, it probably is the inquiring mind. All sides of public questions are open to discussion on the Chautauqua platform and tolerance of differing viewpoints is practiced as part of Chautauqua's tradition** [emphasis mine]. (92)

In this account can be seen the same spirit of acceptance for both difference and sameness apparently present from the moment Lewis Miller imagined such an "idea" and found such a "place." Such innovative social thinking was part of Miller's daily life; not only was he a successful businessman and inventor of farm machinery but he was also the father-in-law of Thomas Edison.

The third category is "force." A "force" is that which "connects" ideas in a "viewing" place--a theatrical space. Its physical devices, such as the "gate ticket" or "pin," can be both "connecting" and "separating" in their aesthetic, tension-creating functions if not in their aims. The devices of art are seldom calming and soothing and completely satisfying. It is in the alteration between tension and relaxation, between centripetal and centrifugal pulls, that much of the driving force in arts forms is situated. A force is an unseen agent, a mystery, something driving the ideas that created the Chautauqua communities, generally known as "assemblies," or gatherings of both like and unlike viewpoints. Binding these gatherings is a "force," which can be spiritual, an unseen presence; it also can be used in the sense of the "force of life." It is expressed as well in the festival ideal and its place, all three interconnected, intertwined elements.

One example of the abstract nature, yet tangible power of "force," in the sense Vincent probably intended, was noticed in 1987 while returning from Chautauqua through the state of West Virginia. Three crosses were standing on a small, steep hilltop. Two smaller crosses on either side of a large one were painted white; the center cross, left unpainted, was much taller. Three crosses on a hilltop: the place, the isolated hilltop; the ideal, a good teacher crucified and the two evil thieves gathered in common bond; the unseen force, that symbol's power in that space with no other artificial signs, framed and set off by the surrounding green mountain and other small hills. The force is those ideas associated with Christ's death. (93) These ideas were the Chautauqua Institution's primary reason for existence; that is, to teach Sunday School teachers more interesting ways of teaching. Underlying this motivation was a questioning of the old methods, a willingness to search for new means of envisioning ideas and teaching the old meanings, which, as Bakhtin said, are not "absolutely dead."(94)

This is a basic idea of a festival's force, that important things can happen when people of different views and persuasions choose to assemble together in their common as well as opposing interests. It is a force of making believe, found within the theater, that surges back and forth like an electrical arc, and literally carries the idea between audiences and artists. Within this metaphor of force is found the particular power of the festival medium for the exchange of information, a medium functionally different from the traditional church sanctuary, a semiotic device where also, as Peirce said, one person may catch another person's idea (see Preface, endnote five).

The festival's message primarily is its physical structure. In a traditional "one-to-many" Sunday School communication model, which Chautauqua's founders placed in question, there is no participation arrangement, no circular seating, and little chance to discuss, to react, to view other group members. The arrangement is that of the shepherd and sheep, leader and followers, the hierarchical "I know" of the teacher/minister who "knows" addressing those who "know not," the "one who sees" and "those who do not see." The festival form not only inverts this ordering of power relations but rather "scrambles" the meaning of traditional physical structures. Potentially the festival's material environment can provide in varying degrees helical and even random processes for social interaction. The Chautauqua amphitheater, open on three sides and essentially circular in its rows of seats, represents such a new ordering of power relations; the lyceum tent on the postcard replicates this pattern. This formal/informal, official/unofficial ordering of physical elements functions as opposing statements, which represent a functional "spatial code" juxtaposed within the meaning-making signification system.

Even in those festivals, such as Ravinia, Tanglewood, or Artpark (Lewiston, New York), where the "indoor" arrangement is similar to the church sanctuary in its order of relationships and hierarchy of those closer to the "one," an informal area surrounds this formal space. One common pattern of the indoor/outdoor venue is the use of space at Chicago's Ravinia Festival, where seats are sold inside the enclosed area while, picnickers on the grass surround the pavilion. This model of inside order versus outside disorder, of privately owned property in the form of reserved seats versus communal property, can be regarded as a semiotic model displaying the dominant group's desired order of relationships. One "pays" more for proximity to the "live" sound source, which is also broadcast over loudspeakers to the picnic grounds. The model represents a "correct" economic and social hierarchy, such as "in/out" institutional arrangements. Its visual ordering becomes the inherent power of the festival in making meaning. The folk, rock, and political festivals of the 1960s, such as Woodstock, had an entirely different spatial nature. It may be that analyses of a wide range of festivals will indicate not only the manner but also the extent to which major arts festivals represent their communities on a larger scale--and in the aggregate the nature of their societies in which they are born and nurtured. The extent to which participants receive embedded messages, or meanings, is extremely difficult to ascertain. However, where a record of negative or positive response to changes in long-standing festival practices exists, then inferences could be made of the degree of meaningful significance attributed by audiences.

Bakhtin's relationships of meaning, homecoming, and festival correspond to Vincent's three elements. "Every meaning," as Bakhtin put it, implying undiscovered meanings, will be expressed in its own festival as a "homecoming," implying a final destination, a relaxation of interpretation. Various meanings can be inferred from festivals by searching for particular signs, especially the repetition of these signs in their infinite forms and masks, that compose an index for their ideals and driving forces.

Festivals express various differences, as the director of "Artpark" suggested in noting that the difficulty [and the pleasure] of studying festivals is that no two are alike. The source of this difference is the form of difference itself encoded in the festival structure. New meanings, then, as Bakhtin's statement suggests, can emerge at some point through a festival format, or can be inhibited by a distorted form. This suggests an as yet uncertain understanding about how festivals might function as one of the devices that humans have invented to make meaning and to sustain and change beliefs, or to block new meanings.

The primary claim has been that "we believe that make- believe makes belief." In other words, the leaders of the festival believe there is a cause and effect relationship between the festival and their intentions. It is not necessary to provide "evidence" that the festival theater actually does make a belief of any kind. What is important is to establish that there is a expectation in the minds of the founders, the managers, the board, and those who participate in many ways that festivals will create beliefs of some kind in the minds of participants.

There is no certain way of proving that this happens, although opinion survey techniques are readily available for approximating ranges of attitudes and beliefs. The only thing that can be certain is intent: the verbal expression of a belief in the power of this theater in the form of a "festival" and in the political effect of the dramatic and performing arts subtexts that are contained. In this sense, the performances, the programming, the number of events, the type of events have to be looked at as subtexts to the overall text of the festival. Surrounding the festival is its context--the community, the urban environment, the geographic environment in which it is located. Context and subtext shift in their meaning; they vary from a literal spatial geographic location to a set of symbolic relationships and signs and markers that define the physical boundaries to the subtexts that are located in various enclosures or containers and relate in some specific ways to the central ideas of the festival.

Comparative Categories

Comparative studies are needed to determine the obvious as well as subtle differences in the major arts festivals of the day and their functions performed. A table of such a comparison of the Charleston and Chattanooga festivals, based on many of the points presented in the preceding chapters, suggests a variety of potential conceptual categories, in addition to the three selected for consideration in this analysis. Very few similarities can be noticed (through 1988):

Category	Charleston	Chattanooga
Sector influence:	Public	Private
Leadership:	Strong mayor	Weak mayor
City Hall role:	Active	Passive
Funding:	More tax	Few tax dollars
Revenues:	Seat tickets	Outdoor, pins
Commercial ads:	Low visibility	High visibility
Primary goal:	Energize city w/arts	Cohesiveness
Origination:	External	Internal
Previous festivals:	None	A few efforts
Resistance:	Private, failed	Private, failed
Defense of festival:	Mayor, college pres.	Foundation
Location:	Multiple	Primarily single
Crowds:	None, last day 6,000	Up to 100,000
Programming	Comprehensive, new, classical avant-garde	Popular, rock, country, some classical
Set formula:	Yes in 1988	0 in 1988
Artistic emphasis:	Yes	0
Artistic Director:	Yes	0
Federal funding:	Yes	0
State funding:	Yes	0
Primary funding:	Tickets, grants	Advertisements, pins, donations
Emphasis:	New art work	Fun, interaction
Tourism:	High priority	Low priority
International:	Yes	0
Popular music role:	Balance offerings	Attract crowds
Critics reaction:	Extremely important	Disregarded
Key effect desired:	Aesthetic	Social, Economic
Replace key person:	Difficult	0

Overall purpose:	Artistic excellence	Riverfront boost
Source of vision:	Gian Carlo Menotti	Conflicting
Est. 1988 budget:	$4 million	$1.6 million
Policy dominance:	Board, artistic dir.	Board, foundation
Arts dominance:	Performing	Performing
Other art forms:	All	Token of types
Chamber music:	Major; sponsored	Minor
Acoustic theaters:	Yes	No
History written:	0	0
Symbol of town:	Yes	Yes
Future changes:	Artistic leadership	New locations
Previous model:	Spoleto, Italy	Spoleto U.S.A.
Poster type:	Different each year	Basically same

Several categories merit special notice: **posters, revenue devices, programs, and theatrical spaces**. Although all the elements listed above are meaningful, these four possess a "defining" character by the extent to which they compress meanings and function simultaneously as iconic, indexical, and symbolic signs.

The "poster" category generated the greatest contrast of meanings between Spoleto Festival U.S.A. and the Riverbend Festival. Differences in the two cities' festival poster philosophy signify a dramatic example of the meaning intended by difference and sameness in these two festivals. On the wall of the Riverbend office in 1988 were all the posters from the beginning--all a similar basic graphic design of stars and sweeping curves, somewhat modified each year but constant in their graphic symbolism of "sameness." It was not until 1989 that a new poster theme of mountain and river evolved.

Spoleto Festival U.S.A., on the other hand, has had a different artist each year, an artist of international reputation, create a poster. Most have been nonrepresentational, and no two are alike except that they are all different and unpredictable. An exhibition of works of the chosen artist is presented during each festival in Charleston's fine arts museum. No other element signifies the idea of diversity more vividly than this. It is not that the Riverbend posters are unattractive; rather that until 1989 they were predictable and unlikely to differ, a significant variation from the spirit of differences found in typical festival practice. It is highly probable; however, that with the graphic pattern now broken, a continuing variation of the mountain and river symbolism could evolve toward original art works that express the uniqueness of the Chattanooga topography as well as the focus on riverfront development.

A second key signifier is the "token for admission to the magical space," which, if it were a device in a folktale, might have been Propp's way of describing the Riverbend pin's function. The Riverbend office has all the pins, and the varieties of official pins, from their first use in the 1983 festival, mounted on an inner office wall. About one-half of the mounting board is filled, leaving room for many years of pins. The pins also are virtually the same, somewhat modified so they can not be used again, but lacking any sign of imaginative design.

This pin collection, like the poster collection, represents an idea of festival dramatically different from the Spoleto pin that "pilgrims" purchase in the Dock Street Theater lobby as a reminder of the Charleston festival experience. This 1988 pin has a metal treble clef signature sign over the Spoleto name; it is an interesting piece of "art."

The Riverbend pin is the most significant signifier in this very complex semiotic web. It is the device by which an increasingly important percentage of the budget is being exploited for psychological effect. When the organizers were discussing alternative methods for financing the festival, they were confronted with a short-term as well as a three-year deadline on funding assistance from the Lyndhurst Foundation. It did not seem fair to begin something with no more than slight hope of its continuation if no more grant money were available. They searched for an alternative to the model of the expensive, limited seating observed in the examples of Charleston and Salzburg.

While we were searching in 1981 for alternative revenue sources, it occurred to me that in an outdoor festival one has a basically unlimited commodity in that the same product, seats--places for viewing--can be sold again and again in varying densities during a festival of several days. With aggressive marketing, a ticket card for the entire period could be sold for perhaps $10 to a hundred thousand people. This could create a budget of a million dollars, and much innovative, original work in indoor and unique venues could be fostered without dependence on the unpredictable whims of wealthy patrons or advertising.

This idea was not accepted by the organizers the first year, although considerable private discussion was held concerning the concept and its implications. However, the second year the new board decided to sell plastic lapel pins for approximately $5 each. The remarkable nature of that choice is that these were not placed in every possible outlet for sale. The board, led by a former conservative politician and successful businessman, (95) decided to persuade local companies to buy quantities of these pins at a reduced rate. These employers, as a good will gesture, could in turn donate the pins to their employees or sell them at a reduced rate. According to the announcement in the May 24, 1986, Chattanooga Times: "Promoters, announcing the schedule for this year's riverfront festival has been finalized, said more than 300 Chattanooga-area companies are expected to purchase admission pins for employees before corporate sales end May 29."

What Chattanooga had was a potentially free and open semiotic entity once again captured by the "patron" approach to the arts, as opposed to a "consumer" arts orientation. The Riverbend "pin" is a prime symbol of the "deep structure" Southern plantation mentality that retains control of the workforce. No more powerful signifier of the ordering of social relationships exists than the three-starred plastic pins that grateful employees wear to the ten-day festival. (96)

The donation of pins by employers to Chattanooga festival goers can be seen as an aesthetically repressive device in its effects if not in its intentions. If point-of-purchase pin containers, similar to the cardboard holders seen in supermarkets, were located in the many purchasing locations throughout the community and region, revenues could double or triple the festival's budget. Possibly the festival would not have required heavy commercial advertising, foundation funding, or even tax dollars. The additional income could extend Riverbend's time by several weeks or even months as in some summer-long festivals. It could generate several million dollars flowing through the community, a significant economic multiplier effect greater than those mentioned by Colin Sturm.

This is the effect that could create more work for artists, if the festival sponsors and leaders were interested in attaining that objective. Yet the solution of one problem often creates new problems; careful research in simultaneous scheduling should be conducted before such a policy is undertaken. Excessive attendance at some events would be one danger, as has occurred at one Riverbend Festival during the Pointer Sisters' appearance, which was attended by a crowd estimated at 50,000 in a fenced area much too small for safety. The area was enlarged after that episode.

Third, the cover of Riverbend's first program pictured the fantasy of local sculptor James Collins, an "air" sculpture called "Confetti Fingers." Its helium-filled slender balloon fingers swirled and gyrated hundreds of feet above the riverfront festival site--like an open hand welcoming everything in the universe--waiting to be cut loose at the final ceremonies. Fearing a flight safety hazard, the Federal Aviation Authority refused permission for it be cut from its moorings and let loose into the sky, and no amount of persuading would change their ruling. "Confetti Fingers," like later Riverbends, did not "fly," but, as often happened, the organizers turned another problem into an opportunity. The giant air sculpture was cut up into pieces for children to carry home as reminders of the first Riverbend.

After that theatrical chimera that was the first Riverbend, the spirit of aesthetic risk-taking diminished, although belief in the power of the festival to achieve commercial effects increased. Recent Riverbends have included little of that exciting first year--no experimental sculpture, new drama, original ballet, film festivals, juried arts exhibits, or related fringe activities. The last original musical composition apparently was in 1985.

Fourth, the spatial arrangements of "theatrical" spaces are semiotic "markers" that differentiate Charleston's and Chattanooga's festival philosophies. After its first year, Chattanooga's Riverbend expanded its activities to include motorboat races on the river (against strong objections by several of the original organizers). Any popular event, such as a triathlon and charity runs, could be included under the Riverbend sponsorship umbrella if it promoted riverfront development.

From the beginning, this focus on the riverfront took a peculiar course. The first year the symphony played several water theme compositions (such as Handel's "Water Music") for the tired spectators waiting on the final night to hear pop singer Roberta Flack. The orchestra, however, was located about 50 feet away from the nearest listener, on a barge tied to the riverpark bank, and the audience could not hear the mostly soft music because of a failed sound system. Another event proposed by horse lovers in 1983 was a three-day event: equitation, cross-country, and stadium jumping. This was rejected because there was no room for it at the river park site and because it would "diffuse" the riverfront focus. That was the same argument several leaders of the traditional arts establishment had used against having the festival when the idea first surfaced the previous spring.

Meaning through spatial arrangement, therefore, is communicated on a variety of levels in these festivals and the multi-sensory models of relationships that they present to participants. To participate with an audience of 100,000 jammed and packed into the relatively small space at the Riverfront Park is to feel the crowd, the diminishment of the individual. To be in a small acoustic space, such as the Charleston's Dock Street Theater or Chattanooga's Tivoli Theater lobby or Chattanooga Choo Choo convention theater entrance hall, with a chamber quartet playing classical or jazz music, is to be in intimate contact with the artists and other members of the audience. Such use of space is a "world" of "difference."

Retrospective

Chattanooga's festival is young by the standards of significant town festivals. It grew out of the private leadership's belief in an organic "heritage" versus an imported "arts" festival in a narrow logic that concluded the city's town festival should be no more than what local people could create or buy. What happened from the original vision of the Riverbend Festival to its evolvement over seven years was that a formula of popular entertainers on each night, much like the Five Nights event, had been found successful in drawing massive crowds to the riverfront, where intense economic development was planned by investors. This created a commercial medium for advertisers and sponsors. It met the goals of commercial development for individual property owners while neglecting other aesthetic possibilities.

In contrast with Charleston and Salzburg, which certainly experienced increased property values, Chattanooga's festival practice represents an excessive subordination of arts and artists to the needs of industrial development. The international festival models that could have been expected, on a smaller scale, to open up Chattanooga to change, and to a climate in which new forms of art would be welcomed and encouraged, were lost in the "rush to the bank" in an overemphasis on the commercial objective originally set forth. The lack of an artistic director to offset these natural capitalistic tendencies to focus on financial growth, given the market-creating power of the festival medium, can be offered as one explanation. At a deeper structural level is an exploitative pattern of the way in which the arts and artists are regarded in this and probably other similar communities.

In Chattanooga, the work of the artist--instead of being respected as an end, a peak of human achievement, a pinnacle of success for civilization--is regarded as a means to the ends of the business structure. It is expected that the presence of a local ballet company, for example, will help bring a Japanese bulldozer manufacturer, such as Komatsu, to town. Apparently, it is not in the community leadership's consciousness or awareness that, if a Japanese bulldozer firm, or any other new business, opens a manufacturing plant in the city, then the added human and financial resources could contribute to more and better ballet. That is to say, Chattanooga's current leaders believe in ballet for bulldozers, not bulldozers for ballet; music for money, not money for music; art for work, not work for art. The present conception of the Riverbend Festival may very well be a necessary stage through which a town arts festival passes, although the example of Charleston suggests otherwise if visionary outside intervention occurs and if a broader view of art and artists is presented to the community by its public and private leaders.

A festival's function as a distorting mirror in times past, and now in modern towns and cities, can be paramount if not consciously checked and guarded against. One justified fear is that the current model of the arts that Riverbend now represents in relationship to the community is unlikely to receive any further innovative direction or restructuring without the presence of an influential and strong artistic director along with a board more sensitive to broader aspects of a town arts festival. However, there continue to be within the festival, depending on one's viewpoint, small signs of new growth, or tokenism, such as the continuing chamber music series that receives modest funding (it lacked a commercial sponsor in 1988). Such "seeds" from Charleston's festival of differences remain within Chattanooga's festival, waiting for a nurturing environment.

Restatement of Claims: Intent, Function, Effect

This comparison of the origins of these two contemporary town festivals suggests their opposing central ideas, essential natures, and primary functions and meanings. It summarizes the broader basis of this study's two aims, the discovery of key elements and functions in the two festivals:

> If several key elements of these two festivals are identified sufficiently, and if their basic social and political functioning appears reasonably clear, then the limited aims of this dissertation will have been realized.

The principal claim is that:

> We shape our festivals; thereafter our festivals shape us. The festival provides a model for accepting differences in life; we learn to tolerate as normal the great range of diversity contained within a festival's time and space, where the new and different are made visible.

Neither ethnography nor history, the study was designed as a selective theoretical interpretation of the significance of embedded meanings in these festivals' untold stories of origin. These stories were used to search for the fundamental idea that emerged from each festival's multiple contexts, which were reflected indirectly in their "stories of origin."

The specific descriptions of the genesis of these two festivals pointed toward two specific types--a Spoleto "arts" form and a Riverbend "heritage" form. These two forms were claimed to represent examples, respectively, of "difference" and "sameness" in the discursive practice of festival. No claim was made about the application of this concept to other festivals, although the intent, functions, and effect methodology could be useful in an extended study of the Charleston and Chattanooga festivals as well as in the analysis of other festivals and similar cultural practices.

This view of difference and sameness was generated by inferences from three major categories of thought around which the Spoleto and Riverbend chapters were organized. These were the three elements mentioned in an earlier quotation from John Heyl Vincent, the Chautauqua Institution's founder: "Chautauqua is a place, an ideal, and a force." Equivalent terms suggested by the research for these categories were: empty space, purpose, and artistic director.

By separating various claims previously advanced into the categories of intent, function, and effect, a triadic template of the inseparable elements of the nature of "festival" can be viewed as functioning as an initial "semiotic template" (97) of this ancient cultural practice. These claims evolve from the materials reviewed in the Spoleto and Riverbend festival chapters and appendix. They also are reinforced by the additional material briefly presented in this concluding chapter. No doubt they will require modification in an extended study of other festivals (as is suggested by the Black Mountain Festival example mentioned briefly in the Preface).

Intentions:
> 1. The intentions of a festival's creators create an essentially theatrical genre of artistic multi-functional structures composed of context, text, and subtext, "artistic" in terms of the medium and effect if not always in terms of intention.
> 2. Festivals are a form of "meaning-making" theater in a bounded space or spaces, which define the type of festival just as the shape of the stage has defined various types of theater.
> 3. The modern festival has evolved into a Brechtian theater that is a "socio-political...effort to oppose and change actual social reality" (Reiss).
> 4. The founders' intentions shape a signifying practice with a clear "unity of action," where the essential structural logic

springs from the degree of the presence or absence of textual differences.

Functions:
1. The festival in general can be viewed as a special art form similar to the traditional structures of the separate performance arts, such as opera, symphony, dance, film, drama, and poetry, but operating with a distinctively different logic that embraces and enhances these genres and also other forms.
2. The possibility of "merry-making," or humans-at-play (homo ludens, Huizinga and Pieper), is a recurring pattern associated with festivals, suggesting that "play," albeit "serious play," and "pleasure" as a broader gratification of the "audience," may emerge as an overlooked function of a festival; however, these two examples do not support such a thesis.
3. Festivals can be viewed as overcoded entities on the threshold between convention and innovation, an unrecognized rule-making operation simultaneously indexical, iconic, and symbolic that allows the social exchange of signs (Eco).
4. The more closed to differences, to variety in performances and activities, then the less the event functions as a festival in the historic sense of the term and the less likely the event is to be labeled a "festival."
5. The festival's ideological and physical space itself functions as a type of "liminal time and space," that is, a social practice existing as an empty space, or gap or overlap among the network of formal institutions and social structures.
6. The festival "operates," or, "functions," whether consciously intended or not by its creators and administrators, as a "container of signifiers" from which the traditional "unity of action," is often absent at the programming "textual" level but appears upon careful examination to be present in the contextual frame.
7. "Serious" festivals are a special type of theatrical time and space where the "new and different" are made visible as during a "pilgrimage."
8. The presence or absence of voices of "difference" now appears to be the key code determining when a social practice is named a "festival."

9. A festival's contextual framing function is its "open" rather than "closed" structure, a characteristic that allows for a multiplicity of signifiers and codes to co-exist.

10. The primary conclusion is: "We shape our festivals; thereafter they shape us." The social theaters we imagine from empty spaces and design from bare festival stages reflect our view of the proper order of things in a manner much like the Renaissance festivals discussed by Strong and Orgel; the festival refracts this order though its contextual frame.

Effects:

1. The festival ordinarily is seen as a collection of discrete performances but, when a larger contextual aesthetic logic is assumed in which the textual elements are juxtaposed, this theater can lead to a new interpretation of social and political meanings.

2. At certain historical moments the artist is endowed with the power of awakening, quickening, and actually forming forces which constitute the local and national identity (Hadamovsky).

3. The festival theater can be seen as a deliberate framing device in which not only context, or "circumstance," but also texts and subtexts are in artistic free play where participating spectators are "addressees" in potential opposition to "senders" (sponsors and performers) in a dramatic "semiotic guerilla war" in the time and space of the festival (Eco).

4. A festival's "multi-functionality" can be a time and space for play with no other purpose (Pieper).

5. A view of "homo ludens," "humans at play," (Huizinga) as yet has no place in this general construction of a political theater that appears to generate its effects from a Darwinian "theater of power."

6. Festivals, as places for openness, conflict, and play, represent unique art forms that not only mirror their world but with little public notice shape its course.

7. Contemporary festivals appear to provide state, corporation, university, and church with an "encyclopedia of universally understood symbols" that compose the contemporary American city festival's "mise-en-scéne" and actively "promote" civic "rulers" wishes and desires.

8. "Contexts" can be the product of the artistic imagination as much as "texts."

Neither laws nor causes, and readily classified in more than one category, these claims are patterns of association that suggest three aspects of a festival's basic nature:

> 1. A festival is the deliberate creation of an artistic text that works within its physical and ideological context to contain contradictory, disparate, opposing, and even warring elements--a primary source of the tension and excitement associated with the idea of festivals.
> 2. A festival could be the general historical class of which theater is a sub-genre, although no festival theory yet exists to support this claim.
> 3. The festival as a communication medium suggests the possibility of a conceptual shift from a one-to-many, linear, ethnocentric sender/receiver communication model to a many-to-many, helical, multi-dimensional, contextual reception/response model.

Four Conclusions: Festivals' Shaping of "Reality," Openness, Conflict, Play

The concluding words of Roy Strong in *Art and Power: Renaissance Festivals 1450-1650* frame the long-range research goal for those interested in the shaping process of societies:

> Few subjects have suffered so much from the modern compartmentalisation of knowledge as festivals. It has fallen between so many stools, those of the historian of art, literature, ideas and political history....[Earlier studies] remain collections of particular events looked at in isolation and as an attempt to establish the subject as a coherent discipline may be said to be a failure. One emerges with no overall picture as to what this stupendous development was. Perhaps the study of festivals can never by its very nature be a coherent discipline without distortion. I opened this book with one modest objective: to make real to the reader Ménestrier's statement that such festivals were `Allegories de l'Estat des temps'. I close in the hope that he by now knows precisely what Ménestrier meant by that definition of what was a unique alliance of art and power in the creation of the modern State. (98)

Yet festivals function as more than an allegory of the times in their intended or unintended function of shaping of social reality. The social theaters we imagine from empty spaces and design from bare festival stages reflect our view of the proper order of things in a manner much like the Renaissance festivals discussed by Strong and Orgel. However, this relational view is "refracted," or modified by the festival medium itself as a type of distorting lens. The participants' unconscious and conscious interpretation of the public performance of the festival ritual can change the very social reality originally reflected through the evolving shape of the festival itself. The physical analogy of a double mirror is not adequate to explain this idea; another metaphor is needed.

Because a festival clearly is a component of the process of human communication, a model of this process is proposed as a tentative template through which to consider the basic arguments of this thesis. An open-ended helical (spiraling) model of the human communication process, (99) rather than the traditional closed circular schematic model, is suggested. Here the linear, functional positions of sender, encoder, channel, decoder, receiver are blurred to the extent that the receiver position is equal, if not primary. This helical "response" model places primary emphasis on the complex nature, often assumed in traditional communications textbook diagrams, of the surrounding context, both ideological and physical. This idea is summarized in the Churchill quote on the "shaping" interplay between buildings and the people in them. In actual practice there is no clear, marked beginning point of a festival as a linear model of information flow implies. It follows that studies of complex signifying practices have a higher probability of useful insight when focusing on definable moments of historical origination, such as the "stories of origin" reviewed previously.

That festivals have their undiscerned meanings and practical social-political as well as aesthetic significance is an underlying assumption. Bakhtin held a view of meanings as endlessly evolving:

> At any moment in the development of the dialogue there are immense, boundless masses of forgotten contextual meanings, but at certain moments of the dialogue's subsequent development along the way they are recalled and invigorated in renewed form (in a new context). Nothing is absolutely dead: every meaning shall someday have its homecoming festival. The problem of great time. (100)

The import of Bakhtin's final provocative idea on the "forgotten contextual meanings" "at certain moments" "recalled and invigorated in renewed form (in a new context)" is found in the special social role given the festival. The festival has a unique communication function in the production of meaning, one that suggests more tourists or more businesses may be "effects" but that such "effects" do not in themselves explain the multiple "reality shaping" functions of a festival.

A second conclusion associated with a festival's contextual framing function is that a festival's basic nature is its "open" rather than "closed" structure, a characteristic that allows for a multiplicity of signifiers and codes to co-exist. This opposition implies that the more closed to differences, to variety in performances and activities, then the less the event functions as a festival in the historical sense of the term and the less likely the event is to be labeled a "festival." As noted earlier, in this sense the logic of festival contradicts the Aristotelian "unity of action" element of drama described in the Poetics. "Disunity of action" would be more characteristic of the sights, sounds, smells, tastes, and touches labeled "festival." This apparent lack of a clear oppositional dichotomy in many festivals is a conceptual problem that is not adequately explained by current theories (101) of ritual and performance ritual. A festival's logic apparently springs from sources other than the official/unofficial, upside-down world of carnival logic proposed by Bakhtin in his work on Rabelais. If carnival is the opposite of the official church world, for example, then it should possess the expected symbolic unity of action in its reversals of the church as a norm, functioning in effect to authenticate the church's authority and power to frame social discourse. Festivals appear to lack this logic of reversal, as can be seen from analysis of the Chattanooga and Charleston festivals, and, in effect, perform the semiotic iconic function of "church."

A third conclusion follows that a festival's basic nature appears to be the deliberate creation of an artistic text that works within its physical and ideological context to contain contradictory, disparate, opposing, and even warring elements--a primary source of the tension and excitement associated with the idea of festivals. Festivals, in Peircian terminology, derive their distinctive features in functioning as sign and sign systems that are simultaneously indexical, iconic, and symbolic, and that are also separately each of these functions, depending on the contextual social and physical environment and intended purpose. No one "sign-function" (102) dominates, as is usually the case in a given art form, possibly with the exception of opera. Therefore, the festival in general can be viewed as a special art form similar to the traditional structures of the separate performance arts, such as opera, symphony, dance, film, drama, and poetry, but operating with a distinctively different logic that embraces and enhances these genres and also other forms.

A fourth conclusion--rising from the problem of play versus work--is derived from the separation of intention, function, and effect in a festival's statements of purpose. Exploring the Charleston and Chattanooga festivals with these categories reveals a glimpse of the nature of the functions of festivals--in the sense of artistic "work" performed as "play." There is a subtle and important distinction between traditional and artistic forms of work and play. Vladimir Propp in his 1963 work *Russkie Agrarnye Prazdniki [Russian Agrarian Festivals]* traced these festivals to the "economic" factor, as Anatoly Liberman noted in his introduction to Propp's *Theory and History of Folklore*:

> Propp's book is not a cheap piece of antireligious propaganda, but a thorough investigation of the festivals....Propp traced the festivals to the economic factor, namely the peasants' struggle for the increase of the land's fertility....True to his pattern of causal hypotheses, Propp rejected all other explanations and disregarded the merry-making itself. "Homo ludens" seems to have been alien to Propp. (103)

Although it is unproductive to search for "causal" patterns when addressing the complexity of a festival, it appears increasingly desirable to consider the possibility of "merry-making," or humans-at-play (homo ludens), as a recurring pattern associated with festivals. (104) Artistic and spectator/participant "play" may be a constant unnoticed festival "function." "Play," albeit "serious play," and "pleasure," as noted previously, as a broader gratification of the "audience," may emerge as an overlooked function of a festival.

As places for openness, conflict, and play, festivals represent unique art forms that not only mirror their world but with little public notice shape its course. A broader semantic frame is needed to explain this perspective.

Toward a Semiotic of Festival

What is the nature and function of a theater that is not an open arena, thrust stage, nor proscenium arch, but properly a "festival" theater, similar to but differing from traditional forms of theater? At one level, a festival theater frames an ideological struggle and makes visible key meanings of a dominant group's encoded values. However, a festival theater creates multiple contextual empty spaces unlike the traditional theater. This makes possible the emergence of many new meanings that can at times threaten a dominant community group's preferred meanings by modifying any traditional sign appearing within the festival's contextual space and time. Through this complex process a festival is used not only to reflect dominant values but also to shape and mold communities in the direction of powerful interests acting "behind the scene."

Unlike the normal closed and bounded corporate structure, a festival's necessarily open structure permits potentially contradictory statements to blend, creating the aesthetic pleasure and tension associated with a "festival" environment. Often here can be seen a logic of both biological and social difference rather than a logic of unity, wholeness, harmony, oneness, sameness. Diverse elements combine to make festival spaces an enduring and powerful theatrical medium of signification and communication, a persuasive medium that competing ideological interests predictably will seek to control and at times exploit.

What perspectives support this "spatial" view of a festival theatrical practice? First, the control of the use of a festival's space is a key element. Ideas about "space" and the "power" in control of that space grounded this study. Festivals had appeared as dense collections of signs--symbolic ritual, activities, and events that are visibly the opposite of empty space. Yet the analytical key was to look at both the presences and the absences in the festival's space.

Second, an unnoticed function of festivals is that they are a special type of theater that can combine all four types of Brook's theaters (deadly, holy, rough, immediate) into another kind of theater unlike traditional physical and ideological forms. The evidence that this can be another form of theater is described by Brook as occurring when, "Sometimes within a single moment, the four of them, Holy, Rough, Immediate and Deadly intertwine." (105) Such a festival theater houses paradox, contradiction, low and high taste, the dull and the exciting, in short, "heteroglossia," to use Bakhtin's term for that which is individual, different, unclassified.

Third, societies have a practical need for theatrical "empty spaces." How can one analyze such complexity in the human communication process? Just as the zero (106) was invented to hold a place where no numerical meaning had been assigned, the metaphor of empty space provides a functional element that reveals the social construct of "theater." The Riverbend festival organizers found in effect that a "dot" instead of a "circle" represented the concept of empty space when an "off-stage" director intervened to prohibit another artistic director. That the Riverbend Festival's artistic character was diminished, however, does not necessarily mean that the space for this meaning is blocked permanently. It means mainly that the community's artists and audiences may not be ready for a "Southern Voices Festival" until the elements of place, ideal, and force combine again at one creative moment in a spirit not of monologue but of dialogue.

The art of power, and its double, the power of art, is bound up in this continuous struggle on public and private "bare stages." The festival theater frames these empty spaces and makes visible the meanings of a powerful group's relational order of ideas and things. These shifting orders of meaning can be seen in comparative studies such as Strong's study of Renaissance festivals. The festival theater accelerates social sign production and transmission by holding a position open for new combinations of elements and possible meanings to be expressed and observed.

From a broad view, an analysis of festivals suggests their role in creating "open" societies that evolve, grow, and adapt. Such societies should possess a healthier character than those less open to discovery or rapid sharing of information. In this sense an unnoticed function of the festival as a unique medium of communication is that festivals are powerful accelerators of information flowing within the semiotic system. "Semiotic," in this sense, is the Peircian definition of a "sign":

> ...something which stands to somebody for something in some respect or capacity. It addresses somebody, that is, creates in the mind of that person an equivalent sign, or perhaps a more developed sign. The sign which it creates I call the interpretant of the first sign. The sign stands for something, its object. It stands for that object, not in all respects, but in reference to a sort of idea, which I have sometimes called the ground of the representamen. "Idea" is here to be understood in a sort of Platonic sense, very familiar in everyday talk; I mean in that sense in which we say that one man catches another man's idea.... (107)

This statement suggests the value of a festival in providing a rich tapestry of signs in which "one [person] catches another's idea" while providing a "ground" for the exchange and "catching" of ideas. A town arts festival, such as Charleston's Spoleto, is more diverse and open in its programming than a heritage festival. It creates more interpersonal connections by bringing persons with diverse interests together. (108)

This study's three primary festival categories--empty space, purpose, and artistic director--represent a beginning effort to create a semiotic of festival, not as a set of fixed scientific laws but rather as a visualization of the repetitive pattern of sign relationships present in the festival theater practice. In festivals are found many associations of many types of signs, as classified by Peirce and others; and thus festivals represent a rich corpus of material not unlike Propp's corpus of folktales but far broader in scope, complexity, and effect. Festivals, as ancient modes of meaning making, can be understood in an indirect manner from their purposes and functions and not from their measurable effects. These three categories can be separated in order to better understand the complexity of social sign processes that festivals represent.

A festival is its own "semiotic" in that it represents itself as a spatial code of meaningful relationships. It reflects the life process itself in a way that no linguistic, static model can adequately represent. No sign exists out of context, semiotic anthropologist Paul Bouissac has said. (109) Therefore, "context" is material and is what bounds "empty space," suggesting that contextual framing is inseparable from any particular sign. In our familiar experience, "theater" can signify any physical empty space (including television sets and computer monitors). Where a theater exists or is built, a potential empty space is opened. In it, any kind of meaning can be expressed in the same way the ancients made meaning. Arithmetical manipulations can be done without the zero; societies can subsist, for a time, without theater. But the zero greatly accelerates symbolic operations by holding a position open for new meanings derived from combinations of other elements. So too does a festival theater accelerate social symbolic operations by holding many positions open for new meanings to be seen.

Umberto Eco has called context or "circumstance" "a revolutionary aspect of semiotic endeavor." (110) This is the social exchange of signs in which "the circumstances can become an intentional element of communication." Eco views this as a tactic of decoding in opposition to a strategy of coding, generating a "semiotic guerilla warfare" that makes it possible "to change the circumstances in the light of which addressees will choose their own ways of interpretation." He says that such a shift would give the addressee "his freedom of decoding...in an era in which mass communication often appears as the manifestation of a domination which makes sure of social control by planning the sending of messages." (111)

In Peter Brook's "I can take any empty space and call it a bare stage" opening statement is embedded the "manifestation of dominance" that Eco says is the strategy of coding that "strives to render messages redundant in order to secure interpretation according to pre-established plans." Or, to use a literary example cited by Eco, in which "sign" should be substituted for "words":

When Alice asks, 'The question is whether you can make words mean so many different things,' Humpty Dumpty's answer is, 'The question is who is to be the master.' Once this point of view is accepted, one might as well ask whether the communicative process is capable of subduing the circumstances in which it takes place.

The "master" of the festival sign, which has so many different meanings, is the unique space in which it is found. Eco's "circumstances" function in similar ways to Bakhtin's "homecoming festival" context and to Brook's theatrical empty space.

To reverse Alice's question: "What other important meanings exist that presently lack words? Words that now are forgotten? Words that are kept `off stage' by the puppeteer?" The festival theater, which in a unique way frames an empty space that continually makes room for lost or forgotten meanings, is one answer to Bakhtin's problem of "great time, an infinite and unfinished dialogue in which no meaning dies." (112) A reply to Humpty Dumpty is that contextual circumstances could be the master in a universe of so many different signs. The master could be neither the puppeteer nor the puppet but their natural theater "in which no meaning ever dies."

From Chattanooga's commercially oriented, downtown business development festivals in the 1950s, 1960s, and 1970s, from Charleston's theaters of power in the 1980s, from the international music festival at Salzburg, and from the peaceful grounds of Chautauqua, one can draw a basic conclusion about an overriding function of these festivals. That conclusion is that festivals of any type, in strong and weak ways, "combine" signifiers in new patterns under high density and compressed time conditions, a primary source of their emotive power. This may or may not be the intent of the planners, and it may not always be the effect of a given festival. Programming at the Riverbend that primarily attracts blacks is not performing its combining function; it has the unintended effect of racial segregation. From this suggested critical posture, informed judgment can begin to assess those cases where festivals group individuals by sameness (class, skin color, etc.) rather than bring them together for reasons other than their social and biological differences.

Societies apparently require devices that connect and bind their citizens into common images and understandings while at the same time protecting their right to differ and to hold divergent views. This seemingly contradictory concept resembles the problem of describing the behavior of light; two separate views are required, a theory of light as particle and as wave, to make sense of observed effects (or the contemporary idea of "wavicles," as Robert Detweiler pointed out in response to this either/or dichotomy). Festivals from primitive times to the Renaissance era through contemporary times have multiple and even seemingly contradictory effects. Quite probably it is the tension that grows out of these contradictory functions that creates the very special atmosphere of openness, of growth, of a degree of newness, of release from tension, that offers an opportunity for various messages to be amplified and framed more powerfully than more traditional mediums of communication permit.

Thomas A. Sebeok has discussed the extreme importance of the mental model that humans and animals have of their "real" world, an insight derived in part from the theories of meaning and modeling advocated by Jakob von Uexhull. (113) Sebeok has noted (114) that when an environment changes and a species' model of the environment does not change, because of denial of reality or other mental disorders or factors, then the species may vanish. It is not possible to understand the modeling functions of the festival without more detailed analysis and invention of new methods for observing and recording such complex entities. But it is possible to state from this functions perspective that with our unique human ability to imagine different realities and to envisage many possible worlds that the models we experience as our "context" do in fact influence and at times strongly shape our knowledge and our templates of reality.

GENERAL BIBLIOGRAPHY

Agee, Warren K.; Ault, Phillip H.; and Emery, Edwin. Introduction to Mass Communications, 8th Ed. New York: Harper and Row, 1985.

Aristotle. Poetics. Translated by L. J. Potts. Cambridge, England: Cambridge University Press, 2nd ed., 1968. First published 1953.

Attali, Jacques. Noise: The Political Economy of Music. Translated by Brian Massumi. Minneapolis: University of Minnesota Press, 1985. From the 1977 edition of Bruits: essai sur l'economie politique de la musique.

Axelrod, Robert. The Evolution of Cooperation. New York: Basic Books, 1984.

Bachelard, Gaston. The Poetics of Space. Translated from the French by Maria Jolas. Boston: The Beacon Press, 1969.

Bakhtin, M. M. The Dialogic Imagination: Four Essays. Edited by Michael Holquist and translated by Caryl Emerson and Michael Holquist. Austin: University of Texas Press, 1981.

_____. Speech Genres & Other Late Essays. Translated, Vern W. McGee. Austin: University of Texas Press, 1986.

_____. Rabelais and His World. Translated by Helene Iswolsky from Tvorchestvo Fransua Rable, Moscow, Khudozhestvennia literatura, 1965. Bloomington: Indiana, 1984. [Written during the 1930s and distilled into a single text in 1940- as a doctoral dissertation for the Gorky Institute of World Literature in Moscow].

Barbour, Sheena, ed. Festivals in Great Britain: A List with Forecast Dates and Policies--1985. Eastbourne: John Offord Publications, 1985.

Barthes, Roland. Empire of Signs. Trans. Richard Howard 1970; New York: Hill and Wang, 1982.

_____. Image, Music, Text. Essays selected and translated by Stephen Heath. London: Fontana Paperbacks, 1977.

_____. Elements of Semiology. Translated by Annette Lavers and Colin Smith. New York: Hill and Wang, 1967. First published in 1964, Paris.

Baydo, Gerald R., editor. The Evolution of Mass Culture in America: 1877 to the Present. St. Louis: Forum Press, 1982.

Benedict, Burton. "The Anthropology of World's Fairs." American Anthropologist, Vol. 87(4), 1-20.

Berger, Peter L. and Luckmann, Thomas. The Social Construction of Reality: A Treatise in the Sociology of Knowledge. New York: Doubleday, 1966.

Berger. Arthur Asa. Signs in Contemporary Culture: An Introduction to Semiotics. New York: Longman, 1984.

Blake, Reed H. and Haroldsen, Edwin O. A Taxonomy of Concepts in Communication. New York: Hastings House, 1975.

Bouissac, Paul. Circus and Culture: A Semiotic Approach. Lanham, Maryland and London: University Press of America, 1985. First published 1976, Indiana University Press.

_____. "The Potential of Semiotics in the Advancement of Knowledge." RSSI, V.4(4), 1985.

Brantlinger, Patrick. Bread & Circuses: Theories of Mass Culture as Social Decay. Ithaca: Cornell University Press, 1983.

Brecht, Bertolt. Brecht on Theatre: The Development of an Aesthetic. Edited and translated by John Willett. London: Methuen, 1964. From the German original Schriften zum Theater published in 1957 in Frankfurt.

_____. Life of Galileo. Translated by John Willett. Edited by John Willett and Ralph Manheim. The Collected Plays, Vol. 5, Part London: Methuen, 1980. From the original 1940 German edition of Leben des Galilei.

Bristol, Michael D. Carnival and Theater. London: Methuen, 1985.

Brook, Peter. The Empty Space. New York: Atheneum, 1984.

Buchler, Justus, editor. Philosophical Writings of Peirce. Dover Publications: New York, 1955 unaltered 1940 original edition.

Clark, Katerina, and Holquist, Michael. Mikhail Bakhtin. Cambridge, Massachusetts and London: Harvard University Press, 1984.

Clarke, Michael. The Politics of Pop Festivals. London: Junction Books, 1984.

Clifford, James, and Marcus, George E., editors. Writing Culture: The Poetics and Politics of Ethnography. Berkeley: University of California Press, 1986.

Cohn, William H. "A National Celebration: The Fourth of July in American History." Cultures (France) 1976, 3(1): 141-156.

Coult, Tony and Kershaw, Baz, editors. Engineers of the Imagination: The Welfare State Handbook. London: Methuen, 1983.

Dance, Frank E. X., ed. "Toward a Theory of Human Communication." Human Communication Theory. New York: Holt, 1967.

Darney, Virginia G. Women and World's Fairs: American International Expositions, 1876-1910 Atlanta: Emory University dissertation, 1982.

Davidson, Philip. Propaganda and the American Revolution-- 1763- 1783. Chapel Hill: University of North Carolina Press, 1941.

Davis, Howard and Walton, Paul. Language, Image, Media. Oxford: Basil Blackwell, 1983.

Day, Arthur R. The Shaw Festival at Niagara-on-the-Lake in Ontario, Canada, 1962-1981: A History. DAI 1983, 43(7): 2157- 2158-A; Bowning Green State University 1982.

Deely, John. Introducing Semiotic: Its History and Doctrine. Bloomington: Indiana University Press, 1982.

Doctorow, E. L. World's Fair. New York: Fawcett Crest, 1985.

Dorson, Richard M. Folklore and Folklife: An Introduction. Chicago: University of Chicago Press, 1972.

Dufresne, Sylvie. "The Winter Carnival in Montreal, 1883-89," or, "Le Carnaval D'Hiver de Montreal, 1883-1889." Urban History Review (Canada) 1983, 11(3): 25-45.

Dukore, Bernard F. Dramatic Theory and Criticism: Greeks to Grotowski. New York: Holt, Rinehart and Winston, 1974.

Dunwell, Wilfrid. Music and the European Mind. New York: Thomas Yoseloff, 1962.

Eco, Umberto. Semiotics and the Philosophy of Language. London: Macmillan Press, 1984.

_____. A Theory of Semiotics. Bloomington: Indiana University Press, 1976.

_____. The Role of the Reader: Explorations in the Semiotics of Texts. Bloomington and London: Indiana University Press, 1979.

_____. Travels in Hyperreality: Essays. Translated by William Weaver. New York: Harcourt Brace Jovanovich, 1985.

Eco, Umberto; Ivanov, V.V.; Rector, Monica. Carnival! Edited by Thomas A. Sebeok; assisted by Marcia E. Erickson. New York: Mouton Publishers, 1984.

Elam, Keir. The Semiotics of Theatre and Drama. London and New York: Methuen, 1980.

Falassi, Allessando. Editor. Time Out of Time: Essays on the Festival. University of New Mexico Press: Albuquerque, New Mexico, 1988.

Frye, Northrop. The Great Code: The Bible and Literature. New York: Harcourt, 1982.

Gallup, Stephen. A History of the Salzburg Festival. London: Weidenfeld and Nicolson, 1987.

Gardin, Jean-Claude. Archaeological Constructs: an Aspect of Theoretical Archaeology. Cambridge: Cambridge University Press, 1980.

Geertz, Clifford. The Interpretation of Cultures. New York: Basic Books, 1973.

Gilbert, Elizabeth Rees. Fairs and Festivals: A Smithsonian Guide to Celebrations in Maryland, Virginia, and Washington, D.C. Edited by Peter Seitel. Washington: Smithsonian Institution Press, 1982.

Goffman, Erving. The Presentation of Self in Everyday Life. New York: Doubleday, 1959.

Gruen, John. Menotti. New York: Macmillan, 1978.

Guthrie, Tyrone, and Davies, Robertson. Renown at Stratford: A Record of the Shakespeare Festival in Canada. Toronto: Clarke, Irwin & Company Ltd.: 1953.

Hadamovsky, Eugen. Propaganda and National Power. New York: Arno Press, 1972. Translated by Alice Mavrogordato and Ilse De Witt. First published in Germany in 1933.

Halle, Morris; Matejka, Ladislav; Pomorska, Krystyna; and Uspenskij, Boris, editors. Semiosis: Semiotics and the History of Culture. Ann Arbor: University of Michigan, 1984.

Hawkes, Terence. Structuralism and Semiotics. Berkeley: University of California Press, 1977.

Hess-Luttich, E., editor. Multimedial Communication, vol. I: Semiotic Problems of its Notation, vol. II: Theatre Semiotics. Gunter Narr, 1982.

Hogarth, William. "Southwark Fair." In Hogarth by David Bindman, p. 85-86. Norwich, G.B.: Thames and Hudson, 1986. Engraving of 1733 work.

Huber, Leonard V., and Belsom, Jack. Mardi Gras: A Pictorial History of Carnival in New Orleans. Gretna, La.: Pelican, 1977.

Hughes, Spike. Glyndebourne: A History of the Festival Opera Founded in 1934 by Audrey and John Christie. North Pomfret, Vt.: David and Charles, 1981.

Huizinga, J. Homo Ludens: A Study of the Play-Element in Culture. 1944; New York: Roy Publishers, 1950.

Hunt, Christopher. "The Official Souvenir Program of Spoleto Festival U.S.A.: 1981." Charleston: David L. Rawle Associates, 1981.

Hunt, Lynn. Politics, Culture, and Class in the French Revolution. Berkeley: University of California Press, 1984.

_____, and Sewell, William H., Jr. "Symbolic Legitimation and Popular Politics in Revolutionary France." Consortium on Revolutionary Europe 1750-1850: Pro. 1979: 281-288.

Irwin, Alfreda L. The Chautauqua Story: Three Taps of the Gavel, Pledge to the Future. Chautauqua: Chautauqua Institution, 3rd ed., 1987.

Jacobson, Romaine. Verbal Art, Verbal Sign, Verbal Time. Edited by Krystyna Pomorska and Stephen Rudy. Oxford: Basil Blackford, 1985.

Jones, Emory Davis. A History of the Southern Literary Festival. DAI 1982, 42(7): 3158-A; University of Mississippi 1981.

Jonson, Ben. Bartholomew Fair. Edited by E. A. Horsman. London: Methuen and Co., 1960 edition of 1614 play.

Krampen, Martin. "Phytosemiotics," Frontiers in Semiotics, John Deely, Brooke Williams, Felicia E. Kruse, ed. Bloomington: Indiana UP, 1986. Jakob von Uxhull's primary work is "Bedeutungslehre", Bios, vol. 10 (Leipzig), Reprinted in Streifzuge durch die Umwelten von Tieren und Menshcen/Bedeutungslehre, by Jakob von Uxhull and Gerog Kriszat (Frankfurt a. M.: S. Fischer Vrlag, 1970.

Kristeva, Julia. The Kristeva Reader. Edited by Toril Moi. New York: Columbia University Press, 1986.

Kundera, Milan. Laughable Loves. Middlesex: Penguin, 1974.

Ladurie, Emmanuel Le Roy. Carnival in Romans: A People's Uprising at Romans, 1579-1580. Translated by Mary Feeney. Middlesex: Penguin, 1981. From the 1979 original French edition of Le Carnaval de Romans, Editions Gallimard, Paris.

Langer, Susanne K. Philosophy in a New Key: A Study in the Symbolism of Reason, Rite, and Art, 3rd edition. Cambridge, MA: Havard University Press, 1941.

Le Bon, Gustave. The Crowd: A Study of the Popular Mind. New York: Ballantine, 1969 edition. First published in 1895 in Paris.

Levi-Strauss, Claude. Myth and Meaning. New York: Schocken Books, 1979.

_____. Structural Anthropology. Translated from the French by Claire Jacobson and Brooke Grundfest Schoepf. New York: Basic Books, 1963.

_____. The Raw and the Cooked: Introduction to a Science of Mythology, Vol. 1. Translated from the French by John and Doreen Weightman. Chicago: University of Chicago Press, 1983. First published in 1964 as Le Cru et le Cuit.

Longo, Gianni. The Making of the Festival. New York: The Institute for Environmental Action, 1981.

Lotman, Yuri. The Structure of the Artistic Text. Translated from the Russian by Gail Lenhoff and Ronald Vroon. Ann Arbor: University of Michigan, 1977. Original text 1971.

Lyotard, Jean-Francois. The Postmodern Condition: A Report on Knowledge. Translation from the French by Geoff Bennington and Brian Massumi. Foreword by Fredric Jameson. Minneapolis: University of Minnesota Press, 1984. From the 1979 French edition, La Condition postmoderne: rapport sur le savoir.

MacAloon, John J., editor. Rite, Drama, Festival, Spectacle: Rehearsals Toward a Theory of Cultural Performances. Philadelphia: Institute for the Study of Human Issues, 1984.

Manning, F., editor. The Celebration of Society: Perspectives on Contemporary Cultural Performance. Bowling Green University Popular Press, 1983.

Maranda, P., editor. Mythology. Penguin, 1972.

March, Richard. "The Ideology of Folklore Festivals in Pre- and Post-War Yugoslavia." Kentucky Folklore Record. 1980 26(1-2): 53-61

Matejka, Ladislav and Titunik, Irwin R., editors. Semiotics of Art: Prague School Contributions. Cambridge, MA: Massachusetts Institute of Technology, 1976.

McDonald, Marcia Ann. A Two-world Condition: The Carnival Idiom and its Function in Four Morality Plays. DAI 1984, 45(12), 3647, Vanderbilt University 1984.

McLuhan, Marshall, and Fiore, Quentin. The Medium is the Massage: An Inventory of Effects. New York: Bantam Books, 1967.

_____. Understanding Media: The Extensions of Man. New York: McGraw-Hill, 1964, 6th printing, 2nd edition.

Meier, Richard L. A Communications Theory of Urban Growth. Cambridge: The M.I.T. Press, 1962.

Meyer, Leonard B. Emotion and Meaning in Music. Chicago: U of Chicago P, 1957.

Miles, Carol E. "Robert Wilson: A Study of His Creative Process," unpublished master thesis, Trinity U, San Antonio, Texas, 1984.

Miller, George A. The Psychology of Communication: Seven Essays. Baltimore: Penguin, 1967.

Mitchell, W. J. T. Iconology: Image, Text, Ideology. Chicago: University of Chicago Press, 1986.

Moffat, Alistair. The Edinburgh Fringe. London: Johnston & Bacon, 1978.

Moore, Wilbert E. Social Change. Englewood Cliffs: Prentice-Hall, 1963.

Morris, Charles. Signification and Significance: A Study of the Relations of Signs and Values. Cambridge, Massachusetts: M.I.T. Press, 1964.

Nagler, A. M. A Source Book in Theatrical History New York: Dover, 1952.

Nattiez, J.J. "Is a Description Semiotics of Music Possible?," Language Sciences Journal, 1972.

Ngugi wa Thiong'o. Decolonizing the Mind. Harrare: Zimbabwe Publishing House, 1987.

Norwich, John Julius. Fifty Years of Glyndebourne: An Illustrated History. London: Jonathan Cape, 1985.

Ogden, C. K., and Richards, I. A. The Meaning of Meaning. London: Harcourt Brace Jovanovich, 1923.

Orgel, Stephen. The Illusion of Power: Political Theater in the English Renaissance. Berkeley and London: University of California Press, 1975.

Patterson, Tom with Allan Gould. First Stage: The Making of the Stratford Festival. Toronto: McClelland and Stewart, 1987.

Peirce, Charles S., and Welby, Lady Victoria. Semiotic and Significs: Correspondence between Charles S. Peirce and Victoria Lady Welby. Edited by Charles S. Hardwick. Bloomington: Indiana University Press, 1977.

Peirce, Charles S. "Logic as Semiotic: The Theory of Signs," Ed Justus Buchler, Philosophical Writings of Peirce. Dover Publications: New York: 1955.

Pettigrew, John and Portman, Jamie. Stratford: The First Thirty Years, Vol. 1 and 2. Toronto: McMillan of Canada, 1985.

Pieper, Josef. In Tune With the World: A Theory of Festivity. Translated, Richard and Clara Winston 1963; New York: Harcourt, 1965.

Piscator, Erwin. The Political Theatre: A History 1914-1929. New York: Avon, 1978. Translated by Hugh Rorrison. Originally published in German in 1929 as Das Politische Theater.

Propp, V. Morphology of the Folktale. Second Edition revised and edited by Louis A. Wagner. Austin: University of Texas Press, 1968. First completed in 1928 and published in English in 1958.

_____. Theory and History of Folklore, ed. Anatoly Liberman, trans. Ariadna Y. Martin et al. 1963; Leningrad: Leningrad U; Minneapolis: U of Minnesota: 1984.

Reiss, Timothy J. The Discourse of Modernism. Ithaca and London: Cornell University Press, 1982.

Reiss, Timothy J. The Uncertainty of Analysis: Problems in Truth, Meaning, Culture. Ithaca and London: Cornell University Press, 1988.

Riverbend Festival: A Comprehensive Evaluation. Urban Initiatives, New York City, in association with Trahan, Burden & Charles of Baltimore, Maryland; Kaminsky & Company of New York and Nashville; and Tatge Productions of New York, 1988. Prepared for Friends of the Festival, Inc.

Rosen, Robert. A Short History of Charleston. San Francisco: Lexikos, 1982.

Rotman, Brian. Signifying Nothing: The Semiotics of Zero. New York: St Martin's P, 1987.

Ruesch, Jurgen and Bateson, Gregory. Communication: The Social Matrix of Psychiatry. New York: W. W. Norton, 1951; 1987 edition.

Saussure, Ferdinand de. Course in General Linguistics. Edited by Charles Bally and Albert Sechehaye with Albert Reidlinger. Translated from the French by Wade Baskin. Bungay, England: Richard Clay (The Chaucer Press) Ltd., 1960. First edition published in Geneva in 1915.

Savan, David. An Introduction to C. S. Peirce's Semiotics. Toronto: The Toronto Semiotic Circle, 1976.

Scholes, Robert. Semiotics and Interpretation. New Haven: Yale University Press, 1982.

Schramm, Wilbur, and Porter, William E. Men, Women, Messages, and Media. New York: Harper and Row, 1982. First published 1973 as Men, Messages, and Media.

Schumann, Robert. "Carnaval, Op. 9," 1834-35. Work for piano. Analyzed in Involvement with Music; William Christ, Richard DeLone, and Allen Winold, authors; New York: Harper's, 1975.

Sebeok, Thomas A. Sight, Sound, and Sense. Bloomington and London: Indiana University Press, 1978. ((P99/S47, Woodruff, Emory).

Segrest, Robert. "The Architecture of the Excluded Middle: Midway- Invisible Writing-Feasts-Vagabonds-Instructions for a Desire Machine-Carnivals-Secret Cities." Paper presented at Emory University's Graduate Institute of Liberal Arts, April 9, 1986.

Shklosvky, Victor; Tomashevsky, Boris; and Eichenbaum, Boris. Russian Formalist Criticism: Four Essays. Translated by Lee T. Lemon and Marion J. Reis. Lincoln: University of Nebraska Press, 1965.

Silverman, Kaja. The Subject of Semiotics. New York: Oxford University Press, 1983.

Steinberg, Michael Philip. The Meaning of the Salzburg Festival: Inventing Cultural Tradition in the First Austrian Republic. DAI 1985, 46(8), 2416, University of Chicago, 1985.

Tachikawa, Ko-ichi. "Revolutionary Festival: The History of Mentalities in the French Revolution," or, "Kakumei Saiten: Furansu Kakumei No Shinsei-shi." Shiso (Iwanimi Shoten) (Japan), 1981 (687): 124-140.

Strong, Roy. Art and Power: Renaissance Festivals 1450-1650. Woodbridge, England: Boydell Press, 1984. First published in 1974 at Splendour at Court: Renaissance Spectacle and the Theatre of Power.

Stubbs, Michael. Discourse Analysis: The Sociolinguistic Analysis of Natural Language. Chicago: University of Chicago Press 1983.

Swiderski, Richard M. Voices: An Anthropologist's Dialogue with an Italian-American Festival. London, Ontario: Centre for Social and Humanistic Studies, 1987.

Telotte, J. P. "Charles Peirce and Walker Percy: From Semiotic to Narrative." Southern Q. 1980 (3): 65-79.

Thibault, Paul J. Text, Discourse, and Context: A Social Semiotic Perspective. Toronto: The Toronto Semiotic Circle, 1986, Vol 3.

Terrasse, Jean. "Political Commitment: the Tableau, the Festival, and Utopia," or, "L'Engagement Politique: Le Tableau, La Fete, L'Utopie." University of Ottawa Quarterly (Canada); 1981, 16(2): 132-143.

Tufte, Edward R. The Visual Display of Quantitative Information. Cheshire, CT: Graphics Press, 1983.

Turner, Victor. From Ritual to Performance: The Human Seriousness of Play. Performing Arts Journal Publications, 1962.

_____. The Forest of Symbols. Ithaca: Cornell University Press, 1967.

_____. Dramas, Fields, and Metaphors: Symbolic Action in Human Society. Ithaca: Cornell University Press, 1974.

_____. Celebration. Washington, D. C.: Smithsonian Press, 1982.

Volosinov, V. N. Marxism and the Philosophy of Language. Translated by Ladislav Matejka and I.R. Titunik. Cambridge, Massachusetts and London: Harvard University Press, 1986. From the 1929 Russian edition, Marksizm i filosofiia iazyka, signed by V. N. Volosinov.

Weingartner, Fannia, editor. Ravinia: The Festival at its Half Century. Ravinia: Ravinia Festival Association and Rand McNally & Company, 1985.

Whisnant, David E. All That is Native and Fine: the Politics of Culture in an American Region. Chapel Hill: UNC P, 1983.

Willett, John. The Theatre of Bertolt Brecht. London: Mutheun, 1959.

Winner, Irene Portis. Semiotics of Culture: The State of the Art. Toronto: The Toronto Semiotic Circle, 1982.

Yoder, Don. "Twenty-five Years of the Folk Festival." Pennsylvania Folklife 1974, 23(Supplement): 2-7.

Young, Judith. Celebrations: America's Best Festivals, Jamborees, Carnivals & Parades. Santa Barbara: Capra Press, 1986.

Zellinger, I. M. Studies of the Idea of Arts Festivals in the 20th Century, with Special Reference to its History in the German-speaking World, or, Studien zur Festspielidee des Zwanzegsten Jahrhunderts mit Besonderer Berucksichtisumg ihrer Geschichte im Deutsche Sprachraum. DAI-C 1984, 45(3): 600; 9/2429; Source: University of Vienna 1982.

APPENDIX A

SPOLETO FESTIVAL U.S.A. MATERIALS

The unique problems of studying the origin of ritual, or the creation of a cultural practice, require explanation. Both Charleston's Spoleto Festival U.S.A. and Chattanooga's Riverbend Festival have multiple "true" stories whose meaning and significance are best detected by listening primarily to the unrehearsed voices of several of those key individuals involved at their genesis or others associated with their later stages.

It appears that for these two festivals their "stories of origin" (or creation myths) can be better derived from transcribed oral history than from written notes or official records that might have been kept before their inception for two reasons. Their founders' "interpretations" of and "feelings" about events probably would not have been written down during these periods of rapid change.

It is unlikely a researcher could read mine or the other Riverbend organizers' rough notes or chaotic files and know much of our versions of the festival's story of origin without talking with me or them. It is the combination of written records, recalled events, and conversations that reveal more of the full story of dimly remembered beginnings that may not have seemed worth preserving during their gestation and birth.

In the early belief that much of the story of a festival's founding would be discovered by searching through yellowed letters, scribbled notes, news clippings, and various proposals, an effort was made in early 1988 to review the official Spoleto files for this study. The festival's first chairman, Dr. Theodore S. Stern, was very much interested and supportive in getting Spoleto's history on record.

However, according to a telephone conversation with the courteous and supportive general manager, Nigel Redden, in early 1988, the Charleston Spoleto office decided not to open its files from the festival's beginning for my review until they could be "vetted." I had explained in a January 1988 letter to Dr. Stern, a former president of the College of Charleston:

> Carmen Kovens [associate director] was very helpful and was to discuss my request to review the early Spoleto files with Nigel Redden and let me know by Feb. 12 [1988] whether I can see these materials. We discussed some of the conditions for access to

what might be sensitive documents, my own thinking being that the academic integrity essential for a credible historical record suggested that free access was the best policy. However, I have no interest in private, confidential personnel and financial matters, only information that bears on the struggle of ideas, philosophies, opinions--such as the Hugh Lane and Nella Barkley withdrawal. There should be no need, then, for anyone to check the early records prior to my study of them. At best, they would corroborate the sequence of events and the names of persons involved during the festival's beginning.

Kovens, who sent a copy of the important Hugh Lane resignation letter, replied that while there was no basic objection to such a review, the staff would have to take the time to review the files and remove any confidential material. By this time the broader implications of the interview with Stern in January 1988, along with a conversation with college archivists, had shifted my thinking to the contribution that oral histories from those most involved in 1975-77 could make to the exploratory nature of this study. Increasingly, it was becoming apparent from the Chattanooga and Charleston cases that original intentions could be masked by later documents written for political, economic, or even personal purposes.
There were other potential sources of information. The College of Charleston library archival staff had the papers of Stern, its former president, who also was the first festival board chairman. But looking through these few records with the archive staff, we discovered to their surprise and mine that little related to the Spoleto Festival. The archive director explained that several proposals had been made to move the festival records to the college library but to date the festival office had not responded. At his request, I agreed to mention this request to the festival office and did so, but no specific response was made to the library archivist's suggestion. It was clear that few of the important private records were available, or within reach, without exhaustive, expensive investigation.
As the story of the festival's creation emerged from conversations with Stern and others at the festival office, as well as from a review of the few public and college library records, I felt that the scholarly task of a dissertation could be served better by taking the first step of relying on the transcribed thoughts of Stern, Wadsworth, and other knowledgeable past and present festival officials. Also, following standard journalistic practice, I felt that if I had reviewed the festival's confidential files under

a general agreement not to disclose protected information, then professional ethics also would prevent using this same material if it were disclosed during the interviews. The need to protect sensitive financial and personnel records is understandable. Possibly a later study will use the available "vetted" materials to compile complete historical studies similar to those of Salzburg and Stratford.

Whether "vetted" histories of powerful cultural institutions that notonly mirror but also shape community life properly serve the public interest is an important matter but lies beyond the scope of this study. It is the case, however, that files I kept as an initiator of the Chattanooga festival are open to anyone and can be used as an indicator of the value of such primary source material. Certainly, however, in analyzing either festival, I would not include any material that would harm anyone as an individual.

Nevertheless, where serious disagreements over purposes, policy, and methods exist, the general community welfare merits an accessible public record. The sunshine of public access is often the best guardian against personal and public error (especially when some of the errors were my own). To insure complete public access and scholarly availability, it is my hope to locate or establish a secure archival center for the festival materials gathered during the past ten years.

Stories of Origin

The following is a transcription of a conversation on February 5, 1988, with Dr. Theodore S. Stern, one of the founders and first board chairman of the Spoleto Festival U.S.A. when it opened in 1977 in Charleston, South Carolina. The interview was taped by me at Dr. Stern's home, 16 Bull Street, in Charleston. Stern approved the transcript and authorized making it public. Afterward, it became apparent that little or none of this information was available from the programs and other materials from the festival press office, which had been gracious in lending special assistance and passes in 1986 and 1988. My questions and comments were not transcribed but are available on tapes. A copy of this transcript was sent to Dr. Stern soon after he approved it.

THE ORIGIN OF CHARLESTON'S SPOLETO FESTIVAL U.S.A.

Remarks of Dr. Theodore S. Stern

A festival reflects the culture of the times, particularly a comprehensive festival such as Spoleto. It reflects all of the different art forms in existence at that time. We have modern dance, classical dance, opera, chamber music, theater, mime--all the existing art forms.

I think it's a matter of interest and history to record that the festival was founded by Gian Carlo Menotti, who was responsible for and the founder of the Festival dei Due Mondi in Spoleto, Italy. The reason for that festival is an interesting story. When Menotti was a student at the Curtis Institute in Philadelphia, his family, who were influential and of affluence in Italy, said, "Oh, don't go to America because that is a wasteland of culture and you'll never *learn anything over there." His mother, who is the driving force for art in the family, discouraged him. But he set his mind on going to Curtis. When he arrived at Curtis Institute, he found that their conception of art and artists in America was completely wrong. He found greater artists in greater numbers and a greater interest on the part of the people than he had in Italy. He said that if I ever attain any prominence, I want to present these young American artists to the world leaders and the culture vultures of Europe. I want them to be able to show their talent to those people and have those people see how talented the Americans are. I guess history will record that from his experience at the Curtis and his desire to compose and his coming in contact with so many young people that he received financial support as well as encouragement from people like Toscanini, Mrs. Edward Bok, the McElheneys, people of Philadelphia who were at that time the Rockefellers, Vanderbilts, and Astors of Pennsylvania. They were the core that provided him with the funds necessary to take American artists to Italy.

From that point on he had to find a place to have this festival. It wasn't the cities because he says, and he said this is true of Charleston as well, that the city must be an art form in itself, that people should walk around the city as well as enjoy the festival, and they tie in together; they're in concert and in harmony. He chose a small town in Umbrian Province, Spoleto, which historians tell us was where Hannibal crossed the Alps and the big battle was at Spoleto. Here is an old, old town that was bypassed by the Twentieth century. It has its original Etruscan walls, original forum, theaters, opera houses; it was the seat of culture of the Umbrian Province. It was destitute, economically completely depressed; people were leaving; there was no industry. The culture which could be presented was nonexistent. So he selected this really depressed area, yes, like a theater that had been empty for many years. It's been the saving grace for Spoleto, Italy, and the Italian government; in fact, the festival in Italy is completely supported by the Italian government. Their budget exceeds the budget of the U.S. festival, and contributions are received from the federal government, the province, and the town of Spoleto, which is now thriving economically and culturally. That was the start. He called it the Festival of Two Worlds, trying to join the culture of Europe--not necessarily Europe--and the United States, the Festival dei Due Mondi.

The United States National Endowment of the Arts in Washington approached Menotti--I believe this was when Nancy Hanks was the head of the National Endowment, and suggested that he establish a Spoleto Festival in the United States. At the behest of then the consultant, I believe, to the National Endowment, Walter Anderson, Menotti was placed in charge of trying to develop a plan to present the festival in the United States. The general feeling of the bureaucracy in Washington was that no festival existed in the Southeastern United States and that this festival should be in the Southeastern part of the United States. Menotti was asked to select a city where this festival could find a home. Walter Anderson prepared a list of several Southern cities, starting with Richmond, Winston-Salem, Charlotte, Charleston, Atlanta--all the way to Miami to Houston and New Orleans. Menotti's agent at the time was Priscilla Morgan, who was very closely associated with Menotti, either as his manager or agent, but I think she worked for Menotti to develop Spoleto, Italy. He asked her to visit these various communities and to pick out those he should look at. She asked the musical director, who was Christopher Keene at the time, to help her in this quest to find a suitable location.

There seems to be some confusion over who actually was responsible for, not the selection of Charleston because Menotti was going to make the final decision, but as to how the Morgan/Keene team would be suitably introduced to the community and its citizens. Alison Harwood, who is a relatively recent newcomer to Charleston, claims that she knew Priscilla Morgan and she told her about Charleston. The fallacy in that one is that I don't think she knew Charleston too well herself. Countess Alicia Paolozzi, who was one of Menotti's initial sponsors in the festival in Italy and who owns two homes in Spoleto and one in Rome, she was a Spaulding of Boston, Massachusetts, recognized for their generosity to the arts, was another person who says she got Morgan and Keene interested in Charleston. However, subsequently, the Countess bought a plantation in Charleston, owns several condominiums in Charleston, and has been member of the board and generous donor of the Festival Foundation and Spoleto USA. She went to school with Frances Edmunds, who is from an old Charleston family and is recognized as the foremost preservationist in the area and perhaps in the United States, having been a member of the board of directors of the National

Trust for Historic Preservation and has received numerous awards. She also feels that she was one of the people who was responsible, having visited the festival in Italy a year before anybody else in Charleston knew of the Spoleto Festival.

Then, Mrs. Rufus Barkley, I'll call her Nella for short, became extremely interested and she headed up a committee to encourage people like the National Endowment, Priscilla Morgan, and Christopher Keene to select Charleston as a place for the festival. She had various committees, of which I was chairman of what you might call a logistics committee. She had a fundraising committee and because of his great influence and political power as well as economic power, Hugh Lane was elected chairman of this committee to try and get the festival here. Frances Edmunds had visited the festival in Spoleto, Italy, in 1975. In 1976, Hugh Lane, Nella Barkley, and Mr. and Mrs. Tom Stevenson went to Spoleto to see really what it was all about. A matter of record is that when Hugh Lane returned to Charleston, he said he would have nothing more to do with it. He did not want to expose the citizens of Charleston to people dancing without clothes and felt that the people who would come to Charleston would be depraved, queers--I think he used those words--and he offered to return all the money that people had donated to this effort. And he did. I think he returned something like a hundred thousand dollars to people because he had misled them. In addition, Hugh Lane said that the festival was not economically feasible and would never be a success. This is part of a letter that he put in writing, which he subsequently has regretted but not denied. He was chairman of the board of the C&S bank. But he was the head of everything here, head of the United Way, you know, he was number one citizen, and he went all over the state to generate these contributions. He does speak to me now, but he'll never admit the festival has done any good. However, the largest contribution we receive from any bank has come from his bank, which he no longer heads, and I don't think banks give money away without getting something in return.

It was at this time that Nella Barkley and Hugh Lane went to a Festival Foundation board meeting in New York, which Frances Edmunds attended. I can only give hearsay information, but I do know that prior to the meeting Mrs. Barkley wrote a letter to the board saying that she would assume the responsibilities of general manager for $20,000 a year, but she wanted full authority, full responsibility for the operation of the festival. That letter was copied to the chairman of the Festival Foundation, who at that time was Ernest Hillman, and Menotti. Frances Edmunds advised me that she had never been more embarrassed at a meeting because they just raked Nella over the coals and showed no respect for Hugh Lane and

Menotti was particularly obnoxious, and said that he was not going to give up any authority, that she wasn't worth the $20,000 she was asking. They left, bitter--this was in September of 1976, maybe August.

NEA must have come up with the idea in 1975; they came to visit in 1975, when I was president of the College of Charleston, and I took them around and showed them all the facilities of the College. They were particularly impressed with the fact that the College and community were working in concert and were enthusiastic about the festival. That was probably in the spring or early summer of '75. This ties in with Frances Edmunds' going over to Spoleto, the visit would have been before she went.

I guess I've gotten ahead of myself with the administrative part, because they had selected Charleston. Going back to the time Christopher Keene and Priscilla Morgan came to Charleston, we gave them the red carpet treatment, this was in the spring of '75. I know that Christopher Keene stayed at the Barkley's home on Sullivan's Island. Priscilla Morgan was placed in a suite at the new Mills House Hotel. I think all in all we impressed them very favorably but they were also impressed with various other cities. They returned, and I guess you can get these details from Menotti, to Menotti and told him of the pros and cons of the various....[inaudible]....

Now to revert back to that meeting. [Menotti was named] composer-in-residence and provided quarters, a house, on the campus, for him and his entourage. As a matter of interest, the first year of the festival, I personally moved with my family to my home on the Isle of Palms and let Menotti occupy the president's house at the College of Charleston. These perks were extremely important. College vehicles were at his disposal. I had seen that having this festival associated with the College of Charleston would be a tremendous advantage to the College; in fact, I think the festival was responsible for the development of our fine arts center.

Menotti was equally impressed with the Dock Street Theater, Middleton Plantation, the closeness of the beaches, and I made arrangements for him to have a house during the festival at Seabrook Island, which his son occupied most of the time. He would go over on weekends, he loved tennis, and play tennis. He is very active during the festival, and has appointments every minute--I would say 18 hours a day, particularly when he directs an opera. Without the College, there would have been no festival, because of the housing situation and the logistic support. Menotti loved the idea of the College, he thought the festival should be near an educational institution, he loved the idea of the historic part of Charleston, and he loved the idea that the Mayor was so enthusiastic and the community that for which he spoke.

Now to revert back to that meeting in New York, which was August of 1976. Nella and Hugh Lane returned to Charleston. Nella wrote a letter resigning and Hugh Lane reiterated his position that he was not going to subject Charlestonians to be a breeding place for undesirables. Now this withdrawal by Nella and Hugh Lane would have been catastrophic had not the Mayor called Menotti and other members of the board of the Festival Foundation and asked them to meet in Charleston.

I recall the meeting extremely well because it was held in the President's house at the College of Charleston in September of 1976. The Mayor had asked if it could be held in the President's house at the College. At that meeting, which was a very vitriolic meeting, in which Mr. Lane walked out with Mrs. Barkley, the Mayor stated that he was convinced that the Spoleto Festival would do a great deal for Charleston, that he disagreed but appreciated the views of the dissidents. He turned to me and he said, "Will you take over?" I said I would never say no to him and I've never turned down a challenge. At that meeting was Frances Edmunds, who did not walk out, and Charles D. "Pug" Ravenel. He was a quarterback at Harvard football and was a presidential White House fellow and he ran for governor, except that he was disqualified since he hadn't lived here long enough, even though he was born here.

The basic question was, "Will there be a festival in Charleston?" And I must say, it was the unanimous view of both the members of the Festival Foundation board and the few Charlestonians that were there that we should have it, and that we should have it next year in 1977. That gave us nine months to prepare for it.

I sort of have a history. The College of Charleston, when I became president, had 432 enrolled. When I left 10 years later, we had 5200 enrolled. The College was bankrupt and I just like that sort of thing. Similarly the Navy Supply Center was just another supply department of a shipyard and I'd been there and it changed to the third largest supply center in the world. I retired from that job to become college president.

Well, you can imagine the tasks that were required. Had I not had the resources of the College to help us, we never would have been able to get through that first year. I thought the most important thing that had to be done was to get a general manager. I was still president of the College, which was my primary responsibility. So we let it me known we were looking for a general manager and advertised it or something. But I remember we had a very good prospect; her name was Christine Reed. She had been assistant at the Marlboro Festival; she had been in charge of Casal's Festival in Puerto Rico. She was from Baton Rouge, Louisiana, and was available. She was...anxious to leave. I went to New Orleans with someone, but I can't remember who I took, to interview her. Then, satisfied, I asked her to come to Charleston.

By December of 1976, she was employed effective Jan. 1. With my wife's complete concurrence, she moved into our home until she could find a place of her own. I had a faculty member who was leaving in February, so she took over the apartment of that faculty member. Office space was catch as catch can. We moved the Spoleto office from pillar to post, whenever there was space available or we needed more space. Initially, she started next to my office, then we moved to a building on St. Phillips Street, which has subsequently been replaced by the fine arts center. Then we moved to Meminger School annex, which had been closed. And finally, to a building owned by the College and occupied by the State Employment Security Commission, which is currently the location of the Early Childhood Education Center. Then we moved to our present location in Marion Square, I think, when Jim Kearny became general manager.

The first festival was one of the most successful festivals. We had the Zulu Dancers, which had appeared at Spoleto, Italy, before, and they were a tremendous hit. We had a dance gala, which featured Alicia Alonzo and Gudenov--I wish I could remember all that, I'll have to go and get that first program. The Zulu dancers and the finale at Middleton Gardens, with fireworks, stand out in my mind as most memorable. At the finale we had the orchestra at the finger lakes and we had the 1812 Overture, and we had the Citadel cadets re-enact the final shelling of Moscow actually firing their cannon, which was followed by a magnificent fireworks display.

To make this thing a artistic success, a social success, and a financial success, certain elements were essential. And Charleston fitted in beautifully. Every opening for every event had a major social party given by a Charleston resident in their home. And these historic homes were open. Some of the parties had four or five hundred people; and most of these homes are beautiful and historic. We paid a great deal of attention to VIPs and contributors. We had at the opening ceremonies a major speaker with the governor and the mayor always attending and some extraordinary event, surprising the audience. One of these was the Flying Wallenders, a circus tightrope group, and we had them go from City Hall over a tightrope to the Federal Building. We always have had puppets, and brass quintets, also singing stars like Esther Hines singing the Star Spangled Banner.

Now, what makes the festival so successful? In three words, Gian Carlo Menotti. His ability, number one, to direct, his knowledge of all of the arts--he always gets the visual artists to do the poster. This year we have a whole Larry Rivers exhibit, and he got Rivers to do the poster for the U.S. and Italy for 1988. The only poster ever done by Henry Moore, the sculptor in England, was made for Spoleto USA, because of his friendship with Menotti. So we have a Henry Moore poster, he's never done a poster. But we have some posters today that are invaluable. I'm the only one who has the first poster from Italy; this is the only one known to exist. Somebody sent this to me, though I have no idea who it is--isn't it something? Menotti says he doesn't have that first poster. When you start, you don't know what to keep. I'm throwing things out everyday. We didn't know what would happen. Hell, we had the leading citizen of Charleston say it could never succeed. But Mayor Riley was just elected to his fourth term, and his opposition ran against Spoleto in 1987, saying that money should be going for the homeless and so forth. But they forgot how much it brings in and how little it costs from the local area.

Now who were our big supporters? And this is something that I think would help you a great deal. Our biggest support right from the beginning was the local newspaper, the Post-Courier, and its publisher, Peter Manigault. The name I'll give you is Frank Jarrell, the art critic, who can go their files, their morgue, and dig up all the old stories, which could be verifying all this that I'm telling you about the history. I remember that meeting that we had at the president's house, if you want the humor in it: My wife was sitting outside the dining room where we had our meeting. She looked out of the window and saw all these TV cameras and reporters outside the house; she stuck her head out and said, "Are you waiting for white smoke or black smoke?" But it was all over the press. They caught Hugh Lane and Nella Barkley leaving and naturally they were waiting to see what was going to happen. The Mayor came out and said that I had agreed to be the chairman and to take over and there was going to be a Spoleto.

Then the job was getting the money to finance it. After the newspaper, one of the big supporters was the Lila Wallace Foundation in New York, the Reader's Digest Foundation; Alice Tulley; all the local banks. I believe our budget for the first year was around $700,000. When you consider that earned income only provides 45 percent of your income, you realize how much money we had to raise. One thing Hugh Lane brought up in his letter is that he was afraid that Spoleto USA would be used to raise funds for Spoleto, Italy. Actually, Festival Foundation raised funds of its own for

Spoleto Italy, which at that time was about $300,000. So what we had was the contributors to Spoleto Italy to contribute to Spoleto USA. As a matter of interest, the Festival Foundation contribution to Italy was not money; it was to send the American artists--the orchestra, the Westminster Choir, the chamber musicians--to Italy and to get them back and to pay their per diem. Contrary to what Mr. Lane had prognosticated, the contribution of Festival Foundation has been reduced to $100,000 or less, with the major contributions coming to the U.S. The Wallace Foundation used to contribute to Italy; now it contributes to the U.S. Alice Tulley still gives $20,000 a year to Italy, but it doesn't come anywhere near supporting chamber music. She doesn't give anything here.

After Christine Reed came, I had to help because she knew festivals but she didn't know people and I had to get a tremendous number of volunteers, fund raisers, hospitality committees. I had to arrange for the theaters, the Mayor was a tremendous help, you see. There was a crisis everyday, and I guess I'm alive today because I was able to shed those things. But I think I've always felt that for every problem there are solutions; the correct thing is to identify them. There's usually more than one solution, too; there's always a problem, one problem, but there are a lot of ways you can solve it. That's my philosophy.

Menotti is very mercurial. I was very close with Menotti, and we still maintain a very close personal relationship. I just came from the christening of his grandson. His son married "Happy" Rockefellers' (Mrs. Nelson A.) daughter; the christening was at the Rockefeller estate in Tarrytown, N.Y. There were a few of his old friends there, and very few new friends, but the whole Rockefeller family. We've never received any support from them. We have received support from the Ford Foundation. Right at the beginning the Ford Foundation was a big help.

You know, an interesting thing I think is that I was the president at first and Menotti the chairman; then later on I became the chairman and he became the founder and chairman emeritus. Replacing me I had Jack Kessler, who developed Seabrook Island, and we used facilities at Seabrook a great deal. He always would provide housing for Menotti and some of the people who came with him, and for VIPs. Kiawah also was a strong supporter; they used to give us money but they also gave us a very big dinner for the board and for the VIPs the night before the opening of Spoleto. Subsequently Wild Dunes has taken it up; Wild Dunes gives our jazz gala.

During those first months of 1977, were you to contact some of the board of the College, a lot of them felt I was spending too much time on Spoleto, but I could see the benefits of it for the College.

And now I think they realize I was right. The festival had a great deal to do with the growth of the College. Certainly it was responsible for the development of the fine arts center. For example, we had the Guarneri Quartet down for Spoleto, and I talked them into coming back to give a concert at the College the following year for I think four concerts.

I don't know what the records will show. If you ask me, and I leave myself out of it, the responsibility for initially setting up Spoleto fell on the Mayor and the College, on both of our willingnesses to never say never and it couldn't be done.

We've never been able to bring the group opposed back in because of the tremendous animosity between Nella and Menotti. Menotti tried to make up to her once when they were on a plane, and she said, "Never, never talk to me again." I think it's bitterness because she had a chance and she's seen the success it's become.

You get this thing going and then come back with the questions you'll develop. You might find some of my statements are not corroborated by others, or that there is a difference and I can tell you why and my impressions. I am very anxious to historically put this on record. I've told everybody how important it is.

Let me tell you a little story to put some humor in this. People have asked me: "How did you get interested in the arts?" and I said, it's very, very simple. I got interested in the arts by ear. My mother would take me by the ear to Walter Damrosch's Young People's Symphony; she would take me by the ear to Ernest Schelling's music; she would take me by ear to the Metropolitan Opera in New York and we sat in a box by Gatti Cazaza; she would take me by ear to Schubert's Theater; she would take me by the ear to the Metropolitan Museum of Art. So I say I got interested in the arts by ear. Now that's a bit of humor but it's true. I think that's why today I feel so strongly that if we would expose the young people, just expose them to art, it'll show up later on. And if you expose them to the arts when they're tempted by drugs or alcohol or things like that, they'll have an outlet for their energies. They'll be interested in reading, in visual arts, in music. I drive up regularly to North Carolina to my farm and I always put on the public radio because I love to listen to the music. I appreciate also the fact that we all go through periods, like I went through the period with the jazz and that sort of stuff, but classical music always remains. I don't object to the people who like the rock music and all that sort of stuff, and the country music. In fact, we have had country music at the festival, we have jazz at the festival.

About the beginning of the festival, it all depends on what your goals are in life. I've always told young people to never set material goals, because you can never achieve them, because you're always changing them. And if you can set your goal as helping others, you will be happier and you'll make other people happier. And the only way to be happy in this world is to have other people happy. And when I see the joy and the pleasure that people get from this festival, I have the satisfaction of knowing that I've come close to achieving what I set out to do. Does that make sense? I tell my own children not to set material goals.

Taking my life as a military person, I'm a devoted American; I love my country. I see its faults but I see its greatness too. And at the College I could see the opportunity to help young people. And in the festival, I see the opportunity to expose a large number of people to something which will be a joy to them and make their life worthwhile.

Charleston was the cultural center of colonial times. And we're just returning it to its former peak condition. The first theater was in Charleston, the first opera in the U.S. was heard in Charleston--there were innumerable firsts, which I think it would be important to look at. I think it can be an educational and a cultural center; education and culture go together.

I think the fact that Charleston itself is so unique, that I wanted to see a festival here to match it, not just another festival. And this could contribute to the well being of our community. And the more I saw of it...let me tell you about a story. I received about the second or third festival a letter from London, from a lady and her husband who had attended the Spoleto Festival and said, "We have just returned from Beirut, Salzburg, Edinburgh, and your festival is second to none. And I enclose herewith a copy of a review in the London Times." I was so touched by that letter that I wrote her back and told her it was unique to receive such a letter and invited her to let me know anytime she was in Charleston. She came here and she bought one of the most beautiful houses and restored it at a cost of $400,000. That woman is still a support of Spoleto, although her husband died. Her name is Denk and her house is located at 15 Meeting Street. Whether that letter would be up in the festival office, I don't know, I certainly don't have it anymore.

You be surprised at the number of people who have come to Charleston as a result of Spoleto, and the number of industries that have made their headquarters here because of the festival. Let me give you an example. The chairman of the board of General Foods, we got them very enthusiastic about the festival, gave us $25,000, and General Foods was just bought out by Philip Morris. He's no longer chairman of the board but he just bought a plantation here in Charleston. Philip Morris gives us $25,000. And General Foods still gives us money. You know who one of our biggest supporters is right now...AT&T. Exxon used to be a very big contributor but they slowed down. We have got different people and groups that support us. Last year without even asking for it, Getty sent us a $15,000 contribution. He had been here. We get Dupont, Amoco, General Dynamics. Dupont gives because Jefferson, who is chairman of the board, is a very good friend of Peter Manigault's and they have a plant here. General Dynamics used to give us very generously and used to sponsor the finale, but Roger Lewis, the former chairman of the board, was a personal friend of mine--he's now retired--but they had a plant here.

Previously "festival" to me meant just trying to fundraise. When you talk Spoleto, they say you know that's a different kind of festival. Number one, it's an international festival; number two, we're not rushing to get Pavarotti, Domingo, or other luminaries--but Menotti has had the ability to select young people who are going to be the Pavarotti's and the Domingo's. People know that they can expect something unusual, different. The Spoleto orchestra--we have 900 auditions, the biggest job of the musical director is to audition. He goes to Curtis, Julliard, Eastman, Bloomington, San Francisco, Dallas. For 90 places he auditions 1,200 people. We have, I think, the greatest orchestra and they're all kids. It gives them an opportunity to expose themselves. Where did Yo Yo Ma get his start? Right here at the chamber music. Emanuel Ax? Here. Look at the international recognition. Menotti's ability to select these people, at least, young singers.... And it's different; they don't know what opera is going to be shown but they know it's going to be different. He's very careful about who directs them, produces them, the designer. Dance, no one knows what's going to be there but they know it's going to be different. And that they most probably will never see it again. The festival meant to me what it meant to Menotti, and I didn't know the extent of it, it meant an opportunity to expose young people, give them an opportunity to show their ability. That's what I thought it was, but I did not know the diversity.

I've been asked about starting a festival many, many times. It comes down to this. You need a Menotti, who's so unusual. He's the only person I know who knows all the arts. I mean, you talk about Leonard Bernstein, what does he know about visual arts? He knows music. Menotti directs, he's a director, producer--he's a genius, and that's why we have a problem in trying to decide what happens after Menotti. We have a planning committee working on that right now. He wants to have an assistant that he can train, but we don't think that will work. I myself am interested, I like the idea myself, but speaking for the board, no. Take somebody like Jerome Robbins and the dance, Charlie Wadsworth and music, someone from California in theater, Beverly Sills in opera--get them as consultants, and have one overall name person to be, not the artistic director but coordinator. Not Kitty Carlyle, see, but somebody who is recognized for interest who could go to a painter, and say, I'd like you to do our poster. Menotti--every orchestra knows him, the theater people know him, the dance people, the opera people, the music people.

Today I'm chairman emeritus of the festival. I think it's dangerous for anybody to be in place too long. I told them at the College I'd be there for ten years. I said to Spoleto, by God I'm getting out. Charlie Way is doing a tremendous job as chairman with Pug Ravenel as president but I don't know if Pug is the right person to be chairman.

Keep in touch with me. I don't have any papers here, most are at the College of Charleston. If I find anything, I'll let you know. I have plenty of blanks about this beginning period; now Susan Sanders told me she has some papers at the College. From '75 to the first festival in '77, right, I think that's the story. No, the idea was not to duplicate the Italian festival, in fact, we've never been able to share productions, which I think is just pathetic. In fact, today I think the only way you can make it financially successful is to share production costs. The opera costs you three to four hundred thousand dollars. If you had Philadelphia, Chicago, Houston, New York, all of them putting one production together and dividing the cost.... Cultural events are not publicly acceptable on television. You have Kennedy Center honors and look at their ratings, even when you honor big name people--Frank Sinatra and Bob Hope and Lena Horne.

***

The following interviews with Spoleto Charleston officials were conducted in Charleston during the May 1986 festival. The complete responses are based on questions presented in writing to Charles E. Wadsworth, Colin Sturm, Nigel Redden, and David Rawle. None of these persons was requested to approve the transcriptions. Follow-up questions are included as appropriate. The complete list of questions was:

1. Who started the festival and why?
2. What is the role of the artistic director?
3. What would Spoleto have been without an artistic director?
4. What might Spoleto become in the future without Menotti?
5. Why is Menotti especially interested in creating festivals?
6. How do, or will, the Italian, American, and Australian festivals differ? be alike?
7. Which are the top arts festivals in the world and how does Spoleto compare with them?

8. What should be the areas of focus of a doctoral dissertation on arts festivals? other types of festivals? fairs?
9. What is the relationship among festivals, fairs, expositions?
10. What is your opinion of Vancouver's Expo 86?
11. What are the main issues and trends facing festival artistic directors today? facing festival managers?
12. Do festivals have a special aesthetic significance?
13. Do festivals have a special economic significance?
14. Do festivals have a special political significance?
15. Is there a special relationship between a festival and its home community?
16. Can festivals be considered an art form? what type?
17. What scholarly work has been published on art festivals and other types of festivals? Who and where? Research centers? What research is needed?
18. What methods can be used to study arts festivals?
19. What is the historical significance of various festivals?
20. Do contemporary festivals follow these patterns, or are they changing? How?
21. Overall, what statement are the three Spoleto's making to their local, regional, national and international audiences?
22. Finally, does Spoleto Charleston differ in any way from other festivals of its type and how?

Charles Wadsworth, artistic director and host for the chamber series, was interviewed at the Dock Street Theater between the morning and afternoon chamber music programs on May 31, 1986.

Q: Mr. Wadsworth, how do you see the nature of a festival after ten years of association with Charleston's Spoleto?

A: This is not for broadcast? This is just for your personal use? [Yes, for the dissertation]. I think it would be more helpful to talk about the special nature of the Spoleto Festival apart from most of the other festivals that I've had any sort of intimate acquaintance with.

To understand this festival it's best for us to go back to the early days of the festival in Italy, because the festival has developed in certain ways, it's changed in certain ways, as it moved to this country. It continues in Italy. The two festivals now have very much the same personality in both Spoleto, Italy, and in Charleston. But Menotti, as he set out to present a festival, and for me what made it the most exciting festival that I know about is that he set out to produce a festival which he was very well aware would not be a sure fire hit. He said if I'm going to be like Edinburgh or Salzburg where all I do is bring in great guest artists, well known orchestras presenting repertoire's that they know is going to be successful, this is not something I'm at all interested in. I feel that the festival must be a creative festival, that it must be willing to take chances, it must be willing to accept the fact of failure, and out of this kind of experimentation you're going to get things which are much more exciting in the long run.

So a great many of the festivals throughout the world do this kind thing where it's a set program and you're bringing in well known quantities and you're playing it safe with the repertoire. Gian Carlo from the very beginning was taking chances on artists who were unknown. He was inviting young people such as--going back to 1958-59--Herbert Ross, who was then a choreographer and developed into one of the most important movie directors. He would bring in Roman Polanski, when he was virtually a kid to direct a performance of Lulu, which is an extremely grotesque work with a lot of sexual aberrations going on there. What, you know, better person--[laughs]--for Gian Carlo to have picked than Polanski, who's had his share of problems? But he got Zefirelli to do some of his first directing.

He asked Jerome Robbins to create Ballet USA, which moved Robbins' career very dramatically. He had Luchino Visconte there directing opera, and got an aspect of that career going. And then he picked on a young man who was still in his twenties; he had gotten to know the talent of Thomas Shippers. Tommy was an unknown quantity in Europe; he had just gotten out of Curtis and he brought Tommy in to be the general music director, artistic director, and Gian Carlo functioned as the overall head of the festival.

The theory was that artists such as Tommy could benefit from exposure to a wide European audience and that it could be have an international flavor, or that European artists working together with American artists to create new pieces. Many playwrights, for instance, wrote pieces for the festival. The "Indian Wants the Bronx" by Horowitz, which was a wonderful play, introduced Al Pachino to Italian audiences. He was an unknown actor at that point. Shelly Winters came over to do some first performances of some early Tennessee Williams plays. We did the first production of "The Milk Train Doesn't Stop Here Anymore."

Q: An unusual juxtaposing of the known and the known, the new and the old?

A: Right. And you had an amazing group of young performers that he brought, hardly an international name among the lot. When he invited me in 1959 to start a series of chamber music concerts in this delicious little seventeenth century theater, which seats about 300 to 35--same as this theater--he said, "I want these concerts to be different. I want you to be sure that you only bring brilliant, gifted young talents to play here, or whatever. And I want you to be sure to find some way that the concerts are informal in nature." At that time, he said to me, "Perhaps there won't be anybody there but myself and a few of the artists working for the festival, but I want to do it anyway. It'll be something in the middle of the day, one hour. I want the concert to be short and perhaps we will eventually have some other people there. But that's not really important. It's really a present for the people of the festival."

And it was true the first few days. We had 20 or 30 people in the audience and it started growing. By the end of the first summer we were getting some nice houses on weekends. The second summer was full on weekends. The third summer we were already getting extraordinary acclaim from everywhere and we were fighting them off. As time went on, it was almost impossible for people to get in. We would have near riots in the lobby. And I would have to come out and speak to the people to try to quite them. Along the way I developed what I think has been an important factor in my end of things in chamber concerts, which made them very different from concerts that went on anywhere else in the world.

I communicated with the people verbally to try to get them into an even more relaxed mood than they might be ordinarily. You have a very important factor in summer festivals particularly in that people are free from work pressures, daily pressures. They're obviously somewhere to have a good time. They're not being locked into a subscription series in New York where they have to fight subways, etc., and they have to go out because they've spent a lot of money and they may rather stay at home and watch the tube or something. So you've got a captive audience, which wants to have a good time. That puts you in a festival situation immediately at an advantage over a normal winter series of concerts.

Q: Is there a feeling of expectation, of release, a carnival atmosphere?

A: Yes, there's an expectation that they're going to enjoy it. Yes, it is that kind of atmosphere. And I wanted to add to that further by getting the people so relaxed that they could open themselves to the performers and to the music and that in turn would create a special feeling among the performers, that they would be able to give in a very free way and enjoy the act of performing.

Q: Doesn't this contrast with the normal framing we would expect of chamber music?

A: Well, it does. I think I've been able to do something of this sort in our regular concerts in New York. I did it in Italy and in Charleston I do it. I have seen people who have no background, no sophistication whatever, come here, like during the first summer, and get hooked. One man, who was very simple--like my father--and on the hottest day would have a vest and a tie and a hat. He came up one day after a concert and said, "I've never heard anything like this before, but this means so much to me I wouldn't miss one of these for anything in the world." That's been my experience.

I don't care whether it's avant garde or early Baroque or the obvious romantics, I think music and the arts must communicate to people on a gut level and it is not an intellectual pursuit--the enjoyment of chamber music, which is considered by many an elitist form. If the people are uninhibited in their listening, then they are going to be able to take the message that the composer intended. The composer is not really interested in how appreciative people are of the devices they've used in getting their feelings down on paper. So this created a special atmosphere in a festival situation, which already gives you one hand up.

For me, it was an incredible opportunity to find artists who I thought were great and then I started combining things into very unusual ways with instruments, voice, percussion, and all sorts of things that would create stimulation in the listener. When I was able to start using these great young people, I brought people who performed for the very first time in Europe such as Morry Pariah, Shirley Verette, Jesse Norman --you should get a list of artist who have been presented in the chamber music; that's probably available somewhere.

Q: It's been difficult to find archival material on festivals that would make this kind of research possible.

A: We're a real example of that. What happens is that because of the condensation, the time frame, and the amount of work you have to do in that time frame, and everybody has busy lives during the winter, so it's all they can do to get things organized for the festival. And you are working on budgets, you have no money, and people are paid very little, you have the bare number of people who can run the festival. So to have what seems at the time extra people around to keep records....

When I got the job at Lincoln Center in 1969, I wanted to know, and I had already presented hundreds of programs, what had been played. The festivals don't keep these records either. Dozens went on to have great careers, but we don't keep track because it seems like one of those extra things at the time than the day to day work. It's too bad; it would be so helpful. Also, the mistakes that were made every summer--to find out what the mistakes have been and how to correct those mistakes so we don't continue making them.

Q: What would you read to learn about festivals? Is there any professional or academic text on the subject? Suppose that in Chattanooga we wanted a book to tell us about festivals, since we had gotten excited about this one. What would we turn to?

A: Except for a couple of people in administration in Spoleto, I'm the oldest living member. Tommy died. All the early people are gone. I'm the only other artist type who's still with it, and I can rely on memory. What we do have, and this you could have access to, are the big souvenir books, at least for the festival in general. That would give you some indication to what's happening in this country. I'm not sure whether they have here a file which has all the early annual books or not.

Q: That's interesting because a British historian, Roy Strong, studied the official programs of Renaissance festivals, many of which were regarded as art works themselves and preserved. Inigo Jones and other artists of some reputation did them and they were thought important. It strikes me as unfortunate that with all our technology and know-how we're losing the visual record, video and audio tapes aren't being edited and kept.

A: The 15th anniversary of the festival in Italy had a very complete book done of all the participants up to that point. I've got that book in New York. That's got some extremely valuable background showing some of the outstanding things that happened during the first years of the festival.

The festival is unique and different from almost all other festivals because from the very beginning Gian Carlo wanted all of the arts to be represented so that the musicians and the actors could all feed off each other's inspirations and it would bring a certain excitement to my work. One summer he had an extraordinary series of poetry readings, so you had Ferlingetti from the West Coast there, and Kerouac, and Ezra Pound on the same afternoon reading from his works. For me to have Ezra Pound coming in my concert--it can't help but create a electricity, or to see Visconte there in the box. We all found we were exciting each other by what we did. I would go to all the opera rehearsals and the play rehearsals and make a point of being at all that. It gave me a feeling about how when a festival is one where things are being created specifically for the festival, really it makes it unique.

Over the years, Spoleto now is a combination of the conventional festival that you have going on all around the world, where you do bring in certain shows and presentations which are already set, such as this year the National Spanish Ballet, which is an extraordinary thing. But that's a company which could be booked anywhere if the place had enough money. It's fun for the people in

Charleston because they probably wouldn't have had a chance to see them.

Q: Does that kind of programming round out Menotti's concept?

A: It's become a way to do a festival and have it be large enough to appeal to all the various disciplines. But at the same time there's a trade off because in the early days you would have three or four different stage presentations, concerts, maybe the poetry readings every day, and a sculpture exhibition around town. We had a extraordinary sculpture exhibition which had works of David Smith, Calder, and Giacometti, and Every Alloway--and the whole town was a great piece by a great contemporary sculpture. But still you would not have anywhere near the activity that you have today, where you have four or five different presentation going on every day of the week.

Q: It's almost as if you reach a critical mass of energy.

A: Well, the only way to keep the ball rolling in the same way that it's been going since we started down here is to have a fair number of things brought in which are pre-made. The role of artistic director. That's an interesting [question] because in the early days there really was only Gian Carlo and Shippers. Gian Carlo was 25 years younger--we started in '58 and he's 75 this year [he was 47]. There was a tremendous amount of energy and he wasn't as busy directing opera all over the world, so that his main activities were the festival in Italy and composing. He and Tommy handled it very well and then they put me in charge of the concerts, which was just one small aspect of the festival. But there was an overall artistic view of what was necessary to give a special profile to the festival. That came from Gian Carlo and his imagination, his faith in brilliant young people, and in the creative arts.

Q: His role as artistic director was special?

A: It was. The Spoleto Festival as we know it would not have what we know unless there had been specifically Gian Carlo.

Q: Can an arts festival be carried off specifically without an artistic director?

A: Not successfully. It could be carried off in my mind maybe financially successful venture by a businessman but to me the festival should be much more than that. It should have some very strong artistic point of view that you're trying to get across. I think you need a creative mind to do that. I mean you could find the manager of a major orchestra who could decide this was a successful play on broadway, let's bring this, and this conductor I've heard was good, we'll have him--you can go down the line and you could put together a festival. You would have an entertaining festival.

You could do it. Whether in the long run you would have the same kind of artistic satisfaction from having attended the festival, from having been involved in it, I would have no interest whatsoever in taking part in a festival which was run by a businessman with just a slight speaking acquaintance with the arts. Those people, that sort, are the kind we want on the board of directors, who can say, "You're the artist. You know what has to be done. We have to raise the money. We know that's what we have to do. We will tell you how much we can raise and how much you have to spend. You can dream and tell us how much you'd like." Then you meet somewhere in the middle.

Q: This is where the dream and the reality come together?

A: Right. Then you come together. Gian Carlo has been throughout the years has been a tough one for business managers to deal with because he has dreamed very big at times with budgets that go way, way out of range. A lot of people get upset. The business managers find they can't handle it, and they jump ship, and we get somebody else. I've seen them come and go and the Peter Principle...some of our fine business managers have gone on to great jobs with important roles at the Washington opera or head of CBS recording, you can go on and on, the arts endowment for dance. Those are three different former directors that come to mind.

Q: But is the artistic director an important focus?

A: It depends on what your aims are. I'm a musician, first of all. I can hear all the best because I live New York during the regular season. So I can see the point of view if you've got a pretty place, it's nice weather, and so forth, and a good place to listen to music or to see theater, then you could bring in attractions. For me that would have very little interest. I want something that is different from what I get in the normal, everyday life of concert and theater going.

Q: If you were studying festivals, what would be the examples of success and failure?

A: Well, that one in Miami was an example of a good healthy failure. He attempted to put on a festival which involved many different disciplines, all 20th century music, in the middle of the summer in Miami with halls as much as 20 or 30 miles apart. I went down to put together all the 20th century budget. He had a huge budget, and he wound up finally covering his deficits through contributions. But it was a struggle. The prices were too high for people in Miami to pay. There wasn't the basis cultural interest. So it was a matter of the wrong place at the wrong time and with the wrong people.

The ones in this country which are the most successful are the ones which usually lean towards one discipline, rather than all the disciplines, as the Marlborough Festival is only chamber music--and you have gifted young people working with their elders who guide them through and they do wonderful things for a small but devoted audience. The Aspen Festival has an educational aim, which has been a very important part of that festival. But it's a glorious place to be in the summer time and they have wonderful distinguished performers. They have a little opera but mostly symphony orchestra and a few chamber concerts. So that festival is restricted. Tanglewood is a great festival but it's all orchestral stuff and its repertoire they've been playing in the regular year; but it's a beautiful place to sit on the lawn and listen to the music.

Q: Does the nature and character of the festival shift according to place and setting?

A: Yes, the place is terribly important in terms of summer festivals.

Q: Are there other festivals like Spoleto?

A: In this country there are not, which really sets it apart because most of the--well, what happens in a place like Tanglewood is that you'll have the Boston Symphony with its great guest artists. Then a couple miles away you have a great summer theater, which is not connected. But people in the area can enjoy various things and have some variety.

Q: What worldwide would be equivalent to Spoleto?

A: Go the Edinburgh Festival or some of the Salzburg Festival and you get then more the kind of festival we are doing here. There at Edinburgh you have, well I don't know the leadership there, but at Salzburg you have Karajan, who is an extraordinarily strong personality who has been guiding that one for a number of years. That's usually the case.

Q: What advice would you have for someone writing a doctoral dissertation on the general topic of festivals? or the topic of festival in general? What might be there to discover?

A: Since festivals are cropping up everywhere, since we got started at Marlborough there must be hundreds of chamber music festivals in Santa Fe, New Mexico, and Euray, Colorado--all of these little burgs are developing special chamber festivals; Santa Barbara has one. It's very exciting and everybody is interested in doing it. But the know how is very limited.

What you've doing could be tremendously valuable. I don't know of any other similar study in the 25 years or so I've been involved. If you could follow this last thing we've been talking about--why some festivals have succeeded and why some have failed--and get the factors together involving naivete on the part of local people regarding board structure, naivete in areas about what is necessary in terms of giving to the arts, that it is not a profit making venture, that serious classical music world is never going to make money.

They look at Pavarotti and Sills and think that's where it's at, and that's not. The cost of putting on Menotti's opera "The Saint of Bleeker Street"--you can't imagine what it cost, it is a glorious production. There's an example of creativity at its highest with Gian Carlo directing that opera with its beautiful design and with all young singers you've never heard of singing so beautifully. The idea of Gian Carlo to have an orchestra made up of young students or people who have just graduated--these hundred people have been called from student bodies all over the country, that to me is one of the exciting things about this festival. There's not that kind of chance taking in other places. I hope you can see it because it would be very illuminating to see what Gian Carlo has done with people with very little experience.

Q: What could I contribute in this study?

A: You could contribute by collecting--I think it's incredible--and gathering information about the types that have gotten into this crazy world and how and why they have been successful, or why they have failed.

Q: Almost as an art form itself?

A: Yes.

***

Nigel Redden, general manager of Charleston's Spoleto, was interviewed May 31, 1986, five months after he arrived from a position with the National Endowment for the Arts.

Q: How was the Spoleto Festival U.S.A. started?

A: The thing that I think is crucial about the history of this festival is that it started for an artistic idea, which was basically to give Italian audiences a sense of what American artists were doing. And that was the Festival of Two Worlds. You can't know the history of the Spoleto Festival without looking at the history of the Festival of Two Worlds. That was started because Gian Carlo Menotti was an Italian who was trained in America but was told by many Italians that America was a cultural wasteland. He wanted to show to Italians that it was not a cultural wasteland. He also wanted to create a kind of sort of artist's colony, that it very much was about artists, artists working together and artists seeing each other's work--that was very much an aspect of the festival. I think it left from that pretty quickly, that is, it became much more a festival about performances, a festival about doing specific events but always the mix was important. And the mix meant that someone who came to play in a play could also see an opera; someone who came to the opera could see a dance performance, and so on. When the festival came to America, it came as a transport but it came with that commitment to artists remaining, although obviously it was no longer a question of proving things to an Italian audience because it was an American audience. It continued to try to do some things that were of interest to a broad group of first rate artists. There also was some economic development, which was an issue here in Charleston. But I think was distinguishes this festival from other festivals, or rather from some other festivals that were started by cities, is that it started with an artistic idea rather than a cultural development idea or even with a place idea. It was very much about artists and it happened to be Charleston rather than, Let's take Charleston and try to figure out what we can do to make something exciting happen in Charleston.

Q: What other types of festivals are there? And what other reasons, such as the place idea, lie behind festivals?

A: Well, the place idea was imposed to some extent on the Festival of Two Worlds, on Gian Carlo Menotti, by the National Endowment for the Arts, which suggested he look to the South rather than to the Hudson River area, where he had initially thought of looking. That is, he had initially thought of looking to Caramoor or some of those places up the Hudson. But the people at the NEA said, Look, there's so many festivals around up there, there's so much arts activity going on outside of New York, that you shouldn't go there; there's no point in putting a festival there. You should go to someplace where there aren't things. And Charleston is sort of ideal in that it has an enormous cultural history. That is the first ballet company in America started here in 1790; the first ballet ever done in America was done here in 1734; the first opera ever done in America was done here; the first theater in America was here--I mean every city has the first something but this has a lot of cultural firsts.

I think one of the other very key things about the city is that it happens to be architecturally beautiful; that is, that this is a place that is an appropriate setting for a festival that celebrates those areas of human imagination that are concerned with beauty and with some of the intangibles of the human spirit. So, that is why it was started here. That's my interpretation. There are other interpretations that are at least as valid, and probably more valid in that I was not involved in this, and others were involved. That is, I think the mayor would have a different tale; I think some of the board members would have a different tale; I think Gian Carlo might have a different tale. The real strength of this festival is for better or worse people have agreed that Gian Carlo Menotti is the artist director, that it has an artistic focus, and that he should be in charge of this thing. It doesn't mean that we don't make compromises, that we do everything that he wants. It doesn't mean that he's happy with everything that we do, by no means. But it does mean that there is a common...a court of last resort...he makes compromises, he does things that he doesn't want to do but he's enough of a realist and enough of an artist to keep the whole thing going.

Q: What is the role of the artistic director?

A: It is the coherence question, that the artistic director, that is, a single mind, can give the festival a coherence that it might not have otherwise. And I think that's very important. Not necessarily that an artistic director has to be involved in every aspect of what's going on. In some ways, an artistic director is very frustrated. I think that a festival, in order to be significant, has to have some idea. Usually the easiest way to embody that idea is through the artistic director. And it should be an artistic idea, not an extraneous idea. If it's economic development, than it becomes an economic festival. If it's to fill concert halls, then it becomes a booking festival. Which all can have their own place and can be good in their own ways.

I think a festival that has an artistic sense has an opportunity to be better than the other because it's serving...I mean there's a kind of integrity that comes with that can't come with something that has nonartistic motives but none the less achieves them through the arts. I mean the arts become a means rather than end. That's my feeling about an artistic director. I don't think it would have happened without an artistic director here. There was talk early on about doing it without any association with the Festival of Two Worlds, without Gian Carlo Menotti, and frankly I don't think you'd be here, I don't think you'd have heard of it. There are 120 festivals in South Carolina; have you heard of any of them...maybe you have, I don't want to speak ill of the others, but I haven't heard of them until I came here.

Q: What will happen after Gian Carlo is no longer connected with the festival?

A: That's a difficult question. Gian Carlo's presence...someone has to be here, and it will be difficult for someone else. And I don't know in what way. I don't think Gian Carlo will be replaced. And I don't think there will be an attempt to replace him...qua him. I think there will be an attempt to have a new artistic director, or I think it should be an artistic director rather than an artistic directorette. I think we'll be a very different festival. I think it will be more different than the Met was in Bing and other and the new director, the stockbroker person. Because I think that this is more malleable than most organizations...it really can be very different from one year to the next.

There are few things that are fixed about it, except that we've going to stay in Charleston. We're going to be a summer festival. We're probably not going to be over 17 days long. We're going to be high arts, whatever that means, and that can mean jazz or circuses or a lot of other things. But it means the arts. I don't know what it would be like after Gian Carlo. I think Gian Carlo sees festivals as a...I think he's an impresario, that's what he feels his role in life is...I think he's an extraordinary impresario. He's been an extraordinarily successful composer, but I think he could have been a hell of lot more so if he hadn't done these festivals.

Q: Why has Menotti put his energy into festivals?

A: I don't know. I'm sure he's been asked that. He doesn't plan to write a book. There are books about him and there probably will be more; I think there have been two biographies at this point, maybe three.

Q: Would you say Menotti is regarded as the most knowledgeable person in the world on the subject of festivals?

A: No, no...I wouldn't say he is regarded as that...and I'm not even sure he is that. I couldn't answer that.

Q: How do the three Spoleto Festivals compare?

A: The one coming up in Melbourne will be in a much larger city, so it's going to be quite different from the Charleston and Spoleto, Italy, festivals. I was brought up on the festival in Italy; I went there when I was 18 and stayed for 5 years...and really came of age in a lot of different ways as a human being...deciding what I was going to do with my life. It was a very emotional and significant time for me and I realize that more and more as I've been here. On the personal level, it's meant an enormous thing to me. So it's hard to take an objective look at the whole concept of these festivals because I feel I'm tied up in them very much personally, even though...I have to say I thought I'd grown away from them--I haven't.

So this festival means a lot more to me than simply a job, a lot more. And its success means a lot more to me and it's importance means a lot more to me. There are advantages to the festival in Italy. Spoleto is a more compact town; it's also got a center, which this town doesn't have. There isn't a place as a tourist that you would go to; in Italy there definitely is. This town, however, has a kind of wealth that Spoleto doesn't have; it's got a kind of caring population, which Spoleto doesn't have. It's got a depth of community involvement that Spoleto never will have. I think the festival belongs much more to Charleston than it does to Spoleto, Italy. The Spoletini are a part of the festival and accept it and expect it, but expect it in they way they expect spring or expect summer. I mean, you don't make summer happen; it happens.

Here, people make this festival happen and don't expect it to happen without a lot of effort of their part. In Spoleto, there's really no office during the off season...just one person who used to be the local English teacher who works out of her home and organizes housing and that's about it. Otherwise, the office is in Rome. It's a very different relationship with the community. There's magic in Spoleto--the cruise ship magic--that I think festivals bring. That is, all these people descend on a place that's beautiful for a specific period of time and they all have these wonderful magical experiences together. And, when they fall in love and when they have affairs and they have fights and they meet people who become lifelong friends and they meet people who are bosom buddies for two weeks and they never see again.

On a human level that's very important; it's extracting you from your daily life. Spoleto, Italy, does it in a way that Charleston doesn't because there is so much community involvement here in Charleston. So there are a lot of people who have ties and continuity. In Spoleto there's very little of that.

And there are advantages and disadvantages to both. There's something wonderful about going to a party for the Scottish Ballet in somebody's glorious house. Members of the board are taking people on boat trips. That adds to the magic for some people...adds to the magic for the board members. In Spoleto...I was 18, I was falling in love every two weeks. I can't compare the two.

Q: What should be the focus of a doctoral dissertation of festivals?

A: I don't know. I feel that the Spoleto Festival is not like other festivals. It's not like the American Dance Festival, which I worked for, or the Jacobs' Pillow Dance Festival. I've put on some festivals myself--one called New Music America and another called New Dance USA. I think this is more like a long drawn-out Robert Wilson piece--a 24-hour, 17-day piece.

Q: A friend of mine, Carol Miles, has worked with him and has created several works of her own. How would an artist, in this case for example, looking for a place to do something new and different approach these kinds of festivals?

A: Basically, in our case they would write to me, rather than GianCarlo, although they'd write to both.

Q: If a festival encourages the new and different to surface, how are artists encouraged to speak out?

A: We approach a lot, half approach and half reaction...half active and half reactive. I think that's the way it's always been here. Gian Carlo is very much a part of the artists' community; the general manager is part of some kind of an artist community.

Q: Issues and trends in festivals, fairs, carnivals?

A: I used to be at the NEA and we'd talk about issues and trends all the time. But when you get here and you're basically trying to...today that woman on the phone was the senator's wife from Orangeville or some place. We have a bill up in the state senate for a line item for the festival and it's extremely important that those people feel that this festival is worthwhile and important and cares about them. The trend is obscured by those details. For example, the reason I was late was because I was having lunch with the people from the Scottish Ballet and they were miffed about the party last night because no one fussed over the chairman of the board...so I was having lunch with the chairman of the board and fussing over him.

That's not long term trend, but it is the absolute reality on which one works. I think the long term trends in a way are misleading. We were talking about the Edinburgh Festival and the impact that the strike on Libya will have it and tourism generally. It's going to have a good deal of impact. Who could have predicted that five months ago? two months ago? Who can predict tomorrow? If the Savannah River nuclear reactor plant blows up, I mean I can tell you that we will have some things to worry about here.

Whether Expo is going to change things operate...I mean, it's been successful...it'll be interesting to be have successful it is in terms of the arts. The LA Olympic Arts Festival was very influential in the way people are thinking of festivals in this country. It's not our way of thinking of festivals; it's a big city way and I think it's the antithesis of what this festival is. I mean, it's a very different concept and I think we can't...everyone is interested in the idea but I don't know why they're interested...cultural tourism is a big issue right now and obviously cultural tourism is something that's gone on in Europe forever.

People, Americans, have gone to Europe for cultural reasons and people have visited America for geographic reasons. They wanted to go to the beach, they wanted to go to the mountains, they wanted to go to the Grand Canyon...they've wanted to visit relatives, visit the Washington monument. But they've not gone to cities because they wanted to see plays, except in New York. They went to Minneapolis when the Met toured there; there was always some cultural tourism but it's become issue and a big money maker in the recent past. So that's a new issue.

Q: What is your background?

A: I've felt the lack of education, that's been a problem, not that I feel there are tools I'm lacking but more because I wish I were more aware of the history of what...I mean, to some extent, there isn't a history because it's going on right now and that history is sort of immaterial. But nonetheless, I've been fascinated by creating an intellectual framework, an intellectual context, within which this thing exists. And I'm not sure there is an intellectual context, but I think it'll be fascinating to develop it, nonetheless. I've never been able read very much about this kind of thing; I just can't bring myself to do it. It's very...I don't know, I just can't bring myself to do it. Q: What would you be curious about in a book, a dissertation? A: I would be interested in fact and figures rather than the intellectual context, because I feel that context...well, I don't read art history books or about the history of contemporary art because I want to make it for myself. What I want to do is to discuss with others what this context is and, frankly, we're a terribly nonintellectual field. We are just decidedly anti-intellectual, I would say. There's a very strong anti-intellectual movement in the arts. I mean, "You do it, and, if you talk about it, then you can't do it." Which is quite a bit different from the European approach, which is much more intellectual, much more political, much more explicit approach.

Q: Do you feel the Europeans see the political functions of their festivals?

A: But I don't think Americans look at political functions at all, whether it is American socialization, whether in terms of blacks and whites or rich and poor or whether in terms of our own development as a sense of place, a sense of people, a sense of where we are in life. Certainly Charleston is a city that has a tremendous sense of its own history, but probably has not much a sense of the artistic, the performing arts elements of that history. One has a sense of the physical history of the place; people know the Blackwell House dates from 1821 or whenever; they don't know there was a series here in this building at one point. There's that kind of history. We very much live in the present. We feel suspicious of the past and feel that we invented ourselves yesterday. To some extent I think that the excitement of the contemporary arts, because we did invent a lot of things yesterday.

Q: Any comment on this list of questions?

A: These questions are very interesting in that they don't deal with any of the facts, figures, how to make it work, which is frankly the thing that all of us struggle with. I can tell you I don't wake up mornings thinking about the artistic vision, though I think it absolutely crucial that it be there.

Q: That's intriguing; because it means that it must be very strong and it is not an issue...it's working. There's an acceptance of what this festival is.

A: Yes, because the consensus is in individuals. That is what has galvanized this community. That is people trust a number of individuals associated with this festival and will take things on faith because of their trust in those individuals, things that they would not take on faith were those individuals not involved. What I mean is generally people think that what they see at the Spoleto Festival is better than they might think if they saw it out of the context of the Spoleto Festival. Or they're prepared to take some radical art in the context of the festival that they would not want to see elsewhere. I was giving a speech yesterday and was introduced by someone who said he was forced to go to a chamber music concert by his wife and that he expected to hate it but he loved it. I think he makes a point of going to things in the festival that he would not go to otherwise. That issue of trust is a very important one. I don't think the people buy into the artistic vision per se; they buy into the fact that there is an artistic vision. Even if they distrust their own taste or, say, I don't like this stuff, they still trust the idea that someone feels this is good...enough.

Q: That leads to the possibility that the NEA might have had more than one reason for thinking this festival was good for the South, one being that there's not that much new art surfacing in the South...

A: No, I think that was the primary reason...

Q: And the effect of this...

A: Well, frankly, I don't think the NEA thinks things through very thoroughly.

Q: Who at the NEA would I talk with?

A: Well, the key person is Walter Anderson, who's now retired. He was head of the music program. He's very charming and a nice man. I knew him when I was at the NEA for a few years. I don't think this country has policies, has politics in the arts. We don't think things through. I mean the glory of the garden, that wonderful English statement about decentralization is now something that could be said here or certainly wouldn't get much attention if it were.

Q: What are your personal plans for shaping the festival?

Q: Do you see broadcasting festival events live on TV or radio?

A: Although I'm eager to have our events put on television, I feel there's something about being in a theater that can't be duplicated anywhere. I think television is a very, very poor second. The exciting thing to me is that relatively few people can come to this. We reach a larger group than the population of Charleston, which is important; when I speak of a small group, I'm speaking of a group larger than our community. It is a large group in its own way but not measured in the millions. I think it's extremely important that we do things that have a kind of intimacy and scale that is human; because I don't think two million has anything to do with the human scale at all. And I don't think it's a question of being elite or exclusive. I think its a question of doing something that is worthwhile. The kind of things we're doing are not things that should be looked at in five minute doses in between flipping channels, having dinner, having telephone calls. That's not what we should be doing because these are serious things that do need to be given serious attention that you can give when you're in the theater. If you devote an hour and a half or three hours to go to a performance, you give it a very different kind of attention span than if you are watching a television set. I think that is something that is crucial for the performing arts, crucial for the arts generally. I think the television sort of demeans things and trivializes; nonetheless, if I can get on TV I'll be thrilled.

Q: There seems to be a lack of archival material?

A: Well, we don't throw anything away...look at my desk. My own feeling on that if given the choice between doing and archiving, there's no choice.

Q: When I was in a position to attempt to explain Spoleto to a community, I found a lack of organized materials. It would have been helpful to have a history, video tapes, and so on, to get across the complexity and the full scale of activity going on.

A: I agree it's very difficult to convey. But I don't think the concept is translatable. I don't think you could do a Spoleto in Chattanooga. I think you can do a Riverbend Festival in Chattanooga. I thought about setting up my own festival rather than doing this, in some city or other...I might do it yet. But I wouldn't want it to be a Spoleto Festival. I would want to do a different festival.

Q: What type of festival would you do?

A: I would prefer to do a festival more like this than like a lot of the others.

***

Colin Sturm, the first managing director of Spoleto Melbourne, Australia, in September 1986, was interviewed in May during Charleston's Spoleto 86.

Sturm: To start from the beginning you've got to make an assessment of the purposes of a festival. The problem from what you have from what you've told me is that you're not going back to basic concepts. A festival has two important foundation stones. They're part of the total structure. Without them both being effective you haven't got a festival that will work. The first part of a festival structure is whether the community wants it. If it's not bubbling up from the community, it's going to automatically fail. You cannot impose something of this sort onto a community from above. It just doesn't work.

If the community wants the festival, and the word festival covers a great number of types of activity, then they're going to help pay for it and they're not going to mind if public monies are put into it. A lot of the infighting that happens can be less intrusive; it will always be there because in a community there are always two sides to what's proposed. You need to set your goal in whatever paper you're thinking about of clearly defining the objectives of the festival.

Q: You would agree that to ask why a festival started is a very important beginning?

A: Yes, Spoleto was started by an idea from Gian Carlo Menotti, which came from his friend, the American composer Sam Barber, who said, when they were both young men, that art should not be just the froth on the top of the main soup, that it should have a concrete, measurable effect in a community. To test that as a premise, they both looked for a town in Italy and in the States--they were looking in both places, but they found quickest a town in Italy which was absolutely on its beam ends. Its population consisted of very elderly and very young people. All the young, middle age groups had to leave because there was no work, no money. Unemployment was something like 60 per cent.

So they thought that if they were going to prove their premise, then the festival would have to do things that in a commercial sense were good. So when they suggested this to the city fathers, they grabbed at the chance to try anything. Therefore, my first point was that the community wanted it, what community there was there. The end result is that Spoleto is a thriving little city as a direct input of the festival. It brings lots of tourism into the place. There's been a great deal of building and regeneration of the medieval buildings has carried out with public money from taxes that the money has generated. So there has been a measurable effect. The improvement in beneficial life style through the arts is enormous.

And in a smaller way, because its effects were not so obviously into grand statistics, which will give you into the country. So that in the USA, although I'm not sure which department it would be, in Australia and in Britain, these statistics are in the department of government that looks after budget, since they're a budget consideration. The multiplier effect in Keynesian economic terms that are available from the arts are surprisingly big. You'll find that the employment possibilities, which for a politician is a big thing, the creation of jobs is quite properly and should be an important vote getter, so that every politician is going to be interested in this. You'll find that there are statistical models everywhere. Local governments if they are at all forward looking will have in their forecasting budgetary processes statistical models of the various types of input that will affect in an improvement fashion their ability to generate income.

Q: So, the primary question is whether the community wants a festival? This would seem to imply that they perceive the need, the benefits, the economics and is that known clearly. Wouldn't that be a key aspect?

A: Yes, the community must want it. If they're not terribly interested, then you won't be able to get money given from private pockets, private in the sense of local people, whatever. And you won't be able to get the important support, which are public monies. No politician worth his salt is going to commit one dollar to a project that hasn't got community endorsement. Politicians are the same the world over; they're looking for votes, the ongoing supply of votes; the pork barrel concept in any language works. Therefore, it's very important for a festival to have a general conception of being good for the community.

The second point that I'd make to you is that the festival has got to be able to raise the money to do the job. Now, a small festival like the Riverbend--I think you said the budget was nearly a million dollars--any community in general terms is going to need between $2 to $4 million dollars to make something happen that is going to be very much up front effective. Just the cost in the USA and Australia, which is going to be too broad a generalization but for this purpose it's enough, and you can't in fact have something that's going to be looked at by people who are not terribly committed unless it is very impactive. It can't be effective in those terms without sufficient money, which then goes the full circle back to there having to be enough people in the community who think it's worth having. So you see my point of that first pair of foundation stones.

Local government, represented by the mayor of Charleston or in your case Chattanooga, both have the same sort of concerns and basically their concerns are the one's I've been talking about--votes and getting those votes in a way the community thinks is worth while. So that where local or state or national government has got clearly in this group mind that there is a benefit, a real benefit, then you're going to get some assistance.

This really goes back to starting the thing off as we have done in Australia for some 15 or 20 years and that is when a festival is put forward to government as being considered for public funding, that there is a proper economic feasibility study done of the impact in all the terms of an economic study of benefits and costs. If there is a plus at the end of the balance sheet, that is, if it's going to put in something more than it takes out, then there's a chance that government might consider it. But if it doesn't come out, if it just comes out even say, then the benefits are not particularly apparent in feet on the ground, down earth principles and it then becomes the sort of festival which is an area grouping of people who are going to put their hands into their own pockets, do a great deal of voluntary work themselves, and probably have a ball. But it'll stay at that particular level.

In Australia, we think of this of the Scout All [Boy Scouts] complex, you know. The Boy Scouts are a nice worthwhile community activity; the parents of the kids get together once a month or whatever--you've got an activity which brings the community together for that particular purpose.

Q: You don't think that's a sufficient purpose for a festival?

A: No, it's too specialized. You see, a general festival--you've got two types of festivals. One which is a carnival, summer festival out in the open, marching girls, sports, swimming, stores selling things in the street--this type of what comes into my mind under the general heading of carnival, which is a great idea. Once a year, usually in the summer time, sometimes a day or a weekend or a long holiday weekend--that's one type of activity. That can be done reasonably cheaply.

But when you start about a festival that means the use of venues, halls, theaters, bring people in from out-of-state, entertainments, and so on, you're then getting into the entertainment business. The entertainment business is a very expensive and very specialized, and, if it's going to work well, almost needing a genius at business. You were saying you that you hadn't had an artistic director. The whole point of having an artistic director is to have somebody who is essentially uninterested in the financial end of things, who is looking purely at what is going to work in a general entertainment sense. And you then have, what I presume you've already got under that system, someone who is a business manager. Now without the combination of the two I think you run a risk.

Festivals are not a subject studied in great depth in England or Australia because it's not going to be of much use to anybody.

There are only about seven major festivals, which are fully blown in administrative terms, in the whole world. These would be the three in England--Wakesford, Edinburgh, and Chichester; there's a number of small ones in the States, one of which is Wolf Trap; there's this one with its three locations; there's a big one in Australia, apart from the one we're setting up, in Adlelaide, which is the capitol of South Australia. It's an international festival.

Of the ones you've mentioned, Salzburg is a very specific festival; it's just an annual event with some specialized operas; it's not what I think of as a broadly based festival. There's one in Canada that I can't remember the name of. There's a marvelous one in France, Aix en Provence. On the fingers of two hands you can come up with all of the top ones, under ten I think.

Of course, the study of those festivals and small ones has been matter of great interest to the economics division of government in that area, both local, state, and federal. Those statistics are probably published every year as part that entity's economic process.

Q: A Salzburg study has used a seven to one economic multiplier. Do you agree with that ratio?

A: I would think that in Keynesian economic terms would be very hard to support. It would treat with a pretty beady eye any multiplier that went much above 2.7 or 2.8. Because in the arts you get all sorts of muddying of the waters by people who are multiple attenders. Say you come here to Charleston to visit the festival. You're one person, but you might have ten activities. So that you as an audience unit are counted ten times. This is in feasibility study terms something that has to be watched very carefully. Similarly, the trickle-down effect to the community in beneficial terms has the displacement factor. By proper statistical analysis, in Keynesian terms, I would imagine that a multiplier of seven, for instance, is double counting the audience number effect. It is also not taking into account properly the displacement effect. What happened is, if you visualize yourself as living here in Charleston, and you decide ten tickets, say at a $100 value, then in your own pocket budget sense instead of spending that $100 on other entertainment or other things, such as replacing a household item costing a hundred dollars, you put it into the entertainment thing. This displacement factor mitigates strongly against the overall beneficial effect. It's where the beneficial effect creates a true plus that you've got something that's measurably beneficial. Therefore, the multiplier effect that anyone comes up with in the arts that's more than the high two's, I'd be casting a pretty beady eye at it.

Q: What got you interested in managing a festival in Australia? What in your background prepared you for festivals? And what will be the artistic nature of that Melbourne festival?

A: Gian Carlo Menotti is our artistic director. He has a very definite opinion on what should be included in a festival. It's very wide ranging but it has its emphasis on opera, ballet, and music. It's not to say he's not interested in the other fine arts, literature, crafts, and so on, but this is his primary interest. Therefore the emphasis of what he puts together has got his personality stamped on it. So the sort of festival we'll have is really rather similar to here in Charleston. There are certain things that push it in one direction or another because there are local requirements. Because unless you can sell the tickets, you are not going to have a festival that will last very long. So you have to look at your market place.

Q: What percentage of tickets will be local?

A: The statistics in general terms, at least the English ones, show that 80 per cent of support for a festival is local. The way they define local varies but it ranges from 50-100 miles. The remainder comes from near but not very far away. Then you classify "far away" as far as you like. If there's going to be a special performance of an opera that I like, and it's going to have a cast that you're never going to see again, I would personally move heaven and earth to get to it. And other people of like mind would come from other parts of the world. But we would be some part of that 20 per cent of "other."

***

David Rawle, public relations agent for the festival, was interviewed May 30, 1986.

Rawle: The festival was started by Gian Carlo Menotti in Italy in 1958 and he always sought to have an Italian festival in American. It was called the Festival of Two Worlds in Italy, always sought a companion festival, looked for a site in America through the National Endowment for the Arts and others was directed to look into the Southeast, came to Charleston, was enormously impressed by it, and was received enthusiastically, and was started by him and the board of Spoleto, Festival dei du Mondi, the festival in Italy.

The artistic director in the case of Spoleto, Gian Carlo Menotti, is also the founder. So it's really his baby. His role is like the gorilla; where does the gorilla sit? anywhere he wants.

I think that each endeavor is a reflection of those who create it and those who help sponsor it and its locale and the interest of that locale. In the case of Spoleto it is a reflection of the artistic direction of its founder and it is a reflection of the Charleston community, which considers itself an art form, if you will, and is celebrating the beauty of its own historic city while also reaching out into new directions as the festival does. It's that sort of combination in the case of Charleston and Spoleto.

The idea was to create a festival in which an entire community could be immersed. It's difficult during the festival to pick up a newspaper, talk to an individual, visit a shop, or watch television or listen to radio without having a sense of Spoleto's presence. That is a joyous celebration of the arts and the festival form provides that.

Q: What is the relationship between festivals, fairs, expositions from your perspective?

A: I think that each endeavor is a reflection of those who create it and those who help sponsor it and its locale and the interest of that locale. In the case of Spoleto it is a reflection of the artistic direction of its founder and it is a reflection of the Charleston community, which considers itself an art form, if you will, and is celebrating the beauty of its own historic city while also reaching out into new directions as the festival does. It's that sort of combination in the case of Charleston and Spoleto.

Q: What are the main issues and trends facing festival artistic directors, managers, or public relations directors?

A: The greatest challenge is to stand up from others and to differentiate yourselves. That requires a focus and the discipline to hold that focus. The special economic significance of Spoleto to Charleston is it has in its nine years contributed about $350 million dollars spending directly and indirectly to this area. Secondly, it has attracted companies that wanted to move here because of the quality of life that Spoleto has helped catalyze. Thirdly, it has helped boost the economic vitality of the other arts organizations. Politically, it has opened up people's minds to a wide variety of ideas and cultural influences because it is so international in its presentation. Aesthetically, it is the perfect complement to Charleston because Charleston itself is an art form.

****

April 2012 – Given the importance of Charleston Mayor Joseph P Riley's leadership and support since Spoleto Festival USA's beginning in 1977, some of his public comments on the festival and what it signifies for his city are valuable in the context of this book. Much of what he has said, such as festival opening ceremony statements, is in the public domain, and the following statement was published on the Spoleto Festival USA press office web page sometime before 2005, according to a conversation with festival public relations director Paula Edwards, March 6, 2012; she in late March emailed and approved the quotation for use. She said the contact person listed had worked in the festival PR office until 2005, so the comments below apparently were posted by the press office in the early 2000's. Again, as he has from the beginning, he stresses "art power," that his city's festival is "a national model of private and public partnership, and a living example of how the arts can revitalize a community."

Conversation with Joseph P. Riley, Jr.
Mayor of City of Charleston, South Carolina
Published around 2000

Question: Mayor Riley, you've been involved with Spoleto Festival USA from its first days in Charleston in 1977. Can you comment on the impact of the Festival on Charleston, and vice-versa? Have the two come together, as Gian Carlo Menotti had hoped, to create an "ideal city"?

Joseph P. Riley, Jr.: As we understood from the beginning, Spoleto Festival USA is something that permeates the city. That's why the scale of the city and its beauty, the tempo of life, were so important. The idea wasn't to have a few events in one building, where people put on their fancy dresses and tuxedos. Rather, it was to be a festival where the arts become a part of the fabric of the city's life. And it has been an extraordinary success. I believe this Festival could serve as a national model of private and public partnership, and a living example of how the arts can revitalize a community.

Q: Can you tell us specifically how the Festival has revitalized Charleston?

JPR: The Festival has been contemporaneous with Charleston's commercial revitalization. Since the Festival began, the city's annual visitation has increased threefold. The Festival now brings $42 million directly into Charleston each year. Through a ripple effect, its annual economic impact is estimated to be more than $100 million. We've now had half a billion dollars of investment and reinvestment in our downtown since 1977, of preserving and renovating our historic buildings, of seeing shops and restaurants and hotels flourish. The result is that Charleston is more beautiful than it's ever been.

Q: Do you feel the impact of the Festival goes beyond dollars and cents?

JPR: Without question. The Festival gives Charleston a priceless opportunity to show itself to the world, and it brings the richness of the world's art and the world's people to our streets and sidewalks. That's the finest revitalization that any city can have.

Q: Mayor Riley, you also witnessed the disputes that led to Gian Carlo Menotti's departure from Charleston in 1993. Can you give us your impressions of that transition?

JPR: I had been greatly worried about the transition for years before that. It was going to happen. It would happen either because Gian Carlo decided to leave or else because of infirmity or death, which come to us all. I always worried, because I knew the Festival was perfect for Charleston, and that it would be a huge loss to our city and to the art world in general if the Festival disappeared from our streets. Frankly, I had hoped the transition would happen on my watch, so I could help Charleston and the Festival get past that difficult period. Now we have done just that. I say it with enormous relief and pride--we have done it. The Festival's future is assured.

Q: What did the city contribute to the effort to keep the Festival in Charleston? And what was your role?

JPR: The city helped in a number of ways. At a time when money was scarce, we were able to provide the Festival with a source of direct funding that was worth close to $100,000. We also wrote off expenses that the Festival owed us, as we should. In addition, we held the Piccolo Spoleto Festival as we do every year, which contributes to the celebratory atmosphere that people expect when they attend Spoleto Festival USA.

As for my own efforts, I see it as my role to be there for the Festival whenever they need me. I just try to make myself available to the Festival's wonderful board of directors and to its general manager, Nigel Redden. It's through their efforts that the Festival achieves such great success.

Q: You just mentioned the celebratory atmosphere that people feel in Charleston during the Festival, and how the city's own Piccolo Spoleto Festival contributes to it. Is this "ideal city" just a Potemkin village, as skeptics might think? Or is there really something behind it?

JPR: It's real. You see, we're very proud of the mingling of the citizens and the Festival's artists. As we see it, the Festival is not an elite series of events, but rather it becomes the city, and the city becomes the Festival. We have all worked hard to make sure that the Festival touches everyone.

That goes back to the first chairman of the board of the Festival, Theodore Stern, who suggested that we hold the opening ceremonies in front of City Hall. They're not held in an auditorium, where you pay admission. They happen in the open air in this wonderful historic district, with the streets closed to traffic, and hundreds upon hundreds of people come. It's a civic event, attended by people from every walk of life. That's the sort of thing that gives Charlestonians the feeling that this Festival belongs to them all.

Q: How does the community demonstrate its support?

JPR: The doors are open. When the musicians are walking down the street, maybe coming from a rehearsal, maybe going to a concert in their formal outfits with their instruments in their hands, you'll hear the citizens saying to them, "We really enjoyed the concert last night," or "It's great to have you here." There's a real feeling of welcoming and involvement.

Q: Again, a skeptic might think that sort of mingling happens in the Historic District, but not in the outlying neighborhoods.

JPR: It's certainly true that the Festival is concentrated in the city's center. But the Festival makes efforts to reach into and involve every part of Charleston, and our citizens have responded with warmth and appreciation. One of the main reasons Nigel Redden organized the *Places with a Past* exhibition in 1991 was to make sure that people in various neighborhoods were touched by the Festival. The artists and the artworks actually came to them, and in many cases citizens from those neighborhoods were drawn into the process of creation. We were very pleased with our involvement in 1997 with the *Human/Nature* exhibition.

Q: When you speak with the mayors of other cities, do you talk about how Charleston and the Festival work together? Do you feel it's a model relationship?

JPR: Spoleto Festival USA has been inspirational to many cities and to many mayors as an example of how the arts can bring about economic revitalization. Of course, there is no other festival that has had such a great impact on a city. But through its example, Spoleto Festival USA has encouraged cities to believe that the arts are developmental, that the arts are not just frills or niceties, that the arts can make cities better and stronger and more economically vibrant. Cities all over are developing arts districts or arts centers, and in large part they have this Festival to thank, because it has shown mayors and city councils that if we invest more in the arts, we will get a high return in terms of the economic and physical and social development of our cities.

***|

APPENDIX B

RIVERBEND FESTIVAL CHRONOLOGY

AND STORIES OF ORIGIN

Note: As mentioned in the author's note, this chronology of Chattanooga's Riverbend Festival origination was taken out of the final draft of the 1990 dissertation for forgotten reasons, most probably to reduce the length at one reader's request. Yet it was written and at first approved to be a part of the formal document. It has been published on the Split Tress Press web page since 1996 but now longer accessible except for the table of contents and book link. It is included to provide context for the preceding more conceptual chapters and for comparison with Dr. Stern's story of origin. Pinpointing the genesis of an idea proves difficult if not impossible, as these two chronologies suggest, since there is always preceding history both remembered and forgotten by choice and by accident. Some of this material is included in the Riverbend endnotes.

And, often there is historical precedent. One does not always expect a grandfather's 1902 dairy to connect with his grandson's 1990 scholarly research. But Walter Clifford Hetzler kept daily journal entries and clippings all his life in Chattanooga, TN. I was surprised when reading my grandfather's journal October 2010 (when I worked on this manuscript at my cousin Carolyn Preische's home in East Hampton, NY) to discover his first hand recollection of an early Chattanooga festival or carnival (similar to the Riverbend Festival that started in 1982):

"During the month of May 1902 the city of Chattanooga celebrated their first major festival which was something in the nature of a fair. At that time the eleventh street was not paved or open for traffic and this street was used for the fair. Beginning at Market Street there were small carnival shows all along the street and many refreshment booths. Where the Patten Hotel now stands there was nothing but a hole or rock quarry, which had been roofed in and converted into a Dante Inferno in which skeletons and unearthly scenes were depicted. **The purpose of the festival was to draw visitors and help business. It was something new and large crowds were drawn to the city.** [Emphasis mine; it's remarkable how much the past repeats itself]. Harry [his brother] had the notion that he wanted to come down to the festival and be off for a few days from work. When he asked for relief there seemed to be no one to relieve him so he told the dispatcher that I could do the [telegraph] work and they let me work for Harry." And that is how my grandfather W. C. Hetzler became a railroad telegraph operator as a young man, later moving along the TAG railway staions with his wife, Anna, formerly Hutcheson, and seven children, eventually settling in Hill City, as North Chattanooga was called then. —March 2012.

Summary: 1987 Riverbend Festival

For this analysis, the methodology used in the "functions" categories for Charleston's festival (Chapter II) can be continued. These categories suggest the basic elements that appear to dominate each city's festival:

Name: Riverbend Festival
Type: Popular entertainment
Model: Spoleto Festival U.S.A., Plum Nelly
Purpose: Bring community together, improve economy, raise awareness of arts
Results: Large crowds, develop riverfront, build pride
Programming: Highlighted popular musical entertainers such as Willie Nelson, Sarah Vaughn with the Chattanooga Symphony Orchestra, "Blood, Sweat & Tears," "Chicago," Arlo Guthrie and Pete Seeger, the "Spinners," the "Judds," a classical chamber trio in residence, and about two dozen other performers
Budget: $1.3 million
Duration: Ten days
Location and theaters: Several acres of a downtown riverfront park plus a few other indoor and outdoor sites
Artistic Director: 0
Management: Self-perpetuating board, hundreds of volunteers and a contracted local management staff
Workers: Hundreds of volunteers, part-time staff
Audience: As many as 100,000 spectators gathered for the most popular concerts, such as "Chicago" in 1987; estimated audience was 250,000
Audience access: $8 plastic lapel pin for all events
Related events: Water skiing and hydroplane motorboat races on the Tennessee River; triathlon; downtown parade
Food: Some two dozen vendors offered food, drinks, and souvenirs

Reaction: City leaders have described the festival as the city's "signature piece." Featured in "Southern Living" as key event
Profit: $75,000 estimated

Urban Context: Other Festival Proposals

From May 1980 to late 1981, various persons in Chattanooga apparently were struggling to fill the city's empty festival space. Of several possible beginning points for the story, it seems wise to acknowledge first that my "dream" to have a town arts festival was nothing very new, although some have said so (see Preface, Slack article). Riverbend's creation myth could have several tellers, each with a different version, each "true." In that respect, it is important to acknowledge other ideas that were in play. These included my awareness:

1. that the community had had downtown arts festivals in the 1970s and did not now have them, that this space was empty, that this category of community activity was absent. Only much later did we learn of the city's spring festivals of the 1900s;

2. that there were others producing commercially successful "arts and crafts" and tourist festivals, such as the local tourist bureau that had its festivals, Nickajack in October and the Chickamauga Lake spring festival;

3. that when I came back from Salzburg in August 1980 and we had a meeting at my home in September, there was talk of different kinds of festivals; Spoleto Festival U.S.A. was the only one of those from which we had materials to review;

4. that later that fall when I talked enthusiastically of my ideas with a UT Chattanooga staff person, I did not realize that she was involved with a downtown arts festival with the Chamber of Commerce and was starting to work on it. This became a source of contention next spring when they were applying for a Lyndhurst grant at the same time as our group, and the foundation director reported we were accused by the Chamber director of plagiarism. However, I believe from private observations that it probably went the other direction and the group picked up on our discussion and ideas, which by necessity were always in the public domain in the hope the festival spark would ignite;

5. that at some time during this general period, the Lyndhurst Foundation's New York consultant Gianni Longo had written for the foundation a five-point strategy for developing the community, one

item of which was a festival, we were told. Later it was discovered that what this strategy mentioned was a city fair and possibly as well a downtown series of outdoor musical popular entertainments in the summer of 1981.

Festival Chronology

The sequence of influences, the process of opening of a new definition of festival, and the larger context of the sources that influenced this one city's creation of a festival are revealed in the succession of festival and festival-related events that follow, condensed for brevity but accompanied by necessary narrative to connect the main events of the story. The list of events, although not complete, includes those activities related to the central arguments of this analysis.

1898-1900s, Annual Spring Festival

During this period, Chattanooga hosted an annual week-long May festival with concerts, parades, bicycle races, flower shows, citizens in carnival dress, and king and queen coronations. These were major events involving towns around the city. A midway carnival occupied downtown city streets. Regional events celebrated the Norwegian god Balfur's arrival in "Spring--the Festival of Nature," a provocative hint of nature's statement of a "festival of differences" when the plant kingdom is in full blossom.

These festivals had several commonalities with the creation, purposes, and programming of the current Riverbend Festival. It appears the only surviving element is the August debutante presentation, the Cottonball Gala. These festivals were unknown to all local Riverbend organizers until March 1988. Then, when several of us read copies of the Chattanooga News-Free Press articles that I had found at the public library, we were struck by the similarity of having had at that time a local man pick up from uncertain sources the idea of having a major town festival for many of the same reasons we had chosen in 1981. It would be trite to say that history repeats itself. But "empty space" theory predicts that the scenic mountain town would inspire imaginative dreaming of cultural artifacts to match those of its natural context. More extensive work in searching for such historic patterns is indicated. [See note at beginning of Appendix B about my Grandfather Hetzler's journal entry on a 1902 Chattanooga festival].

1935: Second National Folk Festival in Chattanooga.

    This event was held in the spring as part of a national resurgence in gathering and performing "authentic" folk ballads and in restoring the "purity" of the "folk," mainly "white folk." In a study of the racist "White Top Folk Festival" of the 1930s in Virginia, Chattanooga's hosting of this event drew comment for its inclusion of black singers:

    Sarah Gertrude Knott, who founded the National Folk Festival in 1934, presented a broad range of performers, including black, who shared the stage with whites. "[The] picture of our folk life today would not be complete," she said, "without the contributions of the Negro." At her second annual festival in 1935, held in Chattanooga, Tennessee--surely as race-conscious an area as south Virginia--Knott's mountain fiddlers and ballad singers shared the program with a thousand-voice black chorus singing spirituals."

    (David E. Whisnant, All That is Native and Fine: the Politics of Culture in an American Region. Chapel Hill: UNC P, 1983, 244).

    I am indebted to Allan Tullos of Emory University's Graduate Institute of Liberal Arts for mentioning this work late in the research for this study. The intentionally racist purposes of "White Top" merit comparison with similar German ideologies of the 1930s. White Top reflects an extreme example of racially exclusive programming and admission to the "white" top of the mountain.

    The image of a thousand-voice black chorus evokes the "sing" festival, "Southern Voices," proposed during the 1981 planning seminars by Doris Hays (presented below). We were very negligent in not doing our homework on past festivals in the city when the formal research was underway.

1950s-60s: Annual spring or fall weekend arts festival sponsored by city's Allied Arts Council; performing and visual arts indoors and outside. Two days.

1972: Last downtown spring arts festival held; closed at request of downtown merchants complaining about lost parking spaces on Saturday. Mayor urges arts to match the city's scenic environment.

    The city's previous downtown festival was the Fall Showcase of the Arts on September 22, 1972. Mayor Robert Kirk Walker's address from the reviewing stand focused on the "energy and spirit generated by the arts." As his communications aide and speechwriter, I was pleased with the editorial in both newspapers to the positive role of the arts in city life.

    But, according to a conversation with Kathy Patten, the chairperson of that event, the downtown retail merchants complained so much about the loss of business during the festival that it was discontinued. All the parking spaces were filled, the merchants complained.

The festival itself was primarily visual arts, including crafts, juried paintings, pottery, and a small amount of performing arts. A few clowns amused the crowd; dancers had a brief presentation, and the Chattanooga Symphony Orchestra played. For nearly a decade no central arts festival of any kind enlivened downtown Chattanooga.

1978: Allied Arts Festival Proposal; no action taken.

A memorandum by attorney Whitney Durand on November 13, 1978, summarized ideas presented by an arts festival committee meeting of the Allied Arts Fund of Greater Chattanooga. The conclusion was that an arts festival both as an artistic event and as a fund-raising venture should be considered, even "though this would entail a significant departure from its [the fund's] present policies." The Fund's policy was not to engage in programming activity.

For a site, a single location at either the University of Tennessee at Chattanooga or a rural site was preferred, although barriers to charging admission fees at UTC were a major obstacle. A rural setting offered scenery and freedom to charge fees but the risk of inclement weather. Other settings included downtown Chattanooga, the Jaycee Fairgrounds, and Chickamauga Battlefield.

The availability of a large number of enthusiastic volunteers was seen as a critical necessity. It was decided that, since the Allied Arts Fund was to receive all the earned funds, it would have to be the chief and perhaps only sponsor. Churches, college students, the Junior League, and arts organizations were suggested for possible workers. Signaling the Fund's view of its relationship to other organizations was the statement that: "Organizations like UTC and the Junior League would be sponsors without contributing front-end money, without receiving financial benefit, and with certain defined roles." The hope was that UTC would provide student drama and musical performances, that the Junior League would provide bookkeeping and budgeting, and that churches could handle food preparation and service (in return for some or all of the proceeds). Another option was to have a Fund member agency, the Chattanooga Arts Council, as sponsor "with the Fund nevertheless receiving the proceeds." The issue was not resolved.

Revenues were estimated at $42,000 from admission charges, food and drink sales, and from commissions on artists and craftsmen sales for a two-day festival bringing 5-15,000 people. After expenses, between $15,000 and $30,000 would remain as profit. The last weekend in September was felt best, judging from the success of Plum

Nelly, Prater's Mill, Ketner's Mill, Gatlinburg and other fairs or festivals. Summer was ruled out because of vacation interruptions.

The type of festival was uncertain. Durand's memo pointed out that "a happy compromise between high quality and lost cost for art and crafts must be reached." The Hunter Museum director, Cleve Scarborough, felt enough artists and craftsmen would participate if many purchasers were possible. Diversity of activity, such as short performances by UTC drama and music groups, the opera association, the Boy's Choir, a ballet group, and a portion of the symphony, was regarded as important. Foreign foods from the Adult Education Council was an idea viewed favorably, but there was no enthusiasm for paid performances such as puppeteers or for carnival "rides" such as merry-go-rounds and ferris wheels. Bingo and balloon-bursting games were not discussed. The consensus was that Plum Nelly (20 miles south on Lookout Mountain, "plum" out of Tennessee and "nelly" out of Georgia) offered a model for suitable art and crafts at satisfactory prices, but there should be more entertainment and an effort to introduce a new audience to the Fund's member agencies.

Soon the Spoleto Festival in Charleston was to shift the emphasis from visual to performing arts. Many of the differences in Menotti's approach to the arts in Charleston, which appears closer to Guthrie's view of a "serious" festival, and Chattanooga's 1978 conception of an "arts and crafts fund raiser" festival can be seen in this one community's idea of a town arts festival in 1978. For unknown reasons, the project was not attempted.

The contrast in the attempted inclusiveness of the 1981 approach and the 1978 "arts and crafts fund raiser" festival is seen in its view of its controlling role: "Organizations like UTC and the Junior League would be sponsors without contributing front-end money, without receiving financial benefit, and with certain defined roles." That hardly would have been a festival of "differences;" it is not surprising that it lacked the broad support needed for a town festival.

1980: May, Chattanooga Times article on Charleston's Spoleto Festival U.S.A.

Several musicians were visiting at my farm, about a half hour south of the city, one weekend morning in mid-May of 1980. Someone called our attention to an article in the Chattanooga Times announcing "Spoleto Festival U.S.A. Opens Friday." After we read it, one respected symphony musician, principal trombonist Art Jennings, then a member of the University of Tennessee at Chattanooga music faculty who now is at the University of Florida, agreed that Chattanooga needed something like this. But he believed the arts leaders would never allow anything of this scale that could not be controlled as were the traditional museum, symphony, opera, or ballet. Having worked as public affairs director for a Chattanooga mayor during the early 1970s and possessing in 1980 (at age 39) the essential optimism of a farmer, salesperson, and teacher combined, I argued that a major festival was possible, one that could have a similar effect on Chattanooga.

The headline that had caught our attention said: "Spoleto Festival U.S.A. Opens Friday." Both community benefits and avant garde programming were given equal weight in the news article. It was a story about the arts and a story about a community, a combination that was proving very potent. The first paragraph summed up most of the elements:

Spoleto Festival U.S.A., an annual multi-arts extravaganza that has drawn worldwide acclaim, has turned this historic city into a cultural mecca and provided the setting for several premiers, including the debut this year of Arthur Miller's first play in a decade.

The 17-day festival begins Friday [the third week in May] with an opening ceremony and the performance that night of Bellini opera "La Sonnambula." The event is expected to draw about 100,000 visitors who will pour an estimated $25 million dollars into the economy.

Charleston Mayor Joseph P. Riley Jr., termed "an advocate of the arts," said:

> The primary value of Spoleto, which I felt originally, would be the case is its intrinsic contribution to the community. The cultural horizons of the citizens of our community have exploded. Spoleto has whetted the artistic appetite of our citizens young and old. The dividends have only just begun to be obvious. The festival, which is operating on a budget of $1.6 million in its fourth year, has turned Charleston into an art form itself. What the festival has done, and continues to do, is to tell the world about the great beauty, architecture, splendor, and ambience of Charleston.

The story reported that Menotti's festival was founded as an American counterpart to the one begun in Spoleto, Italy, 23 years ago (1958). It included opera, theater, film, dance, choral offerings, jazz, country, and mime. Piccolo Spoleto, it said, was a series of mostly free performances in parks, churches, restaurants, theaters, and auditoriums that serve as a showcase for young artists in music, theater, dance, mime, and art; it also provided chamber music concerts, folk music programs, arts and crafts fairs, and innovative theater pieces.

The avant garde programming of Spoleto's "differences" can be seen in the works and in their characterization in the article: Miller's The American Clock--premier; Japanese impressionistic theater event Directions to Servants--controversial; a piece by Jonathan Swift--erotic and shocking, American premiere; Menotti's debut of a children's opera, Chip and His Dog; and composer-arranger Mary Lou Williams performing in the world premiere of a jazz work commissioned by the festival. This mixture of works is seen in dance by Aleksandr Godunov; jazz by Sarah Vaughn, Sam "Lighting" Hopkins, and Dexter Gordon; Verdi's Requiem by the Westminster Choir; pianist Rudolph Fikursny; and an orchestral grand finale at Middleton Place, an eighteenth-century plantation on the banks of the Ashley River. Country music also was included.

In a traditional marketing manner, tickets prices for each event were sold in advance or at the box office and ranged from $2 to $15. This method of using individual seat ticket sales to generate revenues was to be rejected by the Riverbend organizers after its failure the first year; the token used to gain admission into the magical festival spaces was an important key to understanding the differences in philosophy of the two festivals.

1980: May, visit to Spoleto Festival U.S.A., Charleston.

Plans were made to visit Charleston through the press office. I was attending as a communication teacher, and the Spoleto Festival U.S.A. public relations office offered, as it has since then, superb assistance and hospitality. One musician friend accompanied me on the trip. There is a mixture of images from that visit, heightened by the expectations of the news article: visual signs of banners throughout Charleston (which I had never visited), camping near the beach, very hot weather, the role as a tourist, attending opera, ballet in the outdoor garden, chamber music in the Dock Street theater, a play in a small theater, paintings and crafts for sale in outdoor exhibits near City Hall in the streets, formal art exhibits at the private museum--all seen with a growing interest in whether such an undertaking would be possible in my hometown. I saw a city and its festival in the context of the news article I had read and the discussion among the musicians that followed that reading. Also I saw the festival in terms of its potential presence in Chattanooga, continually asking myself whether what I was seeing would have a place in my community. Mayor Riley's comment about the city itself being an art form struck me very forcefully and that concept has not been lost. Other town arts festivals apparently have this same quality in which the city itself becomes the frame, and in effect the "proscenium" arch for this particular type of "theater."

I had been caught in the dream of a festival for Chattanooga; I had been caught up in the powerful emotional currents of Charleston's Spoleto Festival; and I had been caught up in the power of the performing arts; and finally, I had experienced a model of festivals and festivity totally different from any I had seen before.

1980: June, gathering of friends at Sam and Sally Robinson's home, where idea of a local festival was first discussed seriously; the talk elicited interest and letters of introduction for author's visit to Salzburg Festival.

Charleston was having such a success with its new kind of festival, so why not learn from one of the best of all festivals and enjoy a working holiday in Salzburg, Austria? Several friends encouraged me to learn what I could if I traveled there, and letters of introduction were prepared by the mayor's office, the county executive's office, the Chattanooga Times, the Chamber of Commerce, and tourist office, and UT Chattanooga. These proved helpful in gaining interviews and admission to a few of the sold-out events in Salzburg. I decided to take the risk to, as the Seattle poster, with the town's mayor standing from a rear view with his open raincoat put it, "expose myself to art." Personal and professional motives blended, and I do not recall that either motive dominated; romance and festival seemed inseparable then as now, "cruise ship" magic, as Nigel Redden aptly has described the experience.

1980: July, visit to Salzburg Festival, Austria.

If Charleston's Spoleto Festival provided a powerful model of festivals and festivity, then the world famous Austrian festival in Salzburg in 1980 further reinforced the superiority of the performing arts model of "festivalling" over the visual arts model. I knew a report of first-hand experience with an event would have more influence than a report from a book alone.

1980: September, festival planning dinner at my home with arts leaders and a Knoxville opera singer who had worked at Spoleto.

Hoping not to lose the enthusiasm from my exposure to the two festivals during the summer of 1980, I invited some twelve persons to dinner at my farmhouse. Among them were several personal friends: Robert Austin, artistic director of the Chattanooga Opera, and a singer friend; Lynn Grimsley, director of the Allied Arts Fund, and her husband David; Sally Robinson, executive director of the Arts and Education Council, and her husband, Sam; Alex Henderson, a visiting high school friend, and his wife, Virginia; and Howard Alexander, the Chattanooga Steinway piano agent, his wife,

Frances; and Rita Brava, an opera singer from Knoxville who had worked in public relations at Spoleto Festival U.S.A. Brava served as a resource person in answering our questions about the Spoleto experience. We looked at copies of the materials from both Spoleto and Salzburg, although most were from Spoleto because most Salzburg materials were not in English.

A number of suggestions for action resulted, among them the recommendation from Sam Robinson that rather than working with existing arts groups a separate non-profit festival board be created. This eventually became the structure of the original festival. None of the represented organizations responded to the ideas discussed, although the individuals present were to play key roles in winning support the following summer and in making a festival a reality the following summer.

I do not, however, recall anyone else in Chattanooga urging creation of a major town arts festival such as the two I had visited. It seems to me more likely that communities need festivals, possibly certain types of festivals, at various stages of their evolution, more strongly at certain times than at others. If so, I suspect we all were responding more to a felt community need--an empty space--than to the examples of Charleston and Salzburg, powerful though those models were.

In retrospect, it appears that persons desiring to create a town arts festival should focus more on a series of seminars on the idea of festival than on looking at brochures, programs, amateur photographs, and even reports of visits. At the time, I could not conceptualize what I was looking at and could not communicate adequately the differences in what I experienced and the meaning of "festival" in our community.

1980-81: September-April, discussion of idea among friends; interest grew.

We continued to talk about the idea of a community festival of much larger dimensions than any of us had experienced or imagined, but there was no model such as I had experienced easily available to share with various people who were interested. The lack of a downtown festival since 1972 was well known and there was general agreement on the need for another festival of some kind. During these months the tension created by not having resolved some of our plans from that dinner continued to build a network of interested friends and supporters. The subject of festival was in our conversations often during those winter months and spring. I had thoughts of asking for foundation support to develop further research and to find a person or persons who could develop a properly organized proposal for consideration. However, my own teaching, business, farming, and social life prevented any further detailed work on my part.

1981: Discussion with colleagues at University of Tennessee at Chattanooga about university sponsorship of festival; no interest emerged.

In discussions with a university colleague, today only dimly recalled, I learned that the Chamber of Commerce was interested in starting a small downtown arts festival again to promote central city businesses and needs. There was no library reference work on festivals, nor any mention of festivals in my mass communication source books, except possibly in the category of spectacles and as "event marketing." One English department colleague, Dr. Robert Vallier, who also taught the advertising course, and I went through the possibilities of a major festival and his enthusiasm strengthened my hopes during the busy winter months. I also mentioned the idea to the interim chancellor, Dr. Charles Temple, but he said that although he was interested he did not see this as part of the university's mission. However, the new chancellor, Dr. Fred Obear, and his wife, Trisha, were to be key members of the first board of directors that started the festival.

1981: April, a friend, Deanne Werner, encourages action on the idea. Robbins calls Lyndhurst Foundation to suggest a festival, learns of foundation's interest in a citizen-initiated fair as one of five city development strategies, and is given encouragement and numerous suggestions by its executive director.

One April weekend a friend, Frank M. Robbins, III, and I were talking on the front porch of my North Georgia farmhouse, with Chattanooga's smog in view 20 miles away, while his wife was away for the weekend. He and I had worked together on several Arts and Education Council projects since the early 1970s. As we talked, and the festival subject came up as it had done frequently, he said that he agreed with the possibility of a major festival unlike what the town had seen in the past.

If any one person deserves credit for making a town festival dream a reality, it should be Mickey Robbins. His enthusiasm and energy for civic arts projects is legendary in Chattanooga. In his capacity as the next president of the Chattanooga Arts Council, which was the programming arm of the Allied Arts Fund, he decided to call the executive director of the local Lyndhurst Foundation and to discuss possible funding. This was done in late April on a Monday. That evening Robbins called me with great excitement to say that the executive director, Rick Montague, liked our ideas. He said that they also had received a proposal from their community development consultant which mentioned a festival or fair as one of five projects needed to improve Chattanooga. Montague asked that a proposal be prepared and gotten to him immediately so it could be presented at their board's next meeting. He advised Robbins to go first class and not to hold back on what we had in mind.

1981: May 5, first proposal for $1,000,000 "Celebration of Togetherness" festival to Lyndhurst Foundation.

 Robbins and I talked several times during the week and planned a brainstorming session that following Saturday. I will long remember that afternoon when we enjoyed the spring sunshine and the limitless possibilities of "going first class" while sitting in his backyard to draft a proposal for the foundation. We alternated in taking notes as each of us put our "dreams" on paper. Freed of mundane financial concerns, we dreamed big, as all the Riverbend leaders have done since that time. Montague's philosophy and guidance were catalysts then and since for the ideas that emerged as the Riverbend Festival, although considerable disagreement with the substance of his philosophy has been expressed by me and others.

 We reviewed, at Montague's suggestion, the Lyndhurst Foundation annual report of that previous year. Its general guidelines stated that its overall goal was to stimulate broad community support for projects that address neglected, impractical, or invisible needs and that injected something special or out of the ordinary to those aims and interests match the foundation's. The foundation expected results that made recipients more capable, effective, and independent of contributions, which created diversity of support, which encouraged competition in the private sector, and which broadened individual contributions. The duration of support for projects was to be for a limited period of time and those receiving grants should be able to achieve clearly measurable and objective success. We felt the festival concept met all these criteria and in fact the foundation, headed by businessman John T. Lupton, has been the primary and continuing sponsor of the Riverbend Festival since its inception.

 The proposal that Robbins and I wrote in note form that afternoon and typed the next day was also reviewed by Robbins' wife, Eloise, and another friend, Deanne Werner, the professional pianist and opera accompanist who had suggested we "stop talking and act." Through her the "artistic" view was represented at the very outset of the public emergence of the festival idea. We met that Sunday evening at Robbins' house and improved our original draft, which incorporated several suggestions from Montague. From a 1989 view, it appears to have reflected my experience with the two 1980 festivals I visited.

Starting with my 1971 experience in the Chattanooga mayor's office, my primary strategy of public leadership and civic participation has been based on the principle taught in various modern management seminars, which is that "we support what we help create." Basically the strategy is to ask anyone to help with a project if interested, no matter what the person's "station" in life (it is extraordinary how many people are "waiting for a train" to take them to their next destination and only want to be invited aboard). This meant that the more persons involved in generating and giving birth to a community project, the more likely the project to happen because more people would "own" the idea. Yet the risk of this was that it also could evolve in a way differently from what the original proposers had in mind. I felt, as a matter of practical political strategy and tactics, that broad support was more essential than backyard dreaming by a select few if the town were to have a festival resembling anything like the ones I had visited. Hindsight suggests that this philosophy rests on the maintenance of a "creative empty space" for a sufficient period of time to encompass a wide variety of thoughts, inputs, debates, etc.; the ensuing tension has the social effect of cast the imaginative net wider and wider, one in which more and more desires and personal visions are ensnared. This idea grows directly out of Leonard B. Meyers basic theory of music: "Emotion or affect is aroused when the tendency to respond is arrested or inhibited." (*Leonard B. Meyer, Emotion and Meaning in Music* (Chicago: U of Chicago P, 1957) 14).

The ideological struggle between "art for a few" and "art for the many" began at this point. Werner, and another Baylor friend and our volunteer attorney, Nelson Irvine, argued that a few artists could put together a first class festival, while Robbins and I argued that we needed input from many people if we were to have a town arts festival such as those I had visited. This crucial issue was not resolved as late as 1988 in an extensive evaluation that year of the Riverbend Festival.

The ten-page proposal included statements about the city as well as our ideas for a festival. Dated May 5, 1981, we addressed it to the trustees and officers of the Lyndhurst Foundation. The complete proposal, which was never shared widely because, in retrospect, its adoption would have negated the need for the planning grant, which the foundation required to move the process to its own predetermined opinions. We were not sure of our aesthetic or economic reasoning, and the four of us, with the possible exception of Werner, lacked professional experience in the creation of a festival of any kind.

Because the full text was never seen by foundation officials and the early organizers, all of it is included here, where more "empty space" exists for presentation of the complexity of the festival idea. The complete document also is important because I think it captures the basic nature of the festival theater that is being argued. I regard it as the central (but repressed) document that probably would have led to a "festival of differences" had it not been for the Lyndhurst Foundation's intervention in pursuit of its own worthy but excessively private purposes, intentions that are sincere yet impair desirable pluralistic political practices. The proposal opened with a very optimistic view:

May 5, 1981 Foundation Proposal
"Chattanooga has the potential to become a more vibrant and dynamic city in the next few years. New parks, a more active riverfront, the UTC Coliseum, a renovated Tivoli Theater, the TVA Solar Center, and a new Provident complex follow progress already made at Miller Park, the Civic Center, the Public Library, and Fountain Square and suggest a sense of physical momentum. The question, however, is whether the city can reach out and capture a vision of broadbased improvement and vitality or instead fall back on a status quo of social and economic apathy. The history of other cities in similar circumstances suggests Chattanooga could just as easily fall back as move forward.

One of Chattanooga's principal problems is its sociality. Unlike the citizens of many other picturesque cities, Chattanoogans began a mass exodus from downtown at 3:30 every afternoon. By six p.m. the center of the city is virtually deserted. Why? Because very little is happening of interest. The resulting loss of retail and tax dollar is considerable. But beyond the loss in dollars is a loss in community spirit and pride and the loss of a cohesive urban life style and shared interest. By one definition a city is a focus of shared interests and common concerns. A deserted city center is a tangible sign of a citizenry alienated from its city. In short, the potential inherent in Chattanooga's new physical improvements may never take hold if the city remains a social desert. Some have described the Chattanooga community as divided, dispirited, and lacking in broadbased social vitality. We think there is some truth to this view. A key missing ingredient is a set of community activities which physically pull people of different stations in life together.

The purpose of this letter is to propose that consideration be given to funding a comprehensive, community-wide celebration of the visual and performing arts for a five-year period. Much has been done already and is being done to try to improve Chattanooga's "togetherness" activities and amenities. We have much reason for pride in these endeavors. But we think there is considerable opportunity to build on the base of current year-round artistic and cultural activities and the physical and historical attractions of the area. We see considerable potential in a major, well-planned celebration. The returns could be substantial in both a social and economic sense.

Learning from the precedents set by Charleston, South Carolina's Spoleto Festival, and Austria's Salzburg music festival, we see no reason not to create Chattanooga's own "celebration of togetherness with diversity" through a quality of first-rate artistic expression that pulls the community together and attracts substantial regional and possibly national interest. We think it is very important to began the Celebration in the summer of 1982 to capitalize on our share of the estimated 12 million tourists who will visit Knoxville's World Fair in that year. A significant investment could produce both a renewed sense of civic pride and, more practically, measurable economic rewards. Accordingly, we encourage the Lyndhurst Foundation to work with us and other interested Chattanoogans and a variety of organizations in taking the first steps toward making a "celebration of togetherness" (as a temporary title) become a reality as early as the summer of 1982.

We believe the celebration should strive for artistic and cultural excellence and not merely serve downtown business interests alone, as important as this is. The tangible economic rewards of such excellence are large. A recent study by the Johns Hopkins Center of Metropolitan Planning and Research of six cities (Columbus, San Antonio, Springfield, Minneapolis-St. Paul, Salt Lake City, and St. Louis) for 1978-79 showed that arts institutions in those cities generated $209.8 million in direct spending, including restaurant meals and transportation, and $4.1 million in added sales, income and property tax revenues to local governments.

As a tentative theme one aspect of Chattanooga's "celebration of togetherness" is the idea of bringing together at one time and place, possibly at Miller or Riverfront parks, contrasts in musical styles, artists, instruments, etc. For example, Luciano Pavarotti and Loretta Lynn could take turns singing classical leider and love ballads. A rock band and chamber group could be juxtaposed. Istakh Perlman and Stephan Grafelli (the European jazz violinist) and a well-known bluegrass fiddler could alternate in a single appearance and conclude with a joint finale. In addition to this idea, the celebration could bring together, both traditional and innovative, opera, symphony, dance, theater, film, visual exhibits, regional arts (such as story telling, gospel singing, bluegrass music, etc.).

Both indoor and outdoor locations will be needed. Indoor facilities include the Tivoli, Memorial Auditorium, UTC Coliseum, UTC Fine Arts and Theater auditorium, Cadek Hall, Little Theater, Chattanooga Choo Choo, Hunter Museum, churches and schools. Outdoor sites include Miller Park, Riverfront Park, Chickamauga Park, Fountain Square, UTC's Chamberlain Field, the Bicentennial Library,, and even riverboats for "floating musical events" will be needed. And perhaps as architect such as Mr. Longo [the Lyndhurst community development consultant] should consider the merits of an outdoor amphitheater on one of the unused slopes of Cameron Hill.

We see no need to have excessively commercial booths that duplicate the other local arts and crafts fairs. Nor do we see any need to avoid conflicting scheduling of performances within the suggested two-week period. The burden will be on individual artists, supported by effective promotion, to attract audiences by the excellence and popularity of their work. Competition will only enhance the artistic quality, although good judgment should be used to prevent serious overlapping. Local artists will be used as much as possible, and some addition funding may be needed to strengthen local arts organizations. These matter can be dealt with by the professional staff at a later time.

It is difficult to explore fully the multiple facets of this large, complex festival in this letter. Much will depend on the personality and vision of the artistic director. This selection of this individual is the key factor in achieving artistic and financial success. We suggest someone equal in stature to [Gian] Carlo Menotti, artistic director of Spoleto Festival in Charleston. One individual suggested by the assistant director of Szene der Jugend (Youth Festival in Salzburg) during discussions is Andre Previn. Other possibilities are Leonard Bernstein, Beverly Sills, or another dedicated artist of equal standing. This appointment should be made with the full endorsement of the Lyndhurst Foundation board and staff.

The next most important appointment would be that of an administrative director. Possible candidates are Evan Luskin of the Chattanooga Opera Association or Bruce Storey, UTC Sports Arena. A professional advertising and publicity campaign is essential to attract regional audiences needed to offset costs of programming. Much can be learned from the experience of the Charleston, South Carolina, Spoleto Festival, now in its fifth year. A delegation from the Foundation and the proposed Celebration board of directors should attend the 1981 Festival in late May or early June. Reservations had been made for 12-15 persons.

Project Name: Celebration of Togetherness. Note: We prefer "celebration" rather than "festival" because the former term suggests a specific theme while the latter is more general. A "celebration of togetherness" focuses directly on our main goal, which is to create widespread community participation and to bring diverse ethnic, social, religious, and economic groups together. As planning progresses, a more suitable and promotable name can be selected.

Table of Organization: (proposed community leadership)
A. Organizational Committee
1. Rick Montague, Chairman
2. Sid Hetzler, Vice-Chairman
3. Mickey Robbins, Vice-Chairman
4. Sally Robinson
5. Deanne Werner
6. Booker Scruggs

B. Advisory Committee
This group is to be selected in consultation with Mr. Gianni Longo and the staff of the Lyndhurst Foundation. Possible names include: Dalton Roberts, Paul McDaniel, John Franklin, Ralph Kelly, David Beebe, Fred Hetzler, Jim Lewis.

C. Possible staff members
1. Artistic Director: Andre Previn, Leonard Bernstein, Beverly Sills
2. Administrative Director: Evan Luskin
3. Production Manager: Bruce Storey

List of Activities and Proposed Schedule of Events: Rather than attempting to do the work of the artistic director, which involves balancing appropriate programming, availability of guest artists and groups, and budgetary realities, we are attaching a copy of the Spoleto calendar as an example of what is working well now in Charleston and with modification could work here. Many festivals follow a similar pattern in multiple programming, as the brochure from Salzburg indicates. The key point to be gained from a perusal of the Spoleto schedule of activities is that major activities are scheduled at the same time but alternate so as to allow attendance at most activities at some time during the festival. We see the local opera association as one of our strongest artistic offerings and it should be emphasized at the Celebration ("Porgy and Bess" by Gershwin would fit our theme of "togetherness.") Also, the new Civic Ballet offers the talent of an artistic director with international credentials who has participated regularly in the Edinburgh Festival.

Budget: For a general approach to the budget we are inclined to use the Spoleto concept. This festival had a budget last year or $1.6 million, one-half of which was from ticket sales and one-half from foundations, corporate and public sources. Most festivals of this type anticipate one-half of the cost to be born by ticket sales. The Charleston festival reportedly brings 100,000 visitors who spend an estimated $15-25 million in the Charleston economy. Charleston's mayor says the festival has turned the city into an art form itself. This view justifies contributions from federal, state, and local governments (because of the revenue generated) as well as from the private sector (because of the investment return). In reviewing other significant city arts festivals, we find that most experts estimate a 1:7 cost: benefit ratio. Thus, a greater investment produces a greater reward (about seven times for the community). The wisest course here is to work with a total budget with contributions from all public and private sources amounting to $1 million. Most of the funds should go to groups in the performing arts and the quality should be such as to generate substantial regional and national publicity through professional efforts. The leadership exercised by a major Lyndhurst grant should stimulate substantial business, public, and individual support in the early years. Ticket sales should cover one-third to one-half or more in subsequent years. A business-like approach to planning and evaluation should be stressed at all times. Some events should be free while some should subsidize others. We request that Lyndhurst underwrite the festival up to $500,000 per year with the stipulation that this amount be reduced if possible from other sources as outlined above. If the grant is approved, we will apply for tax-exempt ruling from the IRS."

The letter closed with the biographies of the project initiators, Frank M. Robbins III and me, and was signed by the two of us. This proposal represents many of the ideas that were attempted by the first 1982 festival. Even now it seems to have caught the idea of "difference," of juxtaposition of genres, of contrasting styles, of the role of the arts as an energy source--not an "after dinner mint," as Menotti expressed the idea.

The proposal met with favorable reaction from the foundation. We met with the executive director, Montague, and their urban animation consultant, Gianni Longo. It was decided to submit an application grant for approximately $25,000. This would include retaining Longo to research a variety of arts festivals, to provide to travel funds for local officials to visit Charleston's upcoming Spoleto Festival U.S.A., to prepare an audiovisual presentation to communicate the festival idea (this was not accomplished to my regret), and to provide funds for other consultants and expenses to generate broadbased community understanding and support for a major arts festival. This second planning grant letter was signed by Robbins, Deanne Werner, and myself.

Longo, the foundation's community development consultant, had worked with other cities and was an editor of a series entitled Learning from Baltimore and several other cities. Several days previously, he had met with Robbins, Irvine, and me at my home for dinner and for some living-room music-making on my piano, which he was studying in New York. Following that evening of discussion and brain-storming, and preceding preparation of the planning grant, he met with me and explained his five-project community development concept, one being a city fair. This was at a dinner meeting which Robbins, Werner, and Irvine could not attend; each of us had demanding professional obligations and time was scarce for any civic project. Longo said that his "approval of and recommendation of" the grant application was dependent on my taking the primary leadership position. Although I explained my other commitments, and argued that any of the other three organizers or others were better qualified for this project, Longo insisted.

I agreed to take that responsibility until artistic and administrative directors could be appointed under a new board. He accepted this stipulation, about which I felt so awkward that it was not mentioned to the others; it was my intention to propose Robbins for president of the organizing committee. Maintaining silence was a regrettable error and a high price to pay for having a festival in view of the patterns of intervention and conflict that developed.

After this was resolved, we all met and agreed to organize a nonprofit corporation and enlisted what was to be the invaluable support of attorney Nelson Irvine. The four of us then took it upon ourselves as volunteers, although a small legal expense for incorporating was set aside in the planning grant, to shepherd this fledgling idea through its early and tentative steps.

From the theoretical perspective of a empty theatrical space, it appears--in "removing the blindfold," as Kundera put it, "to see what I experienced and what meaning it had"--that in the May 5 proposal and the planning grant proposal we confused the political function of opening up a new space with a more artistic function of filling a defined theatrical space. Yet the entire Chattanooga "mise-en-scéne" itself was a powerful framing device. In this proposal and others as well, the Charleston and Salzburg view of the "city as a stage"-albeit a "bare stage"--became a dominant frame, suggesting the actual "emptiness" of the physical Chattanooga city was itself deeply felt by the festival "dreamers" and others.

It may be more than a coincidence that all four of us--Robbins, Irvine, Robinson, and myself--who were so active in providing the

initial energy for the festival, were amateur or beginner-level musicians. Led by the professional talents of pianist and choir director Deanne Werner at our 1980-82 social gatherings, we would play and sing as much as we would debate what kind of festival we wanted for the town. Music was a basic love of the group and it was natural to share it with anyone who wanted to "sit" in and "jam." This suggests a very close connection between the desire for a party and the desire for a festival, an idea that introduces Chapter I.
1981: May 11, final proposal for $23,000 planning grant to Lyndhurst Foundation for travel to Spoleto, research, consultant from New York.

The foundation, it would appear, could have supported the specific recommendations in the May 5 proposal, which reflect in part some of Montague's suggestions; at his suggestion, we had made specific recommendations. I do not recall the conversations now but somehow the decision was made to withdraw our specific proposals and in their place to request a planning grant. We worked the following weekend at my home in Kensington, Georgia, joined by Deanne Werner and Eloise Robbins, and, rushing to meet the foundation's deadline for its quarterly board meeting, submitted on May 11 the following letter:

Planning Grant Proposal to Foundation
"In reference to our letter of May 5, 1981, and subsequent conversations, we are requesting an urban arts festival planning grant from the Lyndhurst Foundation in the amount of $23,000. The purpose of this grant is to fund travel to other urban arts festivals, research of same, and preparation of an audio-visual presentation and a detailed proposal for consideration by Lyndhurst at its August meeting.

We propose that Mr. Gianni Longo be retained to assist the Project Committee by researching and preparing a full grant application for the type of comprehensive arts festival described in our letter of May 5, an updated copy of which is attached. While one member of the Project Committee has already visited and contacted officials of both the Salzburg, Austria, and Charleston, S.C., festivals, we propose that several community leaders and members of the Project Committee begin the planning phase of this project by attending the finale of the 1981 Spoleto festival on June 5, 6, 7. This will enable some key leaders of the Chattanooga arts community to experience first hand the vitality, artistic significance, and organizational expertise of this established and well-regarded urban festival, which approximates the model of what cold be created in Chattanooga. (See attached article on Spoleto '81 from May 10th Atlanta Constitution.)

The grant will also be used to fund additional travel and research of selected festivals and personal interviews of artistic and administrative personnel connected with these festivals.

The other principal effort is to gather information on a prospective artistic director and necessary administrative staff. Preliminary interviews will be held with potential candidates to prepare for the possible implementation of the final grant."

The letter provided a suggested list of those to be invited to travel to Charleston, which included the organizers, Longo, the mayor and county executive, executive directors of the foundation, Chamber of Commerce, and Tourist and Visitor Bureau, and a city and county commissioner. It requested funds for several visits to other festivals, consultant travel, an audiovisual presentation to accompany the final grant application and for communicating the festival idea, and for Longo's festival research (noting "he is also acquainted with Mr. Gian Carlo Menotti, artistic director at Spoleto"). We indicated our plan to request the required tax-exempt ruling from the Internal Revenue Service:

"The project planning grant will be filed by the Community Foundation or another exempt foundation as sponsor. However, the full final grant will be requested by the newly formed and independent Friends of the Festival, Inc."

1981: May 30, Chattanooga Mayor Charles Rose, his wife, Carolyn, and four festival organizers visit Charleston's Spoleto Festival U.S.A. and meet its leaders.

The strategy to build community support consisted of several separate but related activities. My assignment, political support, was the most immediate because we felt a tour to Charleston's Spoleto Festival U.S.A. was necessary. On short notice, we were able to take then Mayor Charles A. Rose and his wife, Carolyn, to the 1981 Spoleto festival; I had worked with Rose at City Hall in 1971-73. (Rose returned to public office in 1986 as public utilities commissioner; he has been a strong festival supporter.) In making the arrangements I worked directly with Dr. Theodore S. Stern, the very active chairman of Spoleto Festival U.S.A. at the time, and his festival staff. His willingness to extend all assistance to our mayor and our group on such short notice was its own statement of Charleston's new confidence in its much discussed festival of all the arts.

1981: June 5, Friends of the Festival, Inc., incorporates with four officers (Hetzler, president; M. Robbins, vice-president; D. Werner; treasurer; N. Irvine, secretary).

As the project developed during Chattanooga's "revolutionary" summer of 1981, four major strategies for earning public support were planned: gaining financial backing, seeking public support, planning festival research and educational seminars, and searching for potential artistic directors and business managers. Gaining financial control of our grant was at the top of the agenda. First, potential alternative mechanisms for receiving the grant and dispersing the funds were considered. The foundation could not donate funds to other than tax exempt entities. The University of Tennessee at Chattanooga was considered at my request as a faculty member, and the acting vice chancellor was willing to receive the grant, but our committee felt UTC was too costly, unwieldy, and bureaucratic for this type of planning grant. The Chattanooga Arts Council was asked to accept the funds. By this time Robbins was its president but the parent organization, Allied Arts Fund of Greater Chattanooga, and its leadership refused to allow acceptance of the grant for a variety of reasons--one being a plan to cancel the Chattanooga Arts Council. The official reason given was that a festival would diffuse current fundraising efforts toward a planned major capital campaign.

This had the effect that those of us who were active on the arts council, essentially the same group of people with an additional dozen, were unable to act in any official capacity. The decision was to follow attorney Sam Robinson's earlier idea and to create, as promised in the planning grant application letter, a local nonprofit group, Friends of the Festival, Inc. The funds were channeled initially through Longo's New York City firm, the nonprofit Institute for Environmental Action. After the Friends of the Festival was incorporated, within a few weeks a portion of the funds were forwarded to our account, Longo's institute keeping out its portion of more than half for the planned festival research and video presentation. (Irvine did not keep these financial and legal files, he said in 1986, so I assumed this important portion of the record could not be reconstructed; however, he said in May 1988 that he had found these materials.) Longo also discarded his research materials, he said when I asked in 1986; our casualness about keeping what now appears to be such useful historical material apparently is typical of the problem in documenting "stories of origin."

We strongly felt that the combination of outside consultants and local community expertise was essential to raise the level of knowledge about festivals in general and to create awareness of performing arts festivals that was not accessible locally. Neither the university or public library had a comprehensive book of festivals; the best I could find was a reference work listing seasonal and religious festivals.

By this time word had spread about the Lyndhurst planning grant and we began to enjoy the effects of that powerful foundation's support, which I had come to experience as a mixed blessing. Competitive reactions were swift and could have destroyed the festival before it ever got underway. The Chamber of Commerce executive director, for example, objected and accused our group of plagiarizing its own idea for a small downtown arts festival. It is still unknown how this charge could have been justified since Robbins and I wrote the proposal together; it seems appropriate to mention for the record its occurrence, however unpleasant the memory.

Several other key officials in the arts structure objected vigorously to the Lyndhurst Foundation, and attempted to stop its funding of our group but with no success; we were being painted by some as "young turks" rebelling against the all-powerful arts establishment, hardly our intention and in fact opposite to the idea seen in Charleston. My notes show that two individuals within the university argued that this should be controlled by the university and not by citizens who were not professionally trained in the arts, a suggestion that made sense (the first operating president was a UTC music professor) except for the leadership problems within the institution at that time. "Control" of the festival seemed to be the main issue, it now appears, not its potential for imaginative artistic creations of beneficial effects. We surmounted this opposition by using the foundation's influence, and by quickly carrying out our planning grant strategy to gain the interest and support of key community leaders.

The second strategy was for us to visit politicians, financial leaders, and local artists. As mentioned above, my particular assignment was to visit immediately local political leaders and seek their support, based on my acquaintance with them from previous years. Robbins and Irvine were to see financial leaders, and Werner was to see key local artists. This was done quickly; the idea was to offset any negative criticism or counterarguments by the opposition we knew by then to be developing. Our local nature was a crucial factor in this strategy and offset potential criticism that went to fund outside consultants.

It was becoming apparent by then that Longo, for example, had to be kept out of town and out of sight if we were not to be blocked by charges of "foreign" influence, as the Chamber executive director, James Hunt, explained to me when we discussed the source of his accusations of plagiarism. He had little confidence in Longo's efforts and strategy, which threatened the Chamber's traditional dominant leadership role. With the "blindfold" off, it appears a delicate festival idea must have lusty lungs, attentive parents, and a friendly banker to thrive in an environment of sameness where change can be so threatening.

A third major strategy was to fund visits by Longo to several key American festivals and for him to deliver a full report on his evaluation of festivals, and their contributions to communities, in several formats. Longo was able to maintain a connection with knowledgeable festival experts. His summarizing report at the end of the study process was helpful but not as in depth as we had expected for the effort and expense. It did stimulate and force the expanded organizing group to a decision about the direction of a local festival.

On June 30, the executive director of the Lyndhurst Foundation director specified in a letter to the initial four-person board of directors that "the hiring of an artistic director at this time would be a serious mistake":

June 30, 1981, Lyndhurst Foundation Letter
"Dear Mickey, [Mr. Frank M. Robbins, III]
Jack Murrah [assistant to the executive director] and I were talking informally about our lunch yesterday and it occurred to me that we discussed two different aspects of one issue at the same time which probably resulted in my creating an impression which I did not intend.

As Sidney's list indicated, the desire to hire an artistic director is a priority for Friends of the Festival. Yet the actual discussion on that point centered around the Foundation's willingness or encouragement in having you approach other foundations to secure funds to hire that individual; that seems like a good step to take at the proper time. What I failed to address yesterday is my very strong opinion that the hiring of an artistic director at this time would be a serious mistake. I believe that two things, at least, must precede such a move. First, the planning and feasibility study must be completed and its recommendations and implications must be studied thoroughly. Second, but occurring simultaneously, it is imperative that the Board of Friends of the Festival be expanded, broadened and rather dramatically diversified.

While it would appear that actions must begin now in order to ensure that a festival take place in 1982, we greatly prefer that your actions precede on a logical and orderly basis which will ensure that a festival, once created, exists on an annual basis for a number of years. To touch all of the necessary bases properly might--or might not--take quite a while.

In the meantime you can be assured of our strong interest in seeing Friends of the Festival experience long-term success.

I apologize for not dealing with this problem yesterday; it slipped by as we addressed another aspect of this point.

[signed "Sincerely, Rick"] Deaderick C. Montague

cc: Mr. Nelson Irvine, Mr. Sidney Hetzler, Mr. Gianni Longo"

1981: August, four seminars for Friends of the Festival group of about 30 interested persons with festival experts from Baltimore, Boston, and New York; concluded with goal setting workshop. Opened by mayor, county executive, other politicians. Group voted for small "comprehensive" arts festival over "specialized" festival or fair.

The Lyndhurst Foundation's director and his staff were invited to the seminars but did not attend, explaining that it was necessary to avoid the impression of dominating the process. Hindsight suggests that candor would have proved a more effective strategy; today Lupton and the foundation are somewhat more open about their intentions and plans to improve the community. For many years, the foundation's grants had been made by a "Mr. Anonymous," whom all in on the secret knew to be Carter Lupton, a major Coca-Cola Company shareholder and father of the present foundation's leader, John T. Lupton. I had received a $15,000 grant from "Mr. A" for a $30,000 project to improve racial relations in 1968 through the Chamber of Commerce, but we were not allowed to disclose who donated the $15,000 of this amount (even in my 1973 master's thesis on this subject I did not mention the source of our funds). The idea that foundation funds were diverted public funds subject to full disclosure had not become a political issue at that time; in general it seemed that the "golden rule" applied (he who has the gold rules).

By 1981, the foundation had become extremely active under Jack Lupton's leadership, but I do not think it had accepted the public nature and need for public scrutiny of its interventions into the city's political processes at that time--or that it has done so today. The power of private foundations remains a complex social and legal issue nationally for a democratic society. (An Emory University student's forthcoming doctoral dissertation on this subject should prove instructive, possibly enabling a future comparison of foundation functions in Chattanooga and Atlanta, where Coca-Cola money has been crucial in the evolution of both cities).

The foundation's true role became a private joke among the group; the "real" meaning of some very fine cheese left over from one seminar's snacks became known among the group as the "Lyndhurst cheese"; the town has eaten that "cheese" not only for weeks but for many long years, both to its advantage and disadvantage. The general belief among many Chattanoogans is that their scenic town would have become Atlanta except for a handful of powerful people who kept out industries and public agencies that might have increased payrolls and cut into local profits. This probably is more myth than reality, although local news articles of the 1890s reflect much of the self-confidence and "boosterism" of Atlanta in the 1980s. However, the concept of increasing per capita income has never been popular on, for example, Lookout Mountain, which drew M. L. KIng Jr.'s attention in his "I Have a Dream" address as another "place to let freedom ring."

My three years in the mayor's office, along with other experiences, suggest that it is unhealthy to have a community so heavily influenced by decisions made in private by wealthy persons unaccountable to the electoral process. Yet social innovation springs from such sources; a balance of these factors is essential. I have been advised on several occasions not to criticize the foundation or "the festival money might dry up." Would we have had a festival without the foundation, some have asked. My reply always has been that the need was so great that some sort of town arts festival would have emerged, in part as a competitive economic development device and in part because more and more local residents were seeing what could happen with "art power" in towns such as Charleston, an insight which the NEA intended. We knew little about Renaissance festivals but the use of "art power" then was not greatly different, except in the degree of total power exercised by "arts patrons."

Dr. Fred Berringer, new head of the UTC theater department, agreed to lead in planning the seminars and in selecting the speakers. Four meetings were set during the summer at the Chamber's downtown civic forum building, which proved a useful location from which we could adjourn and enjoy two of the "Five Night" concerts. The speakers were Sandy Hillman of the Baltimore mayor's office, Wickham Boyle of the New York City festival office, and Robert L. Lynch, director of the Arts Extension Service of the University of Massachusetts, and creator of the Arts Festival Training Program at the University of Massachusetts.

Longo concluded the fourth seminar with his summary of his firms's research and distributed draft copies of "The Making of the Festival." Berringer skillfully used small group discussion techniques to elicit ideas from each of the two dozen participants attending the seminars and to rank our choices for discussion and voting. In this way we were able to use participatory planning methods to help the group evolve a set of goals and strategies for a local festival that would have the broadest possible support. This was an expression of my own belief in the principle that you support what you help create. I had not explained these ideas; I just practiced them as in past years, when it seemed the necessary course to follow in public leadership positions. With the passage of time it seems this strategy was more exceptional than it appeared at the time.

Longo played an advisory role in arranging speakers, but the primary responsibility was Berringer's, who was paid a modest fee from the grant as a professional to lead the seminar. Not once since then has he participated in the Riverbend planning, which, I presume, is because there has been a complete absence of dramatic work in the festival. He is an extraordinarily talented director and if we had been able to continue the search for an artistic director no doubt Berringer would have been an excellent candidate for what then would have been a part-time position that would not have conflicted with his teaching duties.

At the final seminar understanding chuckles were heard when I passed around copies of an anonymously created description of "Six Phases of a Project": 1) enthusiasm; 2) disillusionment; 3) panic; 4) search for the guilty; 5) punishment of the innocent; and 6) honors and awards for the non-participants. Then, we were at stage one, enthusiasm; all the others would follow in order.

1981: June-September, consultant visits festivals, submits first draft of research, "The Making of the Festival," on September 15 at final seminar meeting.

1981: July, "Five Nights in Chattanooga," $100,000 series of popular entertainers in vacant downtown park.

1981: October, Storey and I attended the "Arts Edge" conference in Pittsburgh; then consulted with New York composer and former Chattanoogan Doris Hays in New York. The following document is from a transcription of her remarks that were taped by her in New York in October and that were shared with the planning group during the October-November sessions. (In 1988 she and playwright Sally Ordway, a former Chattanoogan, were commissioned by the local opera association and the NEA to produce a workshop production of "The Glass Lady," an opera about the local antique glass collection and nine marriages of Anna Houston).

Doris Hays' Southern Voices Festival Proposal

"Hi, this is Doris Hay speaking to you in a disembodied voice. In lieu of being with you in the body, I send you this tape. I'm sitting here late at night in my rather chilly New York apartment, with a cat on my lap trying to keep warm and wishing I were there with you and imagining that it is much warmer in that wonderful more southerly climate.

Here are some of my opinions about an art festival for my hometown, Chattanooga. I have been a performer and composer in many festivals: the Como Festival at Lake Como, Italy; the Spoleto Festival in Charleston, the Fraymusic Festival in Vaun, the May Festival of the resident orchestra in Hague, the Lincoln Center Festival out of doors. Each of these festivals has projected and acquired its particular identity; however, none is near what I see as the right model for Chattanooga.

A Festival is a creature which needs to fit its habitat. And, since it is a creature we make, I think of what kind of creature will be nurtured by the locals--be supported by citizens and in return, full grown, give pleasure to those who make and support it. My creature Festival then, is one which has characteristics of the local scene. It sings. And how! This Festival, then, should always have a chance to sing! Hymn sings, sacred harp sing, blues sing, country music sing, gospel sing, massed chorus sing, special avant garde performance events sings (my kind of singing), orchestra-chorus sing. One of the first and strongest reasons to call this festival "Southern Voices."

When I began my Southern Voices project two years ago, I interviewed southerners mainly to capture on tape the beautiful speech melodies of accent as resource material for taped music. But then I began asking my questions: where are you from, how long have you lived there, and what would you like to change, if anything, about this community. My questions brought forth the variety of opinions and attitudes on friendliness, on neighbors, helping each other, on singing, on church, about economic opportunity, love of the land, and fear and concern about rapid change--those opinions and attitudes which give the South its special face. The South's best art show this rich personality and a festival which shines a strong light upon this distinctive visage and allow it to speak for itself in its various Southern accents can't fail to be heard and attract the attentive air of the larger world about us. When we're listening to ourselves with pride and honest so will the world also listen to Southern Voices.

This festival-creature goes to all parts of the city as I see it--to insurance companies and factories, to the courthouse lawn, to the river bridge, to the mountain parks, to the university campus, to the senior citizen center, and sings, too, with the people where they are. The creature not only sings, of course, it dances and rhymes and paints pretty pictures and makes marvelous, outlandish sculptures and reads outrageously wonderful poems. This festival is of the city and of the region, not laid on it from the outside. It has the accent of many voices of the region. It's not an adopted creature, but one born of the existing cultural institutions: a fifty-year-old orchestra, a vital opera company, and tons of singers, lots of fiddlers, and more composers, writers, performers of all kinds than the majority of the population would know except for the festival celebrating their existence.

For me as creator, my instincts all say yes. Yes, to being part of such a celebration. Robert Frost's poem rings over again and again in my mind every time I'm asked to so something in the South, every time I dream up a piece of music or project which involves my home region. To paraphrase him, "Breathes there a bard who isn't moved to know her work is understood and, happily, more or less approved by her country and her neighborhood."

Celebrating existence of what she has spawned in our region calls on me and others to show our own spiritual creation. My choral events, my orchestra music, or my plays. Sally Ordway's or my poems. Charles Flowers' and my singing Joyce Mathis and Monty Jaffey, that will be listened to by my own neighborhood is a special pleasure in the life of an artist, and a part of the pride of place which this creature-festival can foster. Star performers come and go. They are naturally a part of this festival but the underpinning for that which is already there needs spotlight, aid, support, and moral uplift. Past and present, the existing, and that new to be added to it, all are part of this creature. The past in the form of a living mountain tradition, such as sacred harp and fiddling. The present in the form of commissioned art works.

I see an armada of pleasure boats floating down from Lake Chickamauga, down the Tennessee River to congregate around a steam boat at the wharf by the bridge, and a country music entertainment of a pleasantly rowdy kind by Nashville's tops. I envision my own brain-child, a hundred singers on Cameron Hill, a hundred on the Walnut Street bridge, and other large choruses massed on different promontories ready to start singing their part in a city music festival coordinated by church bells and the telephone network, with local radio broadcasters alerting motorists where to go to see the show and broadcasting the audio result of this special. All the groups will come together to perform their parts in a Choo Choo version under the famous dome to add to the already infinite noisy lunches at that dining spot.

And finally I see lots of fun, good hard work, and a very lasting pleasure from this creature-festival if it does indeed speak with a home-grown accent. Good night!"

1981: November 23, synthesis of research, seminar and visits distributed to all interested persons for comment. Eleven objectives listed.

1981: Nov. 23, final proposal and plan of action presented to Lyndhurst Foundation requesting approximately $60,000 for administrative contract.

Several meetings from November to January were held between foundation and Friends representatives to work out details of the full plan of operation and of the portions that the foundation would support. There was much enthusiasm for the plan that the process had created; it had many fathers and mothers and needed nurturing. Storey's experience with producing Five Nights was valuable and he became the primary spokesperson for the festival group. The four organizers were having some disagreement on nominations for officers and board members, and Storey was active in contacting prospective officers. One problem was finding someone to take my position as president; it was an awkward time and Storey's role as intermediary was valuable in making this transition.

We now had a complete plan to present to the new leaders for consideration, based on extensive research and deliberations. But the new festival lacked a board of directors, officers, and an artistic director. What the Lyndhurst funded was the business manager's position, an action that in retrospect placed unfair obligations on Storey as a businessman to function as de facto artistic director, a function he has had to perform since then in the absence of a qualified artistic director. This person must know, as Menotti does, not only music but also theater to be able to choreograph the complexity of a "festival theater"--what Redden termed an extended Robert Wilson production.

Sometimes the "boss" has to accept criticism for placing an unqualified person in a position; I think the foundation as "boss" had enough input from various sources, including its own consultant, to see the wisdom of including a qualified part or full-time artistic director from the earliest days and that the foundation used poor judgment in this case.

This marked a major turning point in Chattanooga history. Whether Riverbend can evolve from its "fixed" heritage form, which now is a statement of the city's identity in the minds of Chattanooga leaders, is an interesting question that continues to intrigue me, due in part to the foundation's deep questioning of past policy that must have provoked the $100,000 1988 evaluation of the Riverbend Festival. (Tax deductible, nonprofit status also has been a concern of Riverbend's lawyers since its beginning because of the mixture of public and private funds for public and private objectives). Today I no longer worry about the "money drying up for the festival" in making this critique of our well-intended past decisions and actions. The festival now can stand alone financially from its entrance pin income alone if it were to broaden sales to the population within two hours drive, which includes Atlanta, Birmingham, Nashville, and Knoxville. With its extra millions of dollars, it yet could divert traffic from Charleston, as first operating president Walker Breland predicted.

1981: December, board names executive director and contracts with Variety Services production firm to manage festival.

Storey was given the active management of the festival during this period of development. With his usual mixture of humor and rebelliousness, he volunteered without any funds available immediately to coordinate all the activities until a full board could be named. His insights were valuable and I am sure his personal financial contributions toward the making of the festival were as great as had been my personal expenses in visiting the two festivals and using my food brokerage office resources from time to time. Possibly our festival financial contributions by percentage of personal assets were greater by far than the total of all Lyndhurst grants, which were based on the Lupton family assets. It developed that my travel expense was deductible from income because the trips led to a nonprofit corporation; however, I did not know this would be allowed at the time.

1982: January-February, new 24-person board elected a UTC music professor president and artistic director.

This period of matching people with paper plans would make or break the emerging festival. Because of the time and financial constraints on the four of us who originally "initiated" (in quotes because of other influences) the Friends of the Festival group, we continuously searched during the summer and fall months for potential board members and key officers who were interested in our ideas and the seminar's conclusions and proposal as outlined. I did not want to add board members immediately, as Montague requested in his letter, arguing that the next president should choose the officers and board members. And new members were reluctant to make a serious commitment without knowing the new leadership. Already the Variety Services contract had been agreed to in principle; the new officers and board might not feel as strongly committed if they had not participated in these critical decisions. This policy naturally followed from the "we support what we help create" concept.

The possibility of the festival board as a public front for the Lyndhurst Foundation's private community development strategy had not occurred to me then. It may not have occurred to the foundation at that time either, more likely evolving with the sequence of events as the festival "picked up steam" and became a useful vehicle for a variety of civic and foundation purposes. The foundation's records would be needed to reveal this; anticipating an understandable lack of interest in this critique, I have not requested them, although federal freedom of information laws may require public access if the records were requested. For my limited aims here, the available evidence is regarded as adequate for these initial inferences about these events.

A detailed plan of action had been prepared; we thought that we could find in one individual the combination of both artistic director and president of the organization. The influence of the foundation in urging against an artistic director until later in the process was felt by all. It also was clear to those of us most intimately connected with the project that a creative festival with any kind of entertainment quality would require a person with most of the credentials of an artistic director, which would not be found normally in a business manager alone. In addition to perceiving the need for artistically qualified leadership, I was unwilling to take charge of the effort because of my teaching and business obligations as well as because of a lack of arts knowledge. "Knowing when to quit" seems one of my wiser decisions in retrospect; continuing probably would have led to a career choice that at the time I was not prepared to make.

None of the three other organizers would or could take the job. I had had to ask for Robbins' time, which was critical at this juncture, to be made available from his investment company partners, both high school friends uncertain about the merits of time spent on such "artsy" projects. Montague had declined several months earlier. It was becoming difficult to replace myself, and I began thinking about the ancient wisdom of not getting into such things in the first place. But a taste of public service can be emotionally addictive if not financially rewarding.

We first settled with some disagreement on Mai Bell Hurley, an experienced, influential arts leader, a choice which some argued was a necessity due to her enormous power in the community (a role apparently similar to Nella Barkely's in Charleston). But she declined to lead the effort due in part to the planned Allied Arts Fund drive and in part to disagreement with the festival's philosophy. Other familiar civic leaders were discussed also. Our eventual choice, Walker Breland, was a music professor at UT Chattanooga and organist at the First Methodist church. He was very positive about the plans for the festival, was originally from the Charleston area, was familiar with Spoleto, and was a respected musician. We felt he had the institutional support and the time available to lead the community through this initial period. An active civic worker and amateur musician, Lee Parham, agreed to serve as vice-president; Robbins was secretary; Irvine was treasurer. Parham became the mainstay of the festival, and was in all but title the first real leader of the festival. Breland had stipulated that he would take the job as president only if Parham would agree to be his vice-president.

In making the transition to Breland, one incident marred, for me, this transfer from myself as a sort of founder to him as elected leader. He did not want me to serve on the executive committee as past president, a customary practice in Chattanooga arts organizations. This was a step I had assumed was expected after I had worked so hard for a festival when faced with so many other responsibilities. He explained with a peculiar logic that Jimmy Carter had not asked Jerry Ford to serve in his cabinet and that it was not appropriate for me to serve on his new executive committee. I said I was flattered by the analogy, if not in retrospect by the Ford comparison, but thought the situation hardly comparable. I said I had persuaded many people, especially political leaders, to support the festival and it would look as if I were abandoning the project before it was well underway. Nevertheless, he was firm on this and I felt the rejection deeply; it was not unlike Tom Patterson's treatment in Stratford.

I remained on the board as much for appearances after that as for making any real contribution; no doubt, if past actions were any guide, there were "outside" manipulations behind Breland's decision. In fact, I had partially had my way and we had an artistic director who had the real power of the budget, if any money could be found to supplement the Lyndhurst grant. However, in the context of the situation this move in reality was unfair to Breland, who lacked the political power of a Mai Bell Hurley and who had no theatrical artistic experience. At this period we were "makin' do" and any artist was better than none at all, I thought.

I remain convinced his influence, and Parham's, significantly shaped the direction of the festival, not to the extent of a Menotti, because we all lacked a clear understanding of "festival," but at least to the extent of keeping the idea of a "serious" festival alive those first two years. Breland was paid several thousand dollars the second year, apparently with a Lyndhurst grant, but upset all by taking his summer vacation for several weeks just before the festival opened. Probably he also had learned that the script was being written for him; these matters have not been discussed between us. One looks forward to the needed scholarly publication of his interpretation of the events of those days, the local effect of which is something that university tenure should cushion. I, unfortunately, have no such security, except the good feeling that comes from having told the story as I experienced it; if it is not the "whole truth" it is the "truth as I know it" and "let the chips fall where they may" (cliches, like stories of origin, are useful in compressing meanings).

This incident proved to be a forerunner of other management and human relations problems resulting from attempting to mix the duties of president and artistic director in a college professor inexperienced in such large-scale enterprises. I had never mentioned this rejection until several years later, when someone was critical of me for not continuing to work actively on the festival; this person was astounded that I had not been asked to continue in any capacity that I wished since "everybody knew it was your idea."

The six stages of a project best explain the logic of Breland's decision; after that day's luncheon meeting in the basement, a former prison, of the Gazebo Restaurant, I was at stage two, disillusionment. Our dreamed-of first festival of "differences" had lost me along with my insistence on having an "artistic director." I supposed I could have been wrong about that issue until the Spoleto Festival U.S.A. interviews in 1986, when all interviewed expressed amazement that such a festival would be attempted without such a key position filled by a qualified person. That experience, actually beginning with Breland's rejection of me and my thinking, turned my focus to what now are the central ideas of this work. The Riverbend board consistently has dropped any who do not share its riverfront and commercial development objectives; I, on the other hand, consistently have spoken out against the festival's lack of integrity in terms of its original idea and written objectives.

The 1988 evaluation, to recent to be discussed here in detail, supports such criticism, especially the neglect of local artists, but it would take an extraordinary force to change the direction of such a powerful economic engine as the Riverbend Festival has become. It, in fact, has a potentially broader financial base from the "pin" sales than Spoleto Festival U.S.A. One can dream of a Menotti or Charles Wadsworth or Carol Miles or Doris Hays turning Riverbend (and Chattanooga) into a Salzburg of the 2000s. After the civil war, Chattanooga was regarded as one of the world's most scenic cities with its "mountains looking at each other" over the twisting river canyon, a city destined to become a great metropolis (from recollection of a missing old issue of Harper's magazine).

Something happened to block that destiny that the city's natural beauty evoked; I suspect that something relates to why our movement toward the Spoleto model of festival of diversity was resisted by the forces of "unity" and "sameness." One could easily explain the incident I have described as stemming from personal factors, but as the entire story unfolds it appears to me that deeper philosophies were conflicting and that such incidents were only surface manifestations of these structural flaws in the community. A pattern emerges after several such incidents that calls for deeper inquiry than a superficial reading would suggest.

At the most practical level, however, the explanation for my silence, and repressed hostility, after that rejection is that I had helped select Breland; I supported what I helped create, up to the point at which the festival clearly changed its direction several years later. If he changed his mind about taking the apparently thankless job, I might have gotten it back by default, as had happened before when Longo insisted I be president of the committee. That alternative no longer was acceptable because already the time and money put into the making of a festival had adversely affected my food brokerage business and university teaching performance; it was worth it, however, if important lessons were learned and "a good time was had by all." The ancient theological problem of redemption and forgiveness is raised by these reflections. If the record cannot be erased it possibly can be a guide to future ethical dilemmas and social conflicts for me and others interested this and similar stories.

1982: July-August, first Riverbend Festival; three popular music concerts at Engle baseball stadium and in mid-August five days of entertainment, food, air sculpture, etc., at Ross' Landing park on riverfront where city began as loading dock.

For this study, the rest of the story is anti-climatic. Walker Breland, the other officers and new board members took on the job in February and planning proceeded. The festival was held in August 1982. It was preceded by in-home chamber music fundraising events and by three concerts at the local baseball stadium. These included three expensive entertainment groups--the Beachboys, the Commodores, and Rick Springfield--and we expected adequate profits to finance the actual festival at the riverfront. Springfield alone cost $65,000. The Riverbend went into its first actual festival with a large deficit, but with an enthusiastic and excited community. The details of the programming are less important for this discussion the process by which hope was raised in the city and another ideogram of festivals had been presented to the community for potential support, financing, and imagination. The festival was born. Would it be nurtured?

August 1982: Downtown Arts Festival and Fort Wood Festival

Two other downtown festivals were held during the same weekend the Riverbend was held. One was a neighborhood festival with booths, music, poetry readings and so on the tree-lined street of the Fort Wood neighborhood, a national historic district.

The second, in what was the first arts festival in nine years, Miller Park in the city's center served as a stage for music and dance performances; a vacant block nearby housed a circus tent of paintings and sculpture. With a theme of "August Arts: Fun for Everyone," the program also featured musicians, ethnic dance groups, mimes, storytellers, jazz, bluegrass, and a Saturday night performance by the Chattanooga Symphony orchestra. Food booths lined the streets nearby. The participating visual artists, selected by jury, were eligible for several thousand dollars in prizes in categories that included painting, sculpture, photography, fiber, graphics, jewelry, and pottery. The public had the opportunity to purchase the art works during the festival.

Sponsored by the Central City Council for the Chamber of Commerce over a three-day period, it showcased area performers and artists. According to the Chamber president, quoted in a Chattanooga Times article, it was expected to help draw suburban residents downtown: "The festival would not only encourage citizens to come downtown, but will also provide a chance for people to view and purchase valuable art work." The chairman of the arts festival committee announced that the festival promised to promote the idea that the arts are for everyone by bringing a variety of cultural events to the downtown area and offering it free of charge.

The fringe festival developed at Salzburg and the Piccolo started at Charleston (in part to qualify Spoleto for federal funds, according to Longo's report), and it appears the very powerful models of a comprehensive town arts festival create more festival activity rather than less. If the fears of "diffusion" on the part of arts establishment leaders were not allayed, at least the new "festival" medium functioned apparently to encourage "festivalling," just as television coverage of sports increased attendance at sports events.

1982: August, strong favorable public reaction to festival and the whole "festive" city atmosphere.

1982: September, Riverbend lost $100,000 from a budget projecting $1.1 million in revenues and $864,000 in expenses, mostly due to losses from three rock concerts.

The concerts' promoter, Bruce Story, felt these concerts were "a very useful experience," according to a quote in a June 15, 1984

Chattanooga Times feature on the history of the festival. They may have been useful, but they were costly in many ways. The losses proved we were wrong in thinking that "popular" music for high density, outdoor audiences would pay for "classical" music for low density, indoor audiences, to use extreme examples, and that, when admission was charged, the Five Nights "bread-and-circus" model was inappropriate.

Rock concerts were rock concerts, regardless of their purpose; not enough people bought tickets for these three concerts, two of which were held during a heat wave (a fourth, Willie Nelson, was cancelled). However, I know from observation of those efforts (and from 10 years in a professional marketing and sales business) during that summer that competent promotional and marketing had not been executed with an adequate budget. The failure stemmed less from individuals than from flawed concepts and the inappropriate festival structure imposed by the foundation.

1982: October, Lyndhurst promises continued support for administrative needs and programming ideas; board elects same leaders.

1982-1988: The Riverbend Festival continued
"Signs of a festival theater of power" in our town were becoming increasingly obvious to those of us who worked to found the festival originally. My May 19, 1986 letter is important to this interpretation because it illustrates, in context, my first actual awareness of the political, social, and aesthetic conflict between the forces of sameness and difference as I experienced it at that time. The version below includes two paragraphs approved for removal by the newspaper's publisher, Ruth Holmberg. These are sentences that refer to the paper's former managing editor, John Popham, and to the "voices of Lookout Mountain." No explanation for the cuts was given, except for lack of space, when I asked why substantive deletions were made without discussing them with me, which would have been the normal policy when I was a reporter in 1967 for a paper that was first started by Adolph Ochs and still is influenced, if less than in past years, by the New York Times philosophy of journalism. The commentary said:

"Two performing arts events of this past weekend give rise to thoughts about the state of the local arts and about artists in and of Chattanooga.

The Friday night performance of the Chattanooga Ballet company was a tribute to the dancers, artistic directors, parents and board members who created an exciting, moving performance of Ruth Page's "Carmina Burana." This was new, different, original. This was quality as good as much of UTC's Dorothy Patten series. Artistic director Barry Van Curra's original choreography of "Tennessee Homecoming '86" and "Fugitive Visions" showed an inner vision and imaginative personal statement seldom if ever seen in Chattanooga's officially sanctioned "arts for jobs and industry" environment. The young dance company, led by Barry and Anna's fine dancing and also by their extraordinary teaching abilities, is Allied Arts' newest funded member, its first in 14 years. It shows promise of being the only Allied Arts artistic enterprise currently working at fostering original, creative expression by Chattanoogans.

The other new, exciting art work came on Saturday night from an internationally known performer and composer of Chattanooga--Doris Hays, UTC graduate and now New York city resident--premiering her new jazz trio at Emory University's Cannon Chapel in Atlanta as an "Evening of New Music." With singer Janet Lawson and violinist Julie Lieberman of New York, Ms. Hays' trio "Purple Moon" was a joy for the audience. For those of us who have watched her musical direction evolve through difficult contemporary sound statements, it was a deeply moving experience of "accessible" music from a gifted, caring composer who is very conscious of her childhood environment. Ms. Hays' "Southern Voices for Orchestra," which led the symphony's 50th anniversary commemoration a few years ago, has been performed and filmed and enjoyed far beyond Chattanooga. Yet this and the other three original compositions have not been recorded and made a part of our artistic heritage, as the original plan envisioned. It is a significant oversight.

The community has not welcomed nor encouraged new ideas and ways of expressing them by its artists, whose existence seemingly serves to promote economic growth and attract new business. Our leaders talk of arts, not artists. The campaign slogan is a pitch for jobs, not joy. The pledge is for more of the same, not the new, the different, the stimulating. The "new" is not well received in Chattanooga, and it may be that the absence of community leaders, with a few exceptions, at these artistic events speaks eloquently. Who is pushing for our original artists to come home in this special homecoming year and speak their mind? Lyndhurst, Benwood, UTC? Where are our writers, composers, actors, sculptors, painters, musicians and dancers who have left the community? Does the Riverbend Festival spotlight a Doris Hays, a Charley Flowers, a Carol Miles, a Monte Jaffe? How does a town renew itself and see itself anew without the vision of its artists who stay--Hilda Gilkeson, Deanne Irvine, Paul Ramsay, David Pennebaker and others--as well as of those who leave and carry the seeds of their beginnings?

It is Sunday's announcement of the Riverbend Festival schedule that makes this "fear of the new" so clear--the commercial artists, the motor boat races, the events that are fun and that sell pins but that say "more of the same" and "why bother" to some known or unknown artistic talent with a new, untested message or medium. Why does the Riverbend not merit a listing in the New York Times summer music festival section? What is a nearly a million dollars buying for our town? It is an expensive summer "block party," to use one festival president's term. If a Rick Montague had the power six years ago to specify a "promoter" rather than an "artistic director" to shape the Riverbend Festival, then he also has the power to help foster a climate of innovation and support for the "new" sources of artistic energy without which communities stagnate and decline.

It is, in Venture's language, not "places" but "people" who need support and encouragement--not arts, but artists who need nurturing and practical help. If Chattanooga is different and special because of a newsman like John Popham, who came and stayed and spoke his mind on the issues, what would the city be like with the bubbling energy of the multiple voices who left to "speak" in other communities and are not heard here again?

Somehow our leaders must create conditions so that the voices of the "new" and the "different" can be heard and seen here more often. And if our leaders are too set in their traditional ways and too afraid of criticism to foster a creative environment, then it may be time for the political and economic process to change the leadership. Maybe it is wiser to look to city hall and the county courthouse for this leadership, just in case it may need changing, and not to a self-selected few who cannot be voted out of office for spending money on the riverbank instead of on education, health, housing--which is not to say the riverbank is not a potential generator of progress and economic development but to note that it is subject to a public process of decision making and not a secret meeting.

The slogan on my pencil says: "Vision 2000--Turning Talk Into Action." Maybe we need money for more artistic "talk" and less for Venture's fish tanks and other actions."

APPENDIX C

DISSERTATION FRONT MATERIALS

Two Town Festivals: Signs of a Theater of Power
COPYRIGHT 1990

In presenting this dissertation as a partial fulfillment of the requirements for an advanced degree from Emory University, I agree that the Library of the University shall make it available for inspection and circulation in accordance with its regulations governing materials of this type. I agree that permission to copy from, or to publish, this dissertation may be granted by the professor under whose direction it was written, or, in his/her absence, by the Dean of the Graduate School, when such copying or publication is solely for scholarly purposes and does not involve potential financial gain. It is understood that any copying from, or publication of, this dissertation which involves potential financial gain will not be allowed without written permission.

NOTICE TO BORROWERS Unpublished theses deposited in the Emory University Library must be used only in accordance with the stipulations prescribed by the author in the preceding statement.

The author of this dissertation is:
Sidney N. Hetzler, Jr.597 West Cove Road [updated from 1990 to new street post office address] Chickamauga, Georgia 30707

The director of this dissertation is:
Timothy J. Reiss
New York University Graduate School of Arts and Sciences
Department of Comparative Literature 19 University Place, 4th Floor
New York, New York 10003

Users of this dissertation not regularly enrolled as students at Emory University are required to attest acceptance of the preceding stipulations by signing below. Libraries borrowing this dissertation for the use of their patrons are required to see that each user records here the information requested.

Name of User Address Date Type of use / (Examination only or copying)

TWO TOWN FESTIVALS:
SIGNS OF A THEATER OF POWER

By
Sidney N. Hetzler, Jr.
Adviser: Timothy J. Reiss
Department of Comparative Literature
New York University

Approved for the Department:

_____
Adviser

_____
Date
Accepted:

_____
Dean of the Graduate School

_____
Date

TWO TOWN FESTIVALS:
SIGNS OF A THEATER OF POWER

By

Sidney N. Hetzler, Jr.
B.A., Vanderbilt University, 1962
M.S., Boston University, 1973

Adviser: Timothy J. Reiss
Department of Comparative Literature
New York University

A Dissertation submitted to the Faculty of the Graduate School
of Emory University in partial fulfillment
of the requirements for the degree of
Doctor of Philosophy
Graduate Institute of Liberal Arts

COPYRIGHT 1990

Abstract

This semiotic analysis compares the discursive practice of two contemporary town festivals in Charleston, South Carolina, and Chattanooga, Tennessee, as theatrical expressions of a dominant order's power.

It argues the aesthetic, political, and social desirability of festivals of "difference" as opposed to those of "sameness"--"arts" as opposed to "heritage", "serious" as opposed to "bread-and-circus"--and indicates the potentially destructive effect of a festival of sameness.

These and other claims are derived from an analysis of three key categories: the festival's relationship to empty town spaces (its place), its purposes (its ideal), and the presence or absence of an artistic director (its force). These three elements provide the study's conceptual design and suggest, in their interdependence, several conclusions about the nature, function, and meaning of these two festivals.

Charleston's Spoleto Festival U.S.A. and Chattanooga's Riverbend Festival were selected for comparative analysis because Chattanooga's festival sponsors deliberately rejected Charleston's "arts" model of festival for a "heritage" form. The significance of this decision, how and why this change of direction happened, and its meanings are the basic issues explored.

Chapter I constructs the interpretive frame of two basic festival forms and outlines an analytical approach. Chapter II describes key elements in the founding of the Spoleto Festival U.S.A. in Charleston, South Carolina, during 1975-77, based primarily on the recollections of its first board chairman. Chapter III analyzes the founding of the Riverbend Festival in Chattanooga, Tennessee, during 1980-82, through the story of the creation of a citizen's group that was established to sponsor the festival. Chapter IV analyzes a third model of festival, the Chautauqua Institution at Jamestown, New York, in relation to a comparison of key elements of Spoleto Festival U.S.A. and Riverbend, and proposes several conclusions about the nature, function, and meaning of the forms of festival discussed.

NOTES

PREFACE

1. Carolyn Mitchell, Chattanooga Times, June 15, 1984.
2. Charles Slack, Chattanooga Times, June 15, 1984.
3. What perspectives support this view of a distinctive festival theater? "Look at the use of space," University of Toronto semiotician Paul Bouissac advised when asked in 1986 about analytical approaches to the study of festivals. Bouissac, author of <u>Circus and Culture: A Semiotic Approach</u> recalled he had asked his professor, Claude Lévi-Strauss, a similar question about studying circuses. "First study one completely, then a few others, make a few tentative conclusions, then look at other circuses with these views," the influential French anthropologist and founder of structural analysis suggested.

From this conceptual starting point, ideas about "space" grounded the continuing questions, "What is a festival? What does it do?" Personal experience with the genesis of a town arts festival in Chattanooga, Tennessee, during the early 1980s provided the documents and memories to begin to carry out Lévi-Strauss' advice to "study one completely."

4. In Chattanooga, an extensive planning process, funded by an interested local foundation, generated documentation useful for analysis of the Riverbend Festival's birth and gestation.
5. Charles S. Peirce, "Logic as Semiotic: The Theory of Signs," Ed Justus Buchler Philosophical Writings of Peirce, 1940. Dover Publications: New York: Rpt. 1955) 99. The sense of semiotics as the study of signs, intended here and throughout the study, is derived from Peirce's definition of a "sign": "something which stands to somebody for something in some respect or capacity. It addresses somebody, that is, creates in the mind of that person an equivalent sign, or perhaps a more developed sign."

A more general definition of semiotics is the representation and processing of knowledge, a more abstracted model which suggests both human and natural communication and signification processes.

The idea of a triadic template, such as Vincent's "place, ideal, force," generally corresponds (although no precise correlation is claimed) to C. S. Peirce's categories of firstness, secondness, and thirdness, as summarized by David Savan:

Place equals firstness: "Firstness might be called quality space, a space which is occupied by existing qualities. Because Firstness is without relation to physical space, time, or casual conditions, Peirce associates it with the ideas of freedom, novelty, and originality."

Ideal equals secondness: "The crucial idea here is that of brute and obstinate existence, related by opposition and contrast to some other second existence....When we say that experience presents us with hard facts, it is the Secondness of experience that we refer to. So too when we point to something, or refer to something without describing or classifying it, Secondness is prominent."

Force equals thirdness (three categories): "Mediation--whenever two things are connected by means of some third factor, thirdness is the category....Transformation--any principle, function, or law which translates one form into another is a third....Growth and Development--laws are subject themselves to change in accordance with what might be called meta-laws....Peirce understands evolution as just such a hierarchical order of laws....The leading principle of growth is the application of the categories to themselves."

Savan observes: "The categories are not, of course, names of individual things. They are classifications of three aspects of whatever can be known, and they occur always compounded together."

Source: David Savan, An Introduction to C.S. Peirce's Semiotics, from monographs, working papers, and prepublications of the Toronto Semiotic Circle (Toronto: Toronto Semiotic Circle, Victoria University 1976 No.1) 6-9.

6. It was a request for a history of Charleston's festival that revealed the absence of such a record. As one of the founders of Chattanooga's festival, I had kept many of the notes, files, and papers that ordinarily would have been lost. These are available to other researchers. No doubt new documents will come to light as others involved in these historic moments in community life have different stories to tell. However, the evidence presented in this study is as full and complete as constraints of time, funds, and scholarly discourse permit.

7. Jean-Francois Lyotard, The Postmodern Condition: A Report on Knowledge, trans. G. Bennington and B. Massumi, foreword by Fredric Jameson (1979; Minneapolis: U of Minnesota P, 1984) 81-82.

Possibly the most dramatic illustration of Lyotard's idea, as I have paraphrased it, is his willingness to "honor the differences" by including Marxist literary critic Jameson's generally opposing views as a foreword.

8. Milan Kundera, Laughable Loves (1969; Middlesex: Penguin, 1974) 5.

CHAPTER I – The Idea of a Festival Theater

9. This comment was from remarks made by Menotti at a May 20, 1988, press conference in Charleston at the opening of the Spoleto Festival U.S.A.

10. See interview excerpts that follow in Chapter II and Appendix A, especially Theodore S. Stern and David Rawle.

11. Steven Gallup, A History of the Salzburg Festival (London: Weidenfeld and Nicolson, 1987).

Examples of other useful festival histories are:

John Pettigrew, and Jamie Portman, Foreword by Robertson Davies, Stratford: The First Thirty Years 2 Vols. (Toronto: Macmillan of Canada, 1985).

Tom Patterson, founder of the Festival, and Allan Gould, First Stage: The Making of the Stratford Festival (Toronto: McClelland and Stewart, 1987).

Grace Lydiatt Shaw, Stratford Under Cover: Memories on Tape (Toronto: N.C. Press Limited, 1977).

Alistair Moffat, The Edinburgh Fringe (London: Johnston & Bacon, 1978).

John Julius Norwich, Fifty Years of Glyndebourne: An Illustrated History (London: Jonathan Cape, 1985).

Fannia Weingartner, ed., Ravinia: The Festival at its Half Century,(Ravinia: Ravinia Festival Association and Rand McNally & Company, 1985).

Alfreda L. Irwin, Three Taps of the Gavel: Pledge to the Future The Chautauqua Story (1970; Chautauqua: Chautauqua Institution, New York, 1987).

12. From Theodore S. Stern recollections, 1988 interview, Appendix A.

13. Stephen Orgel, The Illusion of Power: Political Theater in the English Renaissance (Berkeley and London: U of California P, 1975) 39-40.

14. Orgel, The Illusion of Power, 40.

15. Orgel, The Illusion of Power, 47-48.

16. A.M. Nagler, A Source Book in Theatrical History (New York: Dover, 1952) 3. Plutarch recounts that Solon warned Thespis that his plays were lies that might find they way into the belief of the people: "If we honor and commend such play as this, we shall find it someday in our business."

17. The concept of "liminality" is that derived from the anthropological work of Victor Turner.

18. Peter Brook, The Empty Space (New York: Atheneum, 1984) 9.

19. Nggi wa Thiong'o, Decolonizing the Mind (Harrare: Zimbabwe Publishing House, 1987) 37-8.

20. Brook, The Empty Space 9.

21. Steven Gallup, A History of the Salzburg Festival (London: Weidenfeld and Niclolson, 1987) 175, 176-7.

22. Elizabeth Mortimer, "The Salzburg Festival," Austria Today (1979).

23. Eugen Hadamaovsky, "Propaganda and National Power," International Propaganda and Communications, introduction by Wilbur Schramm, trans. Alice Mavrogordato and Ilse DeWitt. (New York: Arno Press, 1972) 173-182. First published Oldenburg, Germany, 1933, as a master's thesis.

Hadamaovsky was a deputy to Goebbels and dedicated his work "To the master of Political propaganda Dr. Joseph Goebbels whose brilliant leadership transformed the discredited weapon of German politics into a creative art." This document also explains the strategy and tactics of discrediting "liberalism" in such detail that it could have been the "intellectual" basis of George Bush's 1988 campaign battle plan. The thesis deserves new consideration for its insights into the fascist mentality and its goals of unity and sameness and opposition to "differences."

24. Vladimir Propp, Morphology of the Folktale (Austin: U of Texas P, 1968 revised edition):

Since the tale [like the festival] is exceptionally diverse...the material...must be classified. The accuracy of all further study depends on the accuracy of classification....it must itself be the result of certain preliminary study. What we see, however, is precisely the reverse: the majority of researchers begin with classification, imposing it upon the material from without and not extracting it from the material itself. [5]....it is necessary to place the classification of tales on a new track. It must be transferred into formal, structural features. And, in order to do this, these features must be investigated. [6]....Not a single concrete fact can be explained without the study of these abstract bases. [15]....The historian, inexperienced in morphological problems, will not see a resemblance where one actually exists; he will omit coincidences which are important to him, but which he does not notice. [Emphasis mine]. And conversely, where a similarity is perceived, a specialist in morphology will be able to demonstrate that compared phenomena are completely heteronomous.

We see, then, that very much depends upon the study of forms....undertaken from the viewpoint of abstract, formal problems. Such crude, "uninteresting" work of this kind is a way to generalize "interesting" constructions. [16].

...This makes possible the study of the tale according to the functions of its dramatis personae. [20]

Propp's work suggests the reasoning and process behind the selection of the three basic elements selected for this study "according to their functions:" place, ideal, force and their various equivalents used throughout the analysis.

25. The terms are from a quote on a postcard sold by the Chautauqua Institution in 1987. The quotation, "Chautauqua is a place, an ideal, and a force," was attributed to its founder, John Vincent Heyl.

26. Mikhail Bakhtin, "Popular-Festive Forms and Images in Rabelais," Rabelais and His World. Translated by Helene Iswolsky from Tvorchestvo Fransua Rable, Moscow, Khudozhestvennia literatura, 1965 from the 1940 doctoral original. (Bloomington: Indiana, 1984) 265.

27. One deeper symbolic pattern could be the emergence of the species from the water; this festival becomes then an enactment of that ritual of passage as a return to a point of origin. However, this would be a pattern encoded at the "function" level, one derived from selective interpretation and not one necessarily expressed in explicit goals or observed effects. If this pattern should be found enacted in other festivals, that is, a recurrence of imagery, language, and water-related events, then possibly a significant function of a festival could be identified as a "connector to meanings of ancient, evolutionary beginnings." It cannot be suggested within this study that this actually is a function of a festival; the idea is to point out the potential value of searching for the unnoticed "work" or "function" of a festival.

28. Rufus Triplett, second president of the Friends of the Festival, Inc., quoted in a headline in the Chattanooga Times on or about June 1, 1986.

29. Roy Strong, Art and Power: Renaissance Festivals 1450-1650 (Woodbridge, Suffolk, England: The Boydell Press, 1984) xiii. Splendour at Court: Renaissance Spectacle and the Theatre of Power was used as Strong's 1973 title of the book was revised and expanded in 1984. It is in the sense of his term "theater of power" that the phrase was selected for the title of this work.

30. Umberto Eco, A Theory of Semiotics (Bloomington: Indiana UP 1976) 134.

31. Timothy J. Reiss, excerpt from unpublished course outline for Emory University 1985 summer session seminar, "Toward an Archaeology of the Modern European Theater."

32. Eco, A Theory of Semiotics, 150.

33. Roy Strong, Art and Power, 172.

34. Reiss, "European Theater" course outline.

35. Tyrone Guthrie and Robertson Davies, Renown at Stratford: The First Thirty Years 2 Vols. (Toronto: Clarke, Irwin, 1953) 32.

CHAPTER II -- Spoleto Festival USA

36. In view of the apparent scarcity of world-class examples, it appears a matter of fortunate chance that my visit to Charleston's Spoleto festival provided such a model of excellence. In actuality this was not a random encounter but more a courtship. The National Endowment for the Arts, one of the initiating sponsors of the festival, was as much interested in meeting a budding arts lover like me as I was in getting acquainted with the festival. The NEA intended that a model of a European festival of all the arts be created in the American South, where it was felt such a festival role model would be more unusual.

According to the 1986 interview with the festival's newly-appointed general manager, Nigel Redden, who had worked for the NEA:

> The place idea was imposed to some extent on the Festival of Two Worlds, on Gian Carlo Menotti, by the National Endowment for the Arts, which suggested he look to the South rather than to the Hudson River area, where he had initially thought of looking. That is, he had initially thought of looking to Caramoor or some of those places up the Hudson. But the people at the NEA said: Look, there are so many festivals around up there, there's so much arts activity going on outside of New York, that you shouldn't go there; there's no point in putting a festival there. You should go to someplace where there aren't things. And Charleston is sort of ideal in that it has an enormous cultural history. That is, the first ballet company in America started here in 1790; the first opera ever done in America was done here; the first theater in America was here--I mean every city has the first something but this has a lot of cultural firsts.

37. A few elements of these differing "tales" unfold throughout the narrow limits of this study. Not all are present, especially Menotti's and Riley's stories because of their crowded schedules at festival time. Yet the main direction of their thinking is included in several key quotations from the transcribed interviews in 1986 and 1988. These "stories" reflect basic aspects of the early struggle faced by Riley and Menotti that might not have been revealed in their own words if they

had been available for interviews in 1986 or 1988. No doubt other interpretations will emerge as the festival's archives are made public.

Redden was sensitive to this uncertainty about the analysis of the Spoleto Festival's origin and basic idea: "I think the mayor would have a different tale; I think some of the board members would have a different tale; I think Gian Carlo might have a different tale."

38. Carol E. Miles, "Robert Wilson: A Study of His Creative Process," master's thesis, Trinity U, San Antonio, Texas, 1984: "...Robert Wilson...opted for a radically different way of making theater. Through his longtime practice of splitting apart the elements of the theater--the text, non-verbal sound, decor and lighting--he has created a very personal style of presenting his ideas. His work is based on the visual and aural instead of the verbal. The dramatic value of spectacle by far outweighs the traditional literary dominance found in most Western theater. In his work there are no plots, no traditional characters that interact with each other, no thematic, political, or moral theses to sway the emotions or opinions of the audience, and no representational use of scenery, lighting, and sound. Yet it is theater....Wilson's personal perceptions have created a style that Stefan Brecht has called a theater of visions" [in Brecht's Theater of Visions: Robert Wilson 2-3].

39. Some of Robert Wilson's past associates have demonstrated some of his imagistic techniques. Carol Miles' choreography in the 1988 Charleston Spoleto production of Dvorak's Rusalka was a masterpiece of dramatic effect in the difficult ballroom scene. I am indebted to her for explaining Robert Wilson's concept of non-traditional theatrical forms. Her own directing and choreography, seen on videotape from several of her works in France in 1986-7, in her 1986 Hamlet for the Atlanta Shakespeare Company, and in her The House of Bernard Alba at Theater Emory, Emory University, February 1989, were strong influences on the development of my own "imagistic" festival ideas. A Wilsonian-like "festival theater" staged throughout an entire city was proposed for Chattanooga's festival by Doris Hays, see Chapter III. Possibly one day soon financial support will be granted for Miles own similar proposed production, "City Opera," which is waiting for its own "empty space" and "force."

40. "What is new is art power--the power, as Charleston's energetic 38-year-old mayor, Joseph P. Riley Jr., puts it, `to revitalize a sagging downtown business district, to raise the cultural level of a very wide spectrum of the city's population and to boost civic pride.'" Charles Michener, Newsweek, May 28, 1981.

41. Guthrie, Tyrone, and Davies, Robertson. Renown at Stratford: A Record of the Shakespeare Festival in Canada. Toronto: Clarke, Irwin & Company Ltd.: 1953, vii. Several of Davies' novels, especially

in the Francis Cornish trilogy, use the Stratford Festival as a dramatic device. In the 1988 final book in the Cornish series, The Lyre of Orpheus, the Stratford Festival holds center stage for the restored Hoffman opera production where the action climaxes and many of the threads are woven together. One can see at the festival. The festival is where all the key institutional elements (foundation, university, artists, critics) are gathered for audience and performers alike to interact in one place at the same time.

The function of the festival in fiction and drama is a topic that could not be explored in this study, but it should be included in an expanded analysis of the art of festival. Other examples of the festival/fair/carnival in works of art includes: Brecht's carnival scene in Galileo, the looming presence of the 1939 New York World's Fair in Doctorow's World's Fair, the meeting place of high and low in Jonson's Bartholomew Fair, the rowdy mob scene Hogarth painted in Southwark Fair, and Schumann's disconnected cadences and tonal breaks in the Carnaval concerto.

42. Guthrie, Davies, Renown at Stratford, 31-32.

43. M. M. Bakhtin, Rabelais and His World, trans. Helene Iswolsky (1965; Bloomington: Indiana UP 1984) 265.

44. Roland Barthes, Empire of Signs, trans. Richard Howard (1970; New York: Hill and Wang, 1982) 30-32. Barthes' caption under an overhead map reads: "The City is an ideogram: the Text continues." As such, the City can be a meaningful text like the festivals and angoras it contains.

45. Northrop Frye, The Great Code: The Bible and Literature (New York: Harcourt, 1982). Frye concludes his book with a point relevant to the matter of what is encoded in language code such as the Bible or a serious festival:

Yet perhaps it is only through the study of works of human imagination that we can make any real contact with the level of vision beyond faith. For such vision is, among other things, the quality in all serious religions that enables them to be associated with human products of culture and imagination, where the limit is the conceivable and not the actual. (231-232).

The ancient tie of church and festival remains beyond this study's limits, but further exploration of this central aspect of the festival seems indicated.

46. Strong, Roy. Art and Power: Renaissance Festivals 1450-1650. Woodbridge, England: Boydell Press, 1984. First published in 1974 at Splendour at Court: Renaissance Spectacle and the Theatre of Power, 172. The earlier title provided the idea for the dissertation's title as well as its central concept.

47. Christopher Hunt, "The Official Souvenir Program of Spoleto Festival U.S.A.: 1981" (Charleston: David L. Rawle Associates, 1981) 73.

48. Alessandro Falassi, ed., Time Out of Time: Essays on the Festival (Albuquerque: U of New Mexico P, 1987). From his introduction to Marianne Mesnil's essay, "Place and Time in the Carnivalesque Festival," 184. The importance of the urban environment as a functional element is stressed in this article.

49. Certainly no tabular reduction does justice to any work of imagination. However, this classification scheme provides a useful device for organizing the chaos of a festival into categories for interpretive comparison. In examining the wide array of festival categories on the template, it is clear that categories such as programming, results, management, or critical reaction in themselves merit extensive exploration. Any serious arts festival's programming would itself merit a separate monograph and critical probe, and in fact most available festival histories primarily provide this valuable documentation as chronological lists of performance events and their financing. However, questions of potential deeper significances and social meanings often remain unexplored by these individual festival histories, "collections of studies of particular events looked at in isolation," as Roy Strong observed.

50. Charles S. Wadsworth, interview tape recorded during chamber series break at Charleston's Dock Street Theater during the Spoleto Festival, May 1986.

51. The eleven Spoleto Festival U.S.A. posters form a unique representation of the evolution of this festival and its unpredictable offerings. Each poster differs widely.

52. Wadsworth had visited with the Riverbend organizers in late 1982, when his Lincoln Center chamber society was performing in Chattanooga. He offered several suggestions for associates who could be artistic directors for Riverbend. Now retired from the Lincoln Center organization, he represents a unique musical force in creating popular audiences for American chamber music, while retaining his "downhome" Newnan, Georgia, modesty and humor.

53. This observation was made by an Atlanta ceramic jewelry artist, Dorothy Kimball. She observed a string of colored lights on my 1989 makeshift Christmas "tree," a large palm plant. The comment triggered this idea of the "festive" nature of differences in a more general sense.

54. The festival's first general manager, Christine L. Reed, wrote in the first 1977 program: "There is abundant reason for the appropriateness of Charleston, South Carolina, as the site of Spoleto Festival U.S.A.--its pride in sustaining its own rich aesthetic heritage

of architectural and botanical treasures, its long-time concern for the educational process (the College of Charleston is the oldest municipal college in the United States), the establishment of a repository of its life style (the Museum of Charleston is the oldest museum in the United States), the forming of the St. Cecelia society in 1762 as an outlet for the musically inclined, the first theatre in America built exclusively for theatrical purposes (the Dock Street Theater), and the first opera in this country ("Flora") was performed in Charleston in 1735."

55. John Gruen, Menotti (New York: Macmillan, 1978).

56. Joseph P., Riley, Jr., Mayor of Charleston, Statement in 1978 official Spoleto Festival U.S.A. program guide, 12.

57. Max Reinhardt, "Austria Today," (1979).

58. The emergence of Piccolo Spoleto two years after the first 1977 festival suggests that there were numerous needs that the main festival was not addressing. Piccolo, its several hundred events sponsored by the City of Charleston, probably could be moved to another time of year if it actually were meeting extremely different needs from the main festival. A difference greater than each festival's programming is the cost of both "high" and "low" art, more precisely expensive or free performances, which are highly innovative in the Piccolo offerings. The "big" and "little" festivals appear to be complementary, each drawing their magic and power from their differing purposes, a difference contained within Menotti's aesthetic philosophy.

59. Redden announced at the festival's 1988 news conference that the festival was in the "black," meaning that sufficient "unearned," or grant and donation revenues, had been raised to pay expenses. Considering the festival's early days of large deficits, it was a significant achievement.

CHAPTER III -- Riverbend Festival

60. For this analysis, the methodology used in the "functions" categories for Charleston's festival (Chapter II) can be continued. Although such a chart lacks descriptive power, these categories suggest the basic elements that appear in most festivals as well as the specific features of the Riverbend Festival in 1987:
Name: Riverbend Festival
Type: Popular entertainment
Model: Spoleto Festival U.S.A., Plum Nelly
Purpose: Bring community together, improve economy, present arts

Results: Large crowds, develop riverfront, build pride
Programming: Highlighted popular musical entertainers such as Willie Nelson, Sarah Vaughn with the Chattanooga Symphony Orchestra, "Blood, Sweat & Tears," "Chicago," Arlo Guthrie and Pete Seeger, the "Spinners," the "Judds," a classical chamber trio in residence, and about two dozen other performers
Budget: $1.3 million
Duration: Ten days
Location and theaters: Several acres of a downtown riverfront park plus a few other indoor and outdoor sites
Artistic Director: 0
Management: Self-perpetuating board, a contracted local management staff
Workers: Hundreds of volunteers, part-time staff
Audience: As many as 100,000 spectators gathered for the most popular concerts, such as "Chicago" in 1987; total estimated audience was 250,000
Audience access: $8 plastic lapel pin for all events
Related events: Water skiing and hydroplane motorboat races on the Tennessee River; triathlon; downtown parade
Food: Some two dozen vendors offered food, drinks, and souvenirs
Reaction: City leaders have described the festival as the city's "signature piece." Featured in Southern Living magazine as key event
Profit: $75,000 estimated

61. Of course, in 1980-81 none of us would have thought to articulate such general concepts of "sameness" or the idea of observing the "empty space" as I have employed the phrase, although the idea is present in what Robbins and I wrote on May 5. How could such a completely "foreign" idea of looking at "nothing" surface in the first place? It was not until November 1987, when I was searching for some entry point to writing a final academic essay about Riverbend's meanings, that the concept came to me while reading Peter Brook's The Empty Space, whose implications were discussed in Chapter I. The effect was analogous to that of looking at the surrounding contextual landscape in reverse video. The dark and the light spaces were reversed; in a moment of insight there was nothing, absence, empty space--symbolized by a zero signifying no meaning present--yet this "no thing" became a presence much like a blank space on a grid of elements.

62. Awareness of this "empty space," which of course was not completely empty, began with memory of remarks that I, as the city's public affairs director, wrote for the mayor's welcoming comments at the last Downtown Arts Festival in 1972. He had stressed the vitality

that the arts bring to the city and, an always present theme, called attention to the unusual scenic beauty of mountains, river, and lakes that Chattanoogans should strive to "live up to" and match in our imaginative human works.

63. The sequence of influences, the process of opening a new definition of festival, and the larger context of the sources that influenced this one city's creation of a festival are revealed in part by much earlier efforts.

From 1898 into the early 1900s, Chattanooga hosted an annual week-long May festival with concerts, parades, bicycle races, flower shows, citizens in carnival dress, and king and queen coronations. These were major events involving towns around the city. A midway carnival occupied downtown city streets. Regional events celebrated the Norwegian god Balfur's arrival in "Spring--the Festival of Nature," a provocative hint of nature's statement of a "festival of differences" when the plant kingdom is in full blossom and in full embrace and exchange of differences.

These festivals had several commonalities with the creation, purposes, and programming of the current Riverbend Festival, but it appears the only surviving element is the August debutante presentation, the Cottonball Gala. These festivals were unknown to all local Riverbend organizers until March 1988. Then, when several of us read copies of the Chattanooga News-Free Press articles that I had found at the public library, we were struck by the similarity of having had at that time a local man pick up from uncertain sources the idea of having a major town festival for many of the same reasons we had chosen in 1981. It would be trite to say that history repeats itself. But "empty space" theory predicts that the scenic mountain town would inspire imaginative dreaming of cultural artifacts to match those of its natural context. More extensive work in searching for such historic patterns is indicated.

In 1935, the second National Folk Festival was held in Chattanooga. This spring event was part of a national resurgence in gathering and performing "authentic" folk ballads and in restoring the "purity" of the "folk," mainly "white folk." In a study of the racist "White Top Folk Festival" of the 1930s in Virginia, Chattanooga's hosting of this event drew comment for its inclusion of black singers:

Sarah Gertrude Knott, who founded the National Folk Festival in 1934, presented a broad range of performers, including black, who shared the stage with whites. "[The] picture of our folk life today would not be complete," she said, "without the contributions of the Negro." At her second annual festival in 1935, held in Chattanooga, Tennessee--surely as race-conscious an area as south Virginia--Knott's mountain fiddlers and ballad singers shared the program with a thousand-voice black chorus singing spirituals." Source: David E. Whisnant, All That is Native and Fine: the Politics of Culture in an American Region. Chapel Hill: UNC P, 1983, 244.

I am indebted to Allen Tullos of Emory University's Graduate Institute of Liberal Arts for mentioning this work late in the research for this study. The intentionally racist purposes of "White Top" merit comparison with similar German ideologies of the 1930s. White Top reflects an extreme example of racially exclusive programming and admission to the "white" top of the mountain. However, the image of a thousand-voice black chorus evokes the "sing" festival, "Southern Voices," proposed during the 1981 planning seminars by Doris Hays. When the formal research was underway, we were very negligent in not paying attention to the nature of past festivals in the city. Longo's previous research in a city newspaper insert had esaped notice.

During the 1950s and early 70s, the city's Allied Arts Council sponsored an annual spring or fall weekend arts festival with primarily outside performing and visual arts. The last downtown spring arts festival held in 1972. According to a conversation with the festival's chairperson, Kathy Patten, the downtown retail merchants complained so much about the loss of business during the festival that it was discontinued. All the parking spaces were filled, the merchants complained.

The festival itself was primarily visual arts, including crafts, juried paintings, pottery, and a small amount of performing arts. A few clowns amused the crowd; dancers had a brief presentation, and the Chattanooga Symphony Orchestra played. After that, for nearly a decade no central arts festival of any kind enlivened downtown Chattanooga.

64. The record of the struggle to fill the city's empty festival space is one local example of the power of a "philosophy of sameness" to suppress dissent, diversity, and, differences. Although it was proposed previously that a "theater of differences" could be termed "Menottian," no such specific term for a "theater of sameness" has presented itself. It must suffice to observe that propagandistic "mass spectacles," such as the Nazi fascist versions noted earlier, by their operative nature, cannot allow aesthetic "differences" that threaten values of "unity, oneness, sameness, similarities, harmony."

As Western societies have learned through two world wars, it is the tendency to evolve in the direction of totality--the "single controlling mind"--that the democratic concept of "plurality" and "diversity" is designed to guard against, not under certain conditions always successfully, as the history of Germany in the 1930s suggests. The intellectual bases for two opposing philosophies of human wellbeing, which lacks any simple resolution, seem indicated by this line of reasoning. From this perspective, the Riverbend Festival documents show an evolving ideological process to fill an absence with presence, emptiness with meaning, albeit a meaning that "functioned" to oppose "plurality" and "diversity."

65. In contrast to the formal plan, composer Doris Hays' alternative festival vision now appears as a valuable text that is the forgotten "script" of what a trained artist actually created in response to Chattanooga's empty space.

66. Gianni Longo, the foundation's community development consultant, had worked with other cities and was an editor of Learning from Baltimore, a series that drew lessons from experiences of various cities. Following a meeting for discussion and brain-storming, and preceding preparation of the planning grant, he met with me and explained his five-project community development concept, one item being a city fair. This was at a dinner meeting which the other three organizers could not attend. Longo said that his "approval of and recommendation of" the grant application was dependent on my taking the primary leadership position. Although I explained my other commitments, and argued that any of the other three organizers or others were better qualified for this project, Longo insisted.

I agreed to take that responsibility until artistic and administrative directors could be appointed under a new board. He accepted this stipulation, but when it developed that an artistic director would not be included in the early stages we had to devise new leadership arrangements. The other three organizers could not or would not take the full responsibility. We did not want to expand the board until new leadership was in place. After a few months of discussing the interest and qualifications of influential civic leaders, I was very pleased that we agreed on a popular local university music professor who would take my place and who also could serve in the combined role of president and artistic director. Dr. Walker Breland, who inspired us all by believing that Chattanooga could have just as fine an arts festival as Charleston, took office in early 1982. He and the new board, especially Mrs. Lee Parham, vice-president, performed herculean tasks in creating the first festival by mid-1982.

This partial solution resolved the functional, and by then obvious, need for the knowledge of an artistic director. The two festivals Parham and Breland created had an aesthetic quality lacking in the later commercialized productions. However, it now appears that the policies and decisions that led to this step demanded far too much of this combination artistic/leadership structure just as they did of the promotional firm contracted to manage the festival.

Breland was paid as artistic director the second year in addition to serving as president of Friends of the Festival, Inc. His scholarly analysis of that period would provide a very useful insight into the fundamental issues of art and power, power and art, associated with Chattanooga's new town festival. No doubt a collection of his and other related documents generated by the Lyndhurst Foundation's continuing interest and research grants would provide a valuable anthology for others interested in the creation of a town arts festival, or in the making of any kind of festival.

67. Those who signed the orginal grant application in May 1981 were Deanne Werner, Frank M. Robbins III, Nelson Irvine (attorney), and myself. It may be more than a coincidence that most of us-- Mickey Robbins, Nelson Irvine, Lee Parham, Sam Robinson, and I, who were so active in providing the initial energy for the festival--were amateur musicians. Energized by the talents of versatile professional pianist and opera accompanist Deanne Werner (who later married Nelson Irvine), we would play and sing at our 1980-82 social gatherings as much as we would debate the festival we imagined for the town. Music was a basic love of the group and it was natural to combine music-making and festival "talk sessions" with anyone who wanted to "sit" in and "jam." This suggests a very close connection between the desire for a party and the desire for a festival.

What became the Riverbend Festival first surfaced in discussions at Sally and Sam Robinson's home in June or July 1980, before I visited Salzburg. After that stimulating trip in August, I hosted a dinner meeting at my home in September 1980, when materials from Spoleto Festival U.S.A. and the Salzburg Festival were reviewed by about one dozen persons interested in the idea of a town festival for Chattanooga. The strongest encouragement came from Robert Austin, artistic director of the Chattanooga Opera, and Lynn Grimsley, executive director of the city's Allied Arts Fund.

68. It was not until 1986 that some of the foundation director's private views were accidentally revealed to me in some of the old file notes of Robbins' initial telephone conversation with Montague in early April 1981. The foundation director's responses to Robbins' suggestions during the initial telephone inquiry, based on the actual notes of that conversation, were that the "idea of a festival was great" and that they "were interested in something similar and maybe could tie in."

He said he did not "want to put words in our mouths," but that "something should be submitted with no local sponsorship." "Aim high, go first class, do it right, be comprehensive" were the phrases used. The foundation director was concerned that the community spirit seemed to stop with contributions to the Allied Arts Fund and felt that Chattanooga now had mature arts organizations. He saw Spoleto as "a little of a rip-off" [emphasis mine].

He was intrigued with the "economics of amenities" and urged the group to focus on the economic benefits of a festival. He urged us to get wide ranging, diverse people who could start the ball rolling by the summer of 1982, if we could get the community's support. He was concerned with the fractured community and felt the need for a project to pull everybody together.

I still am puzzled by a leadership philosophy that would view Spoleto Festival U.S.A. as a "rip-off" when that was the primary model we proposed and visited; this seems less tolerance of differing views than secret political manipulation of the "actors on the stage." A healthy debate that included the foundation director and his associates would have been far more useful to the community than such behind-the-scenes maneuvering.

69. I will long remember that afternoon when Mickey Robbins and I enjoyed the spring sunshine and the limitless possibilities of "going first class" while sitting in his backyard to draft a proposal for the foundation. We alternated in taking notes as each of us put our "dreams" on paper. Freed of mundane financial concerns, we dreamed big, as all the Riverbend leaders have done since that time.

70. The June 30, 1981, letter from Deaderick C. Montague was addressed to Frank M. Robbins III, with copies to Nelson Irvine, Sidney Hetzler, and Gianni Longo; it is in the author's Riverbend archives.

71. Apparently the intense desire to have some kind of festival blinded me to the actual political situation. Hindsight suggests the imperative "board diversification" tone of language, for example-- overruled the committee's independent judgment at this moment. Also, except in our few meetings, little continuing public "dialogue" was offered; our only regular contact was through Longo and, later, Storey.

This restriction against appointing an artistic director was received and passed around at one of our weekly Monday meetings at the Gazebo restaurant on Fountain Square. We interpreted this as meaning that any future grant would be withheld if we proceeded to search for an artistic director as outlined in the original proposal. The effect on the group was to inhibit including what seemed to be the primary source of energy and vision in the other festivals visited.

It was clear that major festivals, such as Spoleto, had evolved out of the imagination of a Menotti with bold visions in a receptive environment. I did not see how our festival could fully develop and mature without this kind of person, but we knew we were prohibited from going ahead in that direction. The effect was to move qualified artistic input into later stages of what was in fact a political as well as an aesthetic process in which the functions of artistic vision and local power were intertwined.

72. The foundation was generous in its funding concept if not in its aesthetic insights into the creation of arts festivals. An earlier paragraph in the Dec. 2 contract cover letter noted:

In addition, the Foundation agrees at this time to contribute an additional $70,000 in 1982 for the above-mentioned purposes if Friends of the Festival is able to obtain "up-front" money in an amount not less than $300,000 in additional cash, credit, loan guarantees or as co-signatures on a note with which to book performers. In the event you are unable to attract support of this magnitude from the community prior to March 1, we ask that you refund to the Foundation all of the grant funds which have not yet been spent.

The refund request was not enforced. It was in this context of early deadlines and extreme pressure to find other funding sources that the festival's commercial side of its developing personality developed, which the lack of an artistic director also fostered. The same conditions led to the sale of admission pins and various sponsorships the following year. The implications of the Lyndhurst Foundation's funding policies are encoded in the Riverbend Festival (and throughout the community), and merit more extensive economic and public policy analysis than is possible here.

73. The idea in inviting participants was that you are who you present yourself to be. This was a departure from the usual Chattanooga way of classifying individuals by mountain or ridge altitude level, wealth, neighborhood, and job title. This practice has continued with subsequent appointments to the Riverbend board, excepting black representation. It brought many new persons to leadership positions in the city's performing arts. It was a step in creating a new arts structure in the city, which the foundation's executive director and our group agreed was needed.

We had little choice in creating Friends of the Festival because none of the Allied Arts organizations would accept the foundation grant. This was a destructive step that could have been avoided if there had been more dialogue of all interested parties at the outset. However, several persons in the traditional arts organizations strongly resisted an independent festival at that time.

74. This was an issue discussed in materials from Charleston and Salzburg. The extreme position of a "high art" orientation was expressed in a quotation from Menotti in a New York Times article on May 26, 1981, "I'm not very sympathetic to the tendency to bring art to the people." This is a seeming contradiction in view of his goal of creating a festival in 1958 "for the joy of it" and of making arts the

"main course," but his comment can be taken within the context of Tyrone Guthrie's definition of a "serious" festival, in which artistic expression is goal, not means.

The original idea of juxtaposing artistic elements can be seen in the name of the concluding party for all seminar participants held at one of the member's (Sharon Mills) home. It was called "Bar-B-Q, Beer, Blue Jeans, and Bach" and featured a University of Tennessee at Chattanooga chamber trio and faculty pianist Arthur Rivituso. The spirit of the party led naturally to the spirit of the first Riverbend arts festival (which the Olan Mills company has supported consistently with funds and staff).

"High" and "low" art programming was not mutually exclusive at this beginning phase of the Riverbend Festival, which was funded by the Lyndhurst Foundation planning grant in part as a demonstration of use of the performing arts to generate funds for the festival. Several of these musicales were hosted but were discontinued due in part to lack of staff support.

75. Gianni Longo, The Making of the Festival, (New York: The Institute for Environmental Action, 1981) 22.

76. Longo, The Making of the Festival, 37-38.

77. Longo, The Making of The Festival, 33.

78. "Race" is a problematic, useless term but it reflects the reality of that period, and it remains an active mental category today. It is used reluctantly.

79. Hay is an extraordinarily successful avant garde composer and performer. A sample of her credentials can be seen in a review of the performances at Spoleto Festival U.S.A. in 1981. Allan Kozinn wrote in the Charleston News & Courier on May 30, 1981: "Miss Hays was raised in Tennessee and moved to New York in 1969. There, she has made a considerable career as a pianist specializing in difficult music that uses "cluster" effects, often produced by taking elbows or full arms to the keyboard....She has also earned a reputation as a composer with a flair for multi-media musical and theatrical events, and at Thursday's [Piccolo Spoleto] concert she was featured as a composer, pianist, birdcall blower, synthesist, photographer and water pourer....For the most part, this concert was the first chunk of music I've heard here that was not only composed in the last half of the 20th century, but sounded like it....The Thursday concert, by the way, was well-attended, and it seemed that old and young alike enjoyed the strange variety of things they saw and heard."

A more recent review in the Village Voice (August 16, 1989) by Kyle Gann of Hays' folk opera-in-production, The Glass Woman, contrasted her work to Philip Glass's Fall of the House of Usher, presented July 14-16, 1989, at Alice Tully Hall in the Lincoln Center complex. "...the future of this one is worth keeping an ear out for. If musically conservative, The Glass Woman was 150 times as enjoyable as the Glass House heard two weeks earlier....Hays' fledgling work is a better bet even if the's a woman, even if they've never heard of her, than these assembly-line famous-name extravaganzas that seem to have no artistic impulse behind them whatsoever....Opera America, by investing time, resources, and faith in artists more serious than fashionable, is taking brave steps in that direction."

No other phrases so well capture the essence of the commercial Riverbend Festival that has evolved than "assembly-line famous-name extravaganzas that seem to have no artistic impulse behind them whatsoever."

80. Why did I insist that classical music performances were so desirable in our discussions of Chattanooga's festival? Hays had been my musical inspiration for many years, dating from an evening in 1967 when, after playing in the Memorial Auditorium her obligatory piano pieces as a scholarship winner at the city's Cottonball Gala for debutantes, she and I along with the Robbins went to the Admiral Benbow motel lounge for conversation. When the country music singer stopped for intermission, we persuaded Hays to play some of the Mozart, Bach, and Beethoven she had just played at the Cottonball.

The room was full of persons who probably would not have been assumed to be classical music lovers. They soon stopped talking and drinking and listened as Hays displayed her virtuosity and the lively, sensual power of the music in such intimate quarters. They applauded vigorously after each piece and asked her for more, remaining completely silent during each piece, which she had memorized. Finally, after some 30 minutes she gave the piano back to the now well-rested and obliging country singer. Hays returned to our table to a standing ovation from these "blue-collar" workers who, I've been told for years, will not attend classical concerts because they do not like the music. I have known that belief was nonsense since that night in 1967 in the smokey lounge of the Admiral Benbow.

Sometimes the artist must be brought to the audience. This is an effort not as cost efficient as bringing the audience to the artist in the concert hall for their amusement and edification. This journey to the theater also may not be as likely to bring the magical joy of long-dead improvisational composers such as Mozart and Bach to an appreciative audience who may even have booed if they had known this was "serious, high art."

Is it not a significant and similar semiotic statement of social "hierarchy" that the Riverbend expects its audiences to find it in its riverfront enclosure, rather than for its entertainers to reach out to all parts of the community and present some lively Mozart in the smokey lounges of the city pubs, bars, taverns, homes, churches, businesses? No doubt that would be more expensive, like branch banking. But it truly would be a "music of the masters" outreach.

This 1967 night appears to be for me the actual beginning of the Riverbend Festival's "ideal," the festival-creature that in many ways said I can, I can, I can--but would not move from its tents and mooring at the city's point of origin.

81. The "Proposal for Funding to Establish a Chattanooga Festival," by Bruce Storey of Variety Services, was submitted to the Lyndhurst Foundation, Chattanooga, Tennessee, by Friends of the Festival, Inc., November 23, 1981. It was approved by some two dozen participants in the process during the summer and autumn of 1981, and it represented the collective preferences of the group.

82. Propp, V. Morphology of the Folktale. Second Edition, revised and edited by Louis A. Wagner. Austin: University of Texas Press, 1968, 87-88.

83. "What's New in the Arts." Sidney N. Hetzler, Jr. Chattanooga Times, May 19, 1986.

CHAPTER IV Two Towns, Two Festivals

84. From remarks at a 1986 civic conference in Chattanooga by Deaderick C. Montague, president, Lyndhurst Foundation, Chattanooga, Tennessee.

Deaderick C. Montague was the individual catalyst who made the Riverbend Festival possible so quickly after the idea surfaced in May 1980. Several of us had talked of approaching the Lyndhurst Foundation but it was not until Frank M. Robbins III called Montague in April 1981 that this contact was made. Without Montague's support, as much as several years probably would have passed before enough "believers" would have been found.

Our first proposal recommended him for president of the group. He declined because of his foundation position. By 1988 he had resigned from the foundation and was elected chairman of the foundation-sponsored Chattanooga Venture, a private, nonprofit volunteer group that aims at broad changes in the community, changes that my own set of experiences suggests should come from openly elected political leaders in existing governmental institutions rather than from closed private groups.

Whatever our political positions, there cannot be enough credit given to this thoughtful, dedicated civic worker for not only awarding a planning grant to our group but also for inspiring all of us to aspire to create "excellence" in our festival. Yet we learned that we had in 1981 and in later years different definitions of excellence, conflicting philosophies of community, and divergent approaches toward community change. Although I criticize Montague's philosophy in this study, I in no way criticize him personally.

My convictions about the sameness/difference issue spring indirectly from civil rights events in Boston and Chattanooga in 1968, about which I have written in a 1973 Boston University Master's thesis, "The Feedback Factor in the Communication Process." To my former instructors and later colleagues, Albert J. Sullivan and Otto Lerbinger, I acknowledge a debt that I am repaying in a small way by attempting to transmit portions of their communication philosophies in this work and in everyday living.

85. Excerpts from a 1981 proposal written at the request of festival organizers by New York composer and pianist Doris Hays.

86. Lyotard, Jean-Francois. The Postmodern Condition: A Report on Knowledge. Translation from the French by Geoff Bennington and Brian Massumi. Foreword by Fredric Jameson. Minneapolis: University of Minnesota Press, 1984, xviii.

87. Segrest, Robert. "The Architecture of the Excluded Middle...." Paper presented at Emory University, April 9, 1986.

88. Riverbend Festival: A Comprehensive Evaluation. Prepared for Friends of the Festival, Inc., by Urban Initiatives, New York City, in association with Trahan, Burden & Charles of Baltimore, Maryland; Kaminsky & Company of New York and Nashville; and Tatge Productions of New York, 1988.

89. Alfreda L. Irwin. Three Taps of the Gavel: Pledge to the Future--The Chautauqua Story. Third edition. Chautauqua, N.Y.: Chautauqua Institution, 1987. (ix). From scrapbook II, Mrs. Adelaide L. Westcott, page 7. Lewis Miller's speech on opening night, 1888, The Chautauqua Institution library.

Chautauqua has an extensive library, and I am indebted to its librarian, Alfreda L. Irwin, for assistance in this research.

90. Irwin, Three Taps, 73.

91. It would be enlightening to make some comparison between names of festivals. In the two festivals studied, first was the place, then ideas, then tentative names, "Celebration of Togetherness" festival (function name), then Riverbend Festival (place name). Many of the Chattanooga group's names (one comic came up with "Hetzfest") came from a brainstorming session one evening and focused on the river, suggesting its power as a natural framing device . Chattanooga's festival name signifies a function different from the "foreignness" of Charleston's "Spoleto" name that seemed to alarm some in Chattanooga. However, for Charleston and Melbourne,

"Spoleto" now signifies the idea, not the place. Chautauqua, the Indian name of the lake adjacent to the Assembly's site, now signifies an idea or spirit more than a location; the traveling Chautauqua lyceums expressed the mobile nature of these Assemblies. The "home" place remains the primary model of the "experience," although other assemblies, such as the one on Monteagle Mountain, Tennessee, express the concept in their gate, open-sided amphitheater, and architecture.

92. Irvin, Three Taps, 5-7.

93. Signifieds vary from their signifiers. One reader of this paragraph, who had grown up in New York City, thought it more likely that the Klu Klux Klan had erected these three crosses as a warning to blacks driving into the Southern states.

94. Bakhtin, M. M. Speech Genres & Other Late Essays. Translated, Vern W. McGee. Austin: University of Texas Press, 1986, 170.

95. Jack McDonald.

96. The Riverbend pin signifies more than a mere pass for cheap entertainment and a week of beer and wine drinking and motorboat racing. One of my pins is ceramic instead of plastic; it was given to me by a board member, Sam Robinson, who was one of the early "dreamers." Robinson has been active and valuable as legal council and political adviser since the festival's beginning; he has in fact kept parts of the original dream alive, although we have had long arguments about the particular parts, such as "cohesion," that he supported by ranking them uppermost during our small group session at the final seminar in 1981. He explained that only VIPs, staff, and board members are given the more costly pin, and that it was inexcusable that I had not been given one every year.

The gesture was appreciated, and when I used the "official" ceramic entrance pin in 1988, my experience of feeling set off from "ordinary" pin wearers was much like the first day of wearing the gold bars of an Air Force second lieutenant. Feeling like one of the in-group again, I ran into the new festival president, Margaret Culpepper, one afternoon on the crowded promenade and introduced myself, saying I was happy to see the festival had solved some of the location problems from its early years and that I had never imagined when I was the president of the organizing group that the city's river park would attract so many people. She said she was glad to meet me, but said that the only name she knew from the beginning was a Walker Breland who had been the first president. The shiny official pin lost some of its luster after that encounter; time quickly erases the tracks of pilgrims to its festivals, and I sense that regular festival devotionals are obligatory for the select.

97. See Preface endnote 5, for brief definition of C. S. Peirce's triadic theory of semiotics.

98. Strong, Art and Power, 172-173.

99. Frank E.X. Dance, ed., "Toward a Theory of Human Communication." Human Communication Theory. (New York: Holt, 1967) 295-296.

...the helix presents a rather fascinating variety of possibilities for representing pathologies of communication. If you take an helically coiled spring, such as the child's toy that tumbles down staircases by coiling in upon itself, and pull it full out in the vertical position, you can call to your imagination an entirely different kind of communication than that represented by compressing the spring as close as possible upon itself. If you extend the spring halfway and then compress just one side of the helix, you can envision a communication process open in one dimension but closed in another. At any and all times, the helix gives geometrical testimony to the concept that communication while moving forward is at the same moment coming back upon itself and being affected by its past behavior, for the coming curve of the helix is fundamentally affected by the curve from which it emerges. Yet, even though slowly, the helix can gradually free itself from lower-level distortions.

Dance comments in passing that this geometric form crops up as a descriptive device in a number of disciplines, such as a model of the DNA molecule--the key code of life.

100. 17 M.M. Bakhtin, "Methodology for the Human Sciences," Speech Genres and Other Late Essays, trans. Vern W. McGee, ed. Caryl Emerson and Michael Holquist (Austin: U of Texas P, 1986) 170.

101. 18 John J. MacAloon, ed., "Introduction: Cultural Performances, Culture Theory," Rite, Drama, Festival, Spectacle: Rehearsals Toward a Theory of Cultural Performances (Philadelphia: Institute for the Study of Human Issues, 1984).

Victor Turner, From Ritual to Theatre: The Human Seriousness of Play (New York: PAJ Publications, 1982).

102. Umberto Eco, A Theory of Semiotics (Bloomington: Indiana UP, 1979) 134.

103. Vladimir Propp, Theory and History of Folklore, ed. and intro. Anatoly Liberman, trans. Ariadna Y. Martin et al. (1963; Leningrad: Leningrad U; Minneapolis: U of Minnesota P, 1984) xvii. With chapters on "Honoring the Dead, Ritual Meals, Greeting the Spring, Greeting Songs and Incantations, Plant Cults, Death and Laughter, Games and Entertainments," the agrarian festivals study contains no clear separation by intent, function, or effect categories. Propp's interest in rigorous classification and detection of deep

structural functions (The Morphology of the Folktale, 1928), makes this study worthy of closer attention.

A translation of Propp's opening chapter, "The Commemoration of the Dead," is found in Time Out of Time: Essays on the Festival, ed. and trans. Allesandro Falassi (Albuquerque: U of New Mexico P, 1987) 233-241.

104. 21 See Josef Pieper, In Tune With the World: A Theory of Festivity, trans. Richard and Clara Winston (1963; New York: Harcourt, 1965) and J. Huizinga, Homo Ludens: A Study of the Play-Element in Culture' (1944; New York: Roy Publishers, 1950).

105. 22 Brook, Peter. The Empty Space. (New York: Atheneum, 1984) 9.

106. 23 Mathematics could not have advanced without the invention of the concept of "zero" and a sign for it (Britannica, 1982). Not until the thirteenth century did Europeans adopt the idea of zero, based on Islamic algebra. Most ancient languages used "o" for the position after "9," although the "." was used in Arabic and Kashmir. A metaphor of empty space suggests some undetermined significance about the sign materiality of representing "nothing" or the unknown by a dot rather than a zero. A recent work on this problem, Signifying Nothing: the Semiotics of Zero, is valuable in relating the metaphor of empty space to more general sign theories of meaning.

107. 24 Charles S. Peirce, "Logic as Semiotic: The Theory of Signs," Ed. Justus Buchler Philosophical Writings of Peirce, 1940; (New York: Rpt. 1955) 99.

108. 25 Some self-labeled "town arts festivals" actually function more as central city "urban fairs" when various specific "marketing" functions and effects are revealed. It should be noted in this context that Riverbend did not become a "city fair" as originally outlined by a foundation consultant.

109. 26 Paul Bouissac, lecture, "Semiotics of Performance" seminar, Northwestern University, 1986 International Summer Institute for Semiotic and Structural Analysis.

110. 27 Eco, A Theory of Semiotics, 150.

111. 28 Eco, A Theory of Semiotics, 150.

112. 29 Bakhtin, Speech Genres, 169.

113. 30 Martin Krampen, "Phytosemiotics," Frontiers in Semiotics, John Deely, Brooke Williams, Felicia E. Kruse ed, (Bloomington: Indiana UP 1986) 84. Jakob von Uxhull's primary work is "Bedeutungslehre", Bios, vol. 10 (Leipzig), Reprinted in Streifzuge durch die Umwelten von Tieren und Menshcen/Bedeutungslehre, by Jakob von Uxhull and Gerog Kriszat (Frankfurt a. M.: S. Fischer Vrlag, 1970).

"Umwelt" is the key term for the influence of "modeling" in the sense used here. Krampen explains:

There is a structural correspondence between each living being as an autonomous subject and its own "Umwelt". The term of "umwelt" is difficult to translate into English. It means the subject world of what is meaningful impingement for the living being in terms of its own information processing equipment, sign systems, and codes....The structure of connection between a living being and its "umwelt" is mediated by sign processes...(84).

One example is a walk through a town....Everything witnessed during a walk through a town is geared to human needs....Stairs accommodate ascending legs, bannisters the arms. Each object is given its form and its meaning by some function of human life...(85).

Jakob von Uxhull's approach to biology as a science of life is a holist one: The whole is not explained by the functioning of its parts, but the meaning of the parts is explained according to the plan of the whole, a principle that is not unlike the fundamental proposition of Gestalt theory (95).

114. 31 Thomas A. Sebeok, lecture, "Introduction to Semiotics" seminar, Northwestern University, 1986 International Summer Institute for the Study of Semiotics and Structuralism.

AFTERWORD – May 2012

Part 1
Looking Back and Ahead

These Charleston and Chattanooga festival issues and stories are alive in the 21st century and in 2012, the nature of most festivals being to invite continuous disruption by their diverse programming and liminal venues in various ways, ways not always obvious.

The text has been available on the web since about 1996, and the table of contents and an Amazon page link remain there. Some have found it via web searches and cited it in their own books and articles. But I believe print books remain a superior technology over digital books for scholarly research with broader access in libraries and academic institutions and for working reference material. I tend to go to books on my shelves again and again and thumb the pages, discovering new material and often seeing it differently over time. A print version seemed to better display the two against three conceptual structures that evolved in the academic context of the late 1980's (difference versus sameness; empty space, idea, force). I found no way to improve on these categories in thinking about festival theory and practice.

Those who found it on the web and have wanted to buy it, such as Harry Leopold, an arts leader in Sarasota, FL, now can find it in the more readily shared and readable form of a book. Mr. Leopold was the one who in early 2010 gave me the notion to start thinking of simply publishing the original 1990 thesis unedited. Neither the main festivals' formats nor my views had changed in any significant way.

He emailed me with encouragement in January 2010, saying, after I had emailed him that it could be found online but was not yet for sale and of my efforts to update it, "I thought it was fascinating and well done as is." It had been long enough in gestation and it was time to send it into the world being what it was and is. More could come later. And with luck I would receive needed constructive feedback, such as Reiss's generous insights.

Leopold is involved with Sarasota's new and diverse Ringling International Arts Festival as well as numerous other arts organizations there, as I learned when we met for lunch in 2010 and discussed Sarasota's festivals. He was interested in what the ideas in my dissertation might contribute as new perspectives for Sarasota's cultural life and a possible town arts festival. He passed around copies, he told me March 2012 during a dinner at his lovely home with his talented wife, Victoria, and believes my ideas had some value there for various arts leaders and managers. This includes the city's new, highly diverse Ringling International Arts Festival directed by Mikhail Baryshnikov each October. According to RIAF's web page: "The Ringling International Arts Festival is a six-day cultural celebration of modern music, dance, theater, and visuals arts presented by The John and Mable Ringling Museum of Art with New York's Baryshnikov Arts Center, October 11-16, 2011 at the Ringling Center for the Arts in Sarasota, Florida."

"What do you get," says the 2011 web page, "when you combine one of the country's leading Art Museums with a radical NYC performance space nobly focused on providing precious resources for the creation of new work to the most vital artists in their fields? Come see for yourself when traditional meets radically new at The Ringling International Arts Festival! The world will be watching. The forces at play here have combined to create an event that is all too rare in the US."

Sarasota has one of the liveliest arts scenes, especially in winter, for its size of any city in the world, even some of its old circus energy, and has a magical blend of tradition welcoming disruption, or the new welcoming the old, I'm not sure which...or both—truly differences embracing sameness. The city even has a winter event called "Embracing Our Differences," an annual outdoor art show celebrating diversity in which all can enter quotations, art, objects. I may enter these 117,000 words.

A useful idea, such as "traditional meets radically new," often earns an independent life and rarely do any know its sources, like a river with no clear headspring. Or it is just in the cultural context, the zeitgeist. It is in that same original Riverbend spirit of sharing ideas and alternative perspectives that this book version is offered, particularly about the sensitive role of an artistic director and the "art power" of a city's artistic assets, both local and imported. By their disruptive nature, artistic forces will stimulate struggle, conflict and competition, or "organized surprise," as Charles Wadsworth said in effect. Or, as the Charleston banking leader feared, an arts festival might become a "breeding ground" for deviants and, quite rightly, differences. This is a perfect definition of Spoleto festivals, not as a Darwinian arena of the fittest but as a cradle for delicate cultural organisms best nurtured by a pied piper, a magician like Gian Carlo Menotti, and, today, general director Nigel Redden, who, from all the acclaim, has continued his old boss' alchemy and pipes the parade.

Both the Charleston and Chattanooga festivals have remained remarkably fixed in their formats, although the Chattanooga production, offering leading popular artists if not classical performers, resembled in a small way the whole town model of Charleston for the first few years. It is a mystery why Riverbend changed from a potentially vigorous, even disruptive, comprehensive town festival to riverfront development music concerts and a "block party." After reading Appendix B, Riverbend materials, one might question the usual civic arts leader suspects and powerful foundation leaders; certainly local artists were never again connected as they were at the beginning of the creative process.

Our early Friends of the Festival files, which I was given early on to keep after the first executive director tired of carrying them in his car trunk, and my own documents burned in my home fire August 2007. However, most originals remain at the Lyndhurst Foundation's open archives at the University of North Carolina at Chapel Hill, NC. I've read through most of the early folders and there is rich material there for festival scholars and researchers. The Chattanooga Public Library has a complete news clipping archive. And some of the early leaders have their own files. Having close and open access to local urban history is a strong resource in understanding what led to what over time and in knowing why certain paths were taken.

New York City and Chattanooga writer Rich Bailey speculated about the meanings of Spoleto USA after our visit there in 2005. Writing in Chattanooga's "The Pulse" weekly arts newspaper, he offered some lessons Chattanooga could learn from the Charleston model:

What Can Riverbend Learn from Spoleto?
By Rich Bailey

What's the saying... "How ya gonna keep 'em down on the farm when they've seen Paree?" In my case now, it's "How ya gonna be happy with Riverbend when you've seen Spoleto?"

I started thinking about Charleston, SC's Spoleto festival a year ago [2004] when I met Sid Hetzler, one of Riverbend's founders, and learned some local history I hadn't known. Hetzler was part of a four-person organizing committee that studied Spoleto and other town festivals, hoping to start one in Chattanooga. As Riverbend became a reality but moved away from the festival models that inspired him, Hetzler left the board. He later wrote his doctoral dissertation on "The Idea of Festival," comparing Riverbend and Spoleto.

Hetzler went back to Spoleto this month researching a book on that theme. I tagged along because I'm fascinated by Chattanooga's renaissance and its building blocks. Neither Spoleto nor Riverbend was the sole engine of its city's resurgence, but they set the tempo for the dance early on by using the arts to show the city in its best light. I wanted to see Spoleto because it sounded like a road not taken, a "Riverbend that might have been."

Spoleto is actually two festivals: Spoleto USA, created privately in 1977 to bring world class arts to Charleston, and Piccolo Spoleto, created two years later by the city's cultural affairs department to provide a more accessible and more affordable showcase for local and regional arts. Over the course of 17 days, they bring over 800 performances and exhibits to dozens of venues spread across downtown Charleston.

In three days at Spoleto, just scratching the surface, I saw fabulous modern dance from both the Hubbard Street Theatre of Chicago and the Charleston Ballet Theatre. New York's Mabou Mines theater group staged an over-the-top production of Ibsen's "Doll House," which underscored the play's depiction of constricting female gender roles by casting all the male characters with actors of uncommonly short stature, forcing the female actors to perform on their knees to fit the dollhouse set and to be at eye level with the men. In "Tiny Ninja Theater's Hamlet," Shakespeare's play was performed by tiny plastic ninjas manipulated and voiced by one man. "Kathy & Mo: Parallel Lives" was a very funny Charleston-based two woman comedy show. The Chicago comedy group Baby Wants Candy improvised a consistently hilarious one-hour musical from a single audience suggestion.

The piece de resistance for me came at the Piccolo Spoleto finale, which paired the Charleston Symphony with African drummer Obo Addy of Ghana, performing the world premiere of his composition "Tears of our Mothers" in a city park. Inspired by the mothers left behind when Africans were taken into the slave trade, the piece blends orchestra, African drums and xylophone, African-American choir, and a haunting saxophone solo. The program also included school children who had studied with Addy and local African drummers performing selections from The Lion King with the Symphony, along with a procession of more children costumed as Lion King characters. (At Riverbend, we ask our Symphony to partner with middle-aged rockers doing their greatest hits.)

But the most dramatic difference was in the way the two festivals inhabit their respective downtowns. Much of Riverbend's character comes from the way it funnels massive crowds through a self-contained see-and-be-seen zone, a riverfront-turned-midway complete with carnival rides, food court and car dealers. Because Spoleto spreads its attractions throughout the day and across downtown, its attendees stroll from venue to venue throughout Charleston's renovated downtown, mixing with people going about their daily business, participating in the life of the city, and patronizing local restaurants instead of out-of-town food vendors.

The way Spoleto engages its city finally crystallized my beef with Riverbend: it's a temporary mall in the midst of this vibrant downtown we've created.

Twenty-five years ago, Chattanooga had turned its back on the river and mostly abandoned downtown. As beautiful as our new 21st Century Waterfront is, I think it's wrong for the community's biggest celebration to make it a fenced compound that turns its back on the rest of downtown. Chattanooga needs what Spoleto gives Charleston: an infusion of activity that fills the streets -- not just the venue seats -- with people having a good time.

I don't think it makes sense to scrap Riverbend, but I think it needs a companion festival, like Charleston has in the free or moderately priced events of the city-sponsored Piccolo Spoleto. Imagine dance, comedy and theater spread out all over downtown, incorporating venues like the Tivoli, Memorial Auditorium, and the Theatre Centre into the festival instead of making them go dark. What about putting classical and gospel musicians in churches, or coordinating visual arts exhibits at the Hunter and smaller galleries? (And while we're making changes, let's replace the food court with local restaurants and ditch the jets that fly overhead during the performances.)

Maybe it's time for a new festival to be born. Who wants to be the midwife?

***

Maybe a new "companion" Chattanooga festival has hatched, although it's taken a few decades and lacks a full-time artistic director. Early in 2012 a new Chattanooga festival was announced, called HATCH, short for "History. Art. Technology. Culture. Happenings." An early press release in March from the Waterhouse PR firm reported that HATCH was Chattanooga's first effort at a Spoleto type festival, showing the continuing power of this model's influence. The Lyndhurst Foundation was the lead sponsor, and the Hunter Museum director was the executive director. It included many previously planned arts conferences, concerts, and added support for a smorgasbord of new and previously planned grassroots festivals, such as MakeWorks' 10x10, and the Barking Legs Theater's Cagefest. This partially improvised show celebrated John Cage's 100th birthday with random combinations of music and choreography by six dance groups.

At the Hunter's opening night, choreographer Ann Law's modern dance group, several poets and musicians improvised audience suggestions in one of the museum's galleries along with other performances in the unusually noisy art museum. Clowns amused families outside on the scenic grounds overlooking downtown Chattanooga and the adjoining mountains. As in Charleston, the problem was one of too many choices at the same time. I attended two opening events in Hunter Museum's expansive atrium lobby on the Tennessee River bluff, a perfect venue for "edge" programming. Lee University and Hunter sponsored leading national chamber players as a string octet under the museum's String Theory program, playing works by Shostakovich, Dvorak and Mendelssohn.

Then, just after that sunset chamber concert, we returned to the atrium for Hops at the Opera, an aria-and-local brew celebration of Chattanooga's one tenuous claim to opera fame, Grace Moore, directed with skill and finesse by Harv Wileman. Some of the young singers were excellent, and could begin to fill the gap created by the loss of operas that were produced by the Chattanooga Symphony and Opera Association. It was a perfect spring evening as the setting sun darkened the atrium. HATCH really did feel much like Spoleto's energy, or possibly more like Piccolo Spoleto's diverse small events, as several of us habitual arts lovers who had founded the steamy August Riverbend commented during the interval outside the museum. There were so many diverse streams of unique festivals, performances and happenings that it did feel like an open city festival generating a feeling of excitement with the unexpected mix of old and new.

HATCH did not include any participatory arts or social dancing but some encouraging comments were made about including this next year if it continues; "participatory" is not an idea with any local meaning unless asking an audience for words is the sense.

Zachary Cooper, publisher of Pulse Magazine where Rich Bailey's 2005 Spoleto article was published and mentioned, gave strong editorial support in early March 2012 to the emerging town arts festival's birth:

>...HATCH was just an idea about four months ago and now it's poised to have a significant impact in its inaugural year. There were already major milestones within the 10 days for arts in our community. The 4 Bridges Arts Festival, the Mid-South Sculpture Alliance and the Festival of New Plays. These served as the foundation from which HATCH was born. By building on this foundation, the idea was to establish an annual, large-scale collaborative arts and cultural showcase.
>
> With Daniel Stetson, executive director of the Hunter Museum of American Art, serving as head of the HATCH steering committee, the work began. Organizing partners were coordinated, foundation and corporate support was secured and solid event planning began to take shape. Over the last month or so, the amount of events and exhibits has exploded. This all happened in the span of about 3 months. MakeWorks' 10x10 is a great example of the scale and breadth of HATCH. The installation will establish 100 creative works of art within a 10-by-10 city block area with it all culminating in an exhibition, food, performance and music event on Friday, April 20, at Patten Parkway. And that's just one example of the creativity being unleashed here.
>
> Having just been birthed, HATCH has all the hallmarks of a young child: Bright-eyed, full of energy and curiosity. Ideas and productions rapidly bubbled to the surface as planning progressed....
>
> **Some years ago, Pulse contributor Rich Bailey wrote about the idea of establishing a Spoleto-type art and culture festival here in Chattanooga. He expressed how the leadership and vision that have made that Charleston, S.C., festival such a crown jewel for the region and the country could happen here. Rich's editorial speculated about this within the context of Riverbend, its history and the prospect a dramatic change in Riverbend's direction. HATCH's development has been much more organic than this**

and that's a good thing, as I suspect Rich might agree. That notion is exactly the type of opportunity we have before us. [Author's emphasis].

...HATCH 2012...successfully engaged the creative community, establishing collaborative projects that span multiple days across multiple city blocks....

***

One hopes someone will tell the tale of HATCH's story of origin; committees judge but only individuals create. Mr. Cooper might not know how much the Riverbend Festival idea was organic, if by that is meant local people with their own ideas as opposed to mainly outside influence. But clearly he is encouraging what I would call a festival of differences and diversity, possibly excluding popular music, and very inclusive of many art forms and genres. No doubt HATCH has the financial and arts leadership support that Riverbend was denied, but there is no reason both cannot co-exist and add to the city's cultural resources, unless the financial supporters divert more resources from Riverbend to HATCH as a stronger showcase for the city's new venues and business developments that are making positive national headlines at last. As noted below, Riverbend was losing its only remaining venue beyond its fences, and a major night of its ten-day offerings, when the Bessie Smith Strut street concerts were cancelled by city officials. It is likely the idea of a closed festival will be seriously discussed by the Friends of the Festival board as other models demonstrate their power to create energy and enthusiasm like that generated during the early open Riverbend festivals.

The hot local political issue in March/April 2012 was Chattanooga Mayor Ron Litttlefield's abrupt cancellation, apparently without public discussion or consultation, of Riverbend's 30-year tradition of the free, popular Monday night Bessie Smith Blues and Jazz Strut, now simply called the "Strut." Tens of thousands "strutted" up and down the boulevard, beers and BBQ in hand, and dancing as the mood struck. The mayor and police blamed security concerns from past occasional violence. For the Riverbend management, it long was a night of financial loss with no advertising and little donor revenue.

This was started in the opening year to extend the riverfront park site foot traffic to the black community on MLK Boulevard, formerly Ninth Street, which is nine blocks south of the Tennessee River festival park. Several band stages, currently mostly blues groups, were placed up and down MLK along several East-West blocks, centered by the Bessie Smith Cultural Center. To stimulate walking traffic, bars and restaurants between these points were open along MLK. Currently most restaurants around the Riverbend site lose business during the festival due in part to loss of parking, which is very unusual for a town festival.

Black leaders immediately claimed racism and protested the cancellation. MLK Street businessmen objected to the loss of expected revenues on that Monday evening. Strut lover David Smotherman organized a Facebook "Occupy the Strut on June 11, 2012" page that quickly gathered thousands of members. Friends of the Festival leaders hurriedly met with city hall and black leaders to contain the growing crisis. The mayor remained fixed in his decision to move the Strut inside Riverbend but relented after the Riverbend board refused to move it inside the heavily policed, temporarily fenced park along the riverfront. After considerable public and private pressure, the mayor said he would approve the Strut if three requirements were met: a responsible host group, fences all along the adjoining streets and liability insurance. The Bessie Smith Center, apparently working with the Riverbend director Chip Baker, found an anonymous donor, according to local news reports, and agreed to host the Strut, including fences.

It seems the fenced-in, gated Riverbend model is the norm for the city's leaders, even though the popular Strut was held for three decades without such physical boundaries. I was concerned about the loss of this last remaining tie to the original "open" Riverbend in venues all over the downtown, and published an op-ed piece in John Wilson's online newspaper, The Chattanoogan. To this book's readers, the themes and issues will be familiar. They are an example of how the views presented in this study can decode the underlying ideas and behavior of what is regarded as a festival of sameness.

Moving the Bessie Smith Strut Is Sad News
By Sid Hetzler
Friday, March 30, 2012

Moving the Bessie Smith Strut from MLK street to inside the Riverbend fences is sad, very sad news.

It reflects the mayor's limited understanding of why the Strut was created to move the Riverbend Festival to all parts of the city and open up our festival. It is difficult to imagine that Commissioner Sally Robinson supports this change since she and her husband Sam encouraged the festival director Bruce Story's idea to create this New Orleans street festival to extend Riverbend to the Southside from the primary riverfront park.

The Bessie Smith Strut was the last tie to the original idea of Riverbend as a festival for all arts, all people, all spaces, all venues so that the downtown would come alive again. The City Council should review the mayor's decision and reject it. Friends of the

Festival should think big and make it happen somehow, since the blues bands are contracted, or sue City Hall for reimbursement for contract default.

Riverbend was not at all a big block party for everybody to come, as the mayor believes, but a comprehensive town arts festival like many other cities have without gates, billboards and ads in your face everywhere, bands playing into each other, junk food and booze. But lack of early and ongoing artistic leadership and the critical need for funds changed it into a gated concert event, not a real festival that celebrates some idea and the whole community's talented creators in all genres.

The best example close to us is Charleston, S.C.'s Spoleto and city-run Piccolo festivals, where this city's visionary and practical Mayor Joe Riley believes in "art power," as he calls it. He didn't say "guitar" power.

His philosophy has made his city a mecca for tourists, downtown businesses and artists during the 17-day festival. It was our primary model, along with others studied by our group and advisors. Somehow Chattanooga's politicians, and foundation and business leaders, lost their way and gave us the failed town festival we now have.

With downtown's many new but mostly empty venues, small signs of grassroots creative life all over town, national attention to outdoor sports, high speed web networks, a VW plant, maybe it's time again for some fresh, innovative thinking, the kind of first class, large-scale thinking former Lyndhurst director Rick Montague urged on our small local group that did the early 1981 organizing.

I still believe in that dream of a world class Chattanooga festival celebration that the NY Times' reporters, for example, and critics would cover as they do Spoleto and Bonaroo. I doubt there's ever been one mention of Riverbend in the NY Times, although this tempest in a teapot might attract notice.

Lyndhurst's separate 1981 Five Nights in Chattanooga free downtown park concerts were presented to test whether thousands of citizens could gather without violence. It worked and created confidence in allowing large gatherings. Why not now? We were creating Riverbend the same summer, although there was no direct connection. In Dr. Fred Berringer's final planning seminar, we voted for a festival of all the arts, not just popular or any one genre as now. It appears now virtually all of our city's artists and fine arts organizations are excluded.

Jack Lupton's foundation backed us and that plan then. And that support can return again with a new generation of public and private leaders working together as they once did, even if there was at the time strong myopic arts leadership resistance. As today.

Mayor Littlefield needs to do his homework, as did Mayor Pat Rose in 1981 with our Lyndhurst Foundation grant, and visit Mayor Riley and Charleston's dynamic celebration of *all* the arts, not just the guitar players. Charleston's arts are alive and prospering, Chattanooga's arts institutions are anemic and declining--its opera now history. It's not just the economy. What's missing here is a festival of the whole city, which we started with. My early name for a festival was "Celebration of Togetherness." But it turned into an investor's Riverfront development project and was no longer a celebration of all of us and our creations.

Littlefield's stated security justification of his cancellation of the Strut may not be racist in intent but the effect of the decision leads to racial consequences. It damages the mostly black businesses on MLK. It damages the mayor and police. Any large civic gathering will have security incidents, but many, many cities manage town festivals without putting everybody behind gates and fences monitored by the police. It's like George Bush's over-reaction to 9/11 and the bunker mentality.

It's been a long time since the first Riverbend Festival in 1982 but lots of us remember the work several dozen people put into making it happen with its failures and successes. It most definitely was not the work of an outside consultant. This year the Beach Boys return and who remembers that they were the first of three Riverbend acts in July 1982 at Engel Stadium? The Krystal company sponsored this series as part of their 75th anniversary, I believe. It was meant to raise festival funds but it lost $100,000. It almost doomed the fledgling festival until Lyndhurst and others came to the rescue of Walker Breland and his board of believers.

Maybe this abrupt mayoral decision will be the impetus for a Chattanooga fringe festival to develop all over downtown, even on MLK and in the Tivoli and other venues, including restaurants, which go virtually dark during this failed festival that is long overdue for policy change. Tearing down the gates and fences would be the first step in spreading an "open" Riverbend all over the city once again. Other cities can do it. Why not Chattanooga? Ask the usual suspects, the arts leaders. Or the next mayor. Or help this one save face.

One interesting question is about who owns the Bessie Smith Strut name. Can the MLK street merchants host it if they wish, with a permit? Can the Bessie Smith Cultural Center host a strut on its grounds? Who can stop it if the merchants on MLK join in a celebration of this celebrated blues and jazz singer with a tragic life and ending?

***

For more than two decades the subtle ideas that evolved from this study of festivals have proved their value on my own expanding arts philosophy, in my small festival productions and in my broadened political views. What seemed in 1990 essentially a required academic thesis for an advanced degree appeared 20 years later to offer insights and perspectives of some enduring value for the curious few, my intended readers. At the time I was pleased with the work but had no idea how much it would shape the remainder of my life after age 50. Little did I know that year the fun was just beginning when I lost my Emory student discounts in April but gained my AARP senior discounts in October.

Perhaps the study will benefit other cities considering new festivals or alternatives as well as the scholarly community's continuing dialog about broad cultural frames of social behavior. I do firmly believe the Charleston model offers more civic and cultural benefits as well as economic energy as an example of a comprehensive town festival of all the arts rather than the more narrow popular music concert form such as Riverbend became in the mid-1980's. To repeat Timothy Reiss's conclusion in the Foreword about Charleston's festival, "...Spoleto is simply more critically *productive*, more politically and socially *fruitful*, more aesthetically interesting, moving and provocative, more ethically *generous*."

Avant-garde festivals, such as each of Menotti's Spoleto productions from their beginning in Italy in 1958, and the occasional fringe festivals, always have offered unconventional, disruptive programming that both pleases and angers audiences and critics. Still, enough buy tickets and enjoy the stimulation and the unexpected that keeps the festival alive. As I heard Charles Wadsworth once joke during his informal noon Spoleto chamber music introductions about a play with a nude scene being put on in the same old Dock Theater, "The only thing worse than full frontal nudity is full rear nudity." The now relaxed full house audience erupted in laughter. I had the thought then that unconventional dramatic effect only works when played against the conventional. If all the actors were nude then what would they find to be unconventional? One has only to loosen the imagination. Still, it must be an artistic director, with a board's support, who sets the context for the degree of unconventional material up the point of going beyond the bounds of free speech or potentially illegal material. Or, possibly you "bend" the work to the edge, an always moving point, until you're back at the original and now again amazing production, as for example Mozart's first *Magic Flute* opera might have been.

After Gian Carlo Menotti's son, Francis Menotti, was forced out following the Italian Spoleto's 50th anniversary in 2007, controversy continued about the presence or absence of Menotti's cutting edge philosophy. I have not visited any of the Italian Spoleto festivals and know nothing about them from direct experience. However, Piero Lorenzini, a supporter and set designer at the Spoleto festivals from 1993, wrote of apparent changes in 2009 in "The Affair of the Festival" (see web link below):

> ...the general impression is that of *that* Festival, the Spoleto Festival, Menotti's Festival, very few traces remain....
>
> The *spoletini* knew their Festival well, just as they knew well Maestro Menotti. They knew all about his life, they listened to what he said, they followed his every step as if he was one of them, a relation, a family friend, they praised his decisions, they often criticized him, they loved him and they hated him: but despite the proverbial diffidence of the Umbrians, they were profoundly grateful to the Maestro for what he had done for their town. For the *spoletini* he was not just the father of the Festival, he was the embodiment of a style, which was unique, remarkable and unrepeatable. In early Spring, strolling through the streets of the town, the question on everyone's lips was: "Has the Maestro arrived? Did you see him? Are there auditions at the Teatro Nuovo? For what opera? Is there going to be a Festival this year?" All of which was a sign that the town was beginning to burgeon and would soon bloom in all its glory.
>
> Maestro Menotti was truly Spoleto's magician. He could change the physiognomy of the town, transform it into a crescendo of emotions and lead its inhabitants, its life and its stones into a dream-world. For 50 years. I know that this sensation is still strong in the hearts of many *Spoletini*, but the feeling today is that what remains of *that* Festival – and of Maestro Menotti – is little more than a handful of sand running through our fingers.

But Menotti's creative role as the city's magical Pied Piper, as this book's flutist Papageno cover image suggests, or its Prospero, is now lost, Lorenzini argues, to "...an absolute power that has gone so far as to deny the existence of anyone who might have a different point of view":

> To conclude, a final reflection on the new poster [2008] of the Festival [see link below] designed by Bob Wilson. Someone has said that, like his work in the theatre, it is rather too minimalist, and this is perhaps true. To my mind, however, the use of the word "minimalist" is a way of avoiding another interpretation, more provocative perhaps, which could be summed up in the phrase "always the same self-imitation". I have no hesitation in saying that Wilson's poster is a precise mirror-image of what the new politicized management of the Festival represents. That is to say, it is the re-proposal of a cultural and aesthetic formula which today is feeble and drained of its original essence, a formula that had every reason to exist in a particular historic period (I refer to the 1970s), but which is now manipulated for the convenience of politics and power, with the precise intent of standardizing cultural dogmas that mask a profound incapacity for creativity.
>
> It is of course a sign of the times, but also the consequence of a form of politics, tentacular and omnivorous, that professes itself in favour of renewal and continues to call itself progressist, with shouts from the rooftops that increasingly resemble a litany and to which nobody listens any more. That same kind of politics which, having kept under its control for decades every kind of cultural activity in the area (from theatres, festivals and museums, to conservatoires and art schools), is incapable of the slightest creative impulse of any significance, having detained – narcissistically, and for too long – an absolute power that has gone so far as to deny the existence of anyone who might have a different point of view.

[Source: "The Festival Affair" ("Il Caso Festival"), Piero Lorenzini, June 2009, http://www.spoletofestival.it/ilcasofestival.en.htm].
[Spoleto Festival, Italy web link: http://www.festivaldispoleto.com].

No doubt this view is very much open to debate by Spoleto Festival Italy partisans. However, within our difference/sameness context, a review of the current Spoleto Festival's archives shows what seem to be each of the posters for 2008-10, a gold ball with varying arrangements of the word "Spoleto," something like the sameness of the Chattanooga Riverbend's 30 years of similar posters. Lorenzini sells Spoleto posters from his collection and sold me a 1993 Luzzati Spoleto Italy festival poster (like the one used on this book's cover with the Luzzati Museum's permission). As a set designer, I expect he understands festival poster art in a deep way. Such strong differences of opinion and division merit consideration of international scholarly conferences on the politics, philosophy and influence of festivals.

This idea of a general tendency toward diversity, strongly resisted by the forces of sameness, is very complex, and more sensed than understood in ordinary language. The special language of semiotics can be useful in revealing hidden patterns. The given order, any dominant discourse, or sameness of any kind, strongly resists any disruptive force or technology, at times to the point of death for the disrupters.

Yet disrupters do carry their day at times, as, for example, did spiritual leaders such as Jesus, Mohammed or Buddha (later interpretations often becoming their own "sameness" impervious to change), or as did political movements such as the American colonists under George Washington. Other disrupters include the Gutenberg press, which led to individuals reading, and interpreting without a priest or spiritual go-between, the Bible in their own language; a focused corporate chief such as Steve Jobs with his once-disruptive, now closed Apple Computer company; or visionary, forceful leaders from within such as Abraham Lincoln and Franklin Roosevelt. I suspect that Barack Obama will continue to respond to the times as did these predecessors and be equally well regarded if he is re-elected.

Extremists of any doctrine or dogma often are a threat to peace and harmony. Yet they are effective disrupters in their own guerilla warfare way with real political results, as can be seen from the American military's 9/11 response with attacks on Iraq and Afghanistan and internal "bunker mentality" security measures. With the real threat of nuclear power in the hands of suicide fighters, there seems to be no resolution other than extinction of the threat accompanied by extreme defensive measures that diminish individual freedoms. Where the balance lies is an unresolved political question.

The difference~sameness [sign equals 'embraces'] relationship offers insight into the powerful motivation driving fanatical suicide bombers, who again and again attempt to destroy those unaware of, opposed or deviating from their dogmatic faith, not unlike the Catholic Spanish Inquisition or the New England puritans burning witches at the stake for not embracing the "true faith" of the moment.

It is a useful first interpretation, if not complete explanation, of long patterns of human defiance of "sameness," such as King Henry VIII's rejection of papal authority in his search for a son and heir, as a step on the modern path to degrees of individual choice versus institutional coercion. That England ended up with Elizabeth seems exceptionally fortunate from our differences premise, and not just because she was female but forged into a political diamond. This road leads to the Protestant reformation, which to a degree tolerated Papists, unlike the reverse (and was pushed along by the new printing press much like the "Arab spring" in 2011 was kept at high boil by social media devices as much as military aid).

It sheds light on that global and cruel struggle also fought in WWII over "Hitlerism," as an alarmed Franklin Roosevelt called National Socialism early on after hearing the mad but brilliant Führer's speeches on news radio broadcasts. Hitler's kind returns again and again in history; a festival can be no more than a propaganda spectacle for the authoritarian mind, by definition opposed to individual differences and ideas and behaviors. These two leaders best symbolize the difference / sameness binary political opposition. Contrasted with FDR's openness, Hitler was "an absolute power that has gone so far as to deny the existence of anyone who might have a different point of view."

Was Nazi genocide only a matter of degree of sameness destroying deviation/difference/diversity or some unique madness? Is Mr. Lorenzini's view of current Spoleto dei 2Monde cultural policy the first domino falling back toward a 1930s German mind-set? It seems impossible that the Italian Spoleto Festival and leadership would go in this direction; "denying someone's existence" is not the same as snuffing them out permanently. Still such an accusation is a sign not to be ignored. Behaviour and opinion are thought to be separate modes but the answers are not clear. There are very high stakes in global play for "difference" to "embrace sameness" before the very idea of tolerance for opposition is extinguished, a true existential reality for each individual facing hard choices in life and politics.

It seems necessary that democratic leaders see the Hitlerism "sameness" threat early and contain it as a social cancer, yet allow its existence as ideas if not behaviors within a democratic society—a judicial and legislative challenge of the first magnitude. Germany and several unforgetting European countries have chosen to outlaw certain Nazi symbols, such as the "Seig Heil" upraised salute; America has not under its free speech laws.

But Americans have not, as yet at least (except for native Indians and many Japanese during WWII), directly experienced the horror of, as the German minister's story goes, having had to resist *"sameness"* by becoming the "last one to go to a camp when there was no one left but me," he having seen Jews, gypsies, gays, cripples, unionists, communists, any "difference" deemed "impure," etc. all taken away to concentration camps and gas chambers. All that was "over there" for we Americans; some even deny any of it ever happened, including Iran's president, as if 20 million deaths could be erased with some six million of them Jewish.

Protestant minister Martin Niemöller's meme bears repeating in this context (see Wikipedia, "First they came...") as well as the Wiki discussion about his church's reluctance to become involved in politics and oppose Hitler's party, which, as with the arts as we have seen, insisted on the supremacy of the state over religion and all social life:

> First they came for the communists, and I didn't speak out because I wasn't a communist.
> Then they came for the trade unionists, and I didn't speak out because I wasn't a trade unionist.
> Then they came for the Jews, and I didn't speak out because I wasn't a Jew.
> Then they came for me and there was no one left to speak out for me.

Such is the price of ignorance and apathy when either church or state attempts tyranny. When, if at all, should the church take a political stand? It depends on the situation and nature of the threat to fundamental individual freedoms. According to the Wiki page, "Historian Harold Marcuse...found a 1976 interview in which Niemöller referred to a 1974 discussion with the general bishop of the Lutheran Church of Slovakia. The 84-year-old Niemöller recalled in 1976":

> There were no minutes or copy of what I said, and it may be that I formulated it differently. But the idea was anyhow: The communists, we still let that happen calmly; and the trade unions, we also let that happen; and we even let the Social Democrats happen. All of that was not our affair. The Church did not concern itself with politics at all at that time, and it shouldn't have anything do with them either. In the Confessing Church we didn't want to represent any political resistance *per se*, but we wanted to determine for the Church that that was not right, and that it should not become right in the Church, that's why already in '33, when we created the minister emergency federation...we put as the 4th point in the founding charter: If an offensive is made against ministers and they are simply ousted as ministers, because they are of Jewish lineage (*Judenstämmlinge*) or something like that, then we can only

say as a Church: No. And that was then the 4th point in the obligation, and that was probably the first anti-antisemitic pronouncement coming from the Protestant Church.

It is difficult for most people to know when to resist, or whether to go along with changing times and trends and how to interpret the daily news or their minister's sermons. This often hidden struggle between the extremes of sameness or difference is a condition society apparently must accept as ongoing without ignoring either its consequences or the terrible costs of the dominance of the extreme sameness discourse. At a point one questions the practical limits of democracy and secret ballot voting; our freedoms must not be destroyed by majority rule, as happened in 1920's Germany and Italy. Society must at some point judge, as was done at Nuremberg and today by the World Court, when opinion crosses the line into unacceptable, punishable crimes against humanity.

One good example of a small step in this direction, although it would be denied, was failed 2012 American presidential conservative candidate Rick Santorum's proposal to take down the centuries-old American wall between church and state. This position ignored the very practical reasons for such barriers when they were enacted in practice and law to protect choices of faith even if facts signified other meanings under various interpretive theories, such as Darwinism or scientific reasoning. I've learned that terms such as "liberal" or "conservative" can have very different meanings when applied to concrete, specific problems in daily life, and prefer other levels of abstraction or actual examples in this discussion. Some of my own ideas, or actions, could be classified by either of these labels; it really depends on the person making the classification...very relative and a waste of time it would appear...until it comes time to vote and choices are very limited to either/or candidates. Such is the nature of democracy in the 21st century and complex questions about self-government.

It may be that, as in post-WWI Germany, social complexity, hard economic times, information and technology jobs impact, wealth disparity and unnamed anxiety are increasing political support for sameness dogma with its control obsession. And, too, the percentage of poorly educated democratic populations that requires simple certainty and blind faith over open-ended ambiguity, evidentiary reasoning and skepticism may be growing enough to dominate the political discourse and elections so that the "center cannot hold." It seems the uneducated must be educated, as a first step, with the sunshine of publicity focused on all kinds of private educational institutions that place into question a religion-neutral America's rights and freedoms amendments. These legal issues may not receive a full, fair resolution under the current Republican Supreme Court.

The difference~sameness idea clearly is seen in women's claims to have full control over their bodies and reproductive rights without having to obtain church, business, state or anyone's approval. Several clever female state legislators have proposed equal controls over man's reproductive rights, such as a vasectomy or ED medicine, to show with humor and irony the gender unfairness of such so-called "right to life" anti-abortion and even anti-contraception legislation. One cannot question the sincerity of "lifers" or "non-lifers." But whether the American constitution protects individual choices under the law is the real question as yet unanswered by the political and legal process. Every public or private leader should think through such deep issues and take a stand to justify their reputation, tenure, rank or wealth. Barack Obama's May 2012 public support, if not personal agreement, for the right of same gender couples to marry legally under state law is an example of protecting differences of individual choices and paying a political cost. North Carolina voters had disapproved, along with 32 other states, an amendment allowing same gender marriage in early May, thus raising the question of the legality of such state laws under the federal Constitution. No doubt this will go to the Supreme Court as angry same gender couples fight under the equal rights amendments and other provisions.

These are hot button political issues. For example, at the inclusive, influential Chautauqua Institution, one of the extended summer festivals studied, I asked the press officer in 2009 whether a divisive radio talk show host such as Rush Limbaugh would ever be invited to speak. He said such a person would be too extreme for their program. After reflection, I came to believe there is value in learning bitter, even threatening, realities by inviting the extremes into a speaker's "tent," even a Hitler or a Limbaugh, for an intelligent audience's sharp questions with coverage by national media. Limbaugh lies, and Hitler's dependence on lies plus brute force, eventually catch up with them, or so we all hope...or most of us, excepting those neo-Nazis in that small hostile band of opposing viewpoints that American democracy protects.

The cost of eventual discovery of Hitler's true purpose, whose evil is hard to capture in ordinary language, was extreme in lives and national resources on all sides given the determination of a powerful "sameness" to retain control at all costs in order to gain "Aryan" racial purity and egotistic personal political power. One has only to hear observant, watchful, experienced Winston Churchill's wilderness speeches of the 1930's to grasp national political reluctance to face such uncomfortable realities, costs and consequences. We think we have learned a lesson from the very near destruction of Britain due to Prime Minister Neville Chamberlain's wishful thinking about Hitler's intentions and promises. The probability that WWII could have turned out differently for the democracies should keep the very subtle, complex questions of difference and sameness alive for all generations.

One hesitates to project such a broad political outlook that grew from study of two town festivals. Yet the issue needs to be put before the reader for consideration as a possible larger context. The more I've thought through the difference~sameness idea, the more I've considered modifying the phrase to: "Differences embrace sameness; sameness **destroys** difference." For me this is just words; for many, many Americans it is a matter of guns, even in churches, in statehouses and on college campuses. Only at air terminals is the passenger gun prohibited everywhere, clearly proving the power of federal law over the 2nd amendment, which has its social costs and personal benefits. A Google search of the two terms shows many varied approaches to the meaning of difference and sameness. And Amazon lists many books on various aspects of the difference and sameness relationship. But none could be found with the emphasis here on the unending struggle between the two forces and the real threat of the historic power of sameness. Call it evil; call it bad; call it whatever it is on the Hayakawa abstraction ladder; it exists.

These broad views evolved slowly from my 1980 visit to the Charleston, SC Spoleto Festival USA, when I had minimal comprehension of what I was seeing and experiencing. A decade before I had worked for Chattanooga Mayor Robert Kirk Walker as press spokesperson and speechwriter. When you write speeches for three years for a mayor, you have to think like a mayor; you have to find the middle ground that holds together all of your citizens, not just your supporters; you have to feel the real need, with blacks burning their own buildings, for a celebration of togetherness; you feel the community need for an open town festival and for an open, unfenced Bessie Smith Strut down MLK Boulevard; you have to find ways to show love to those downtown Chattanooga gangs who don't rap about it like their ghetto blues singer did—a real challenge yet before most mayors.

Maybe former Harlem, NY music educator David Darling and his Music for People musicians could come teach Chattanooga's teenage gang members, as we did for a few placed in Project Straight Talk, and neighborhood leaders too, how to make their own music and actually become performers, rather than be attention seeking protestors, at the Strut and elsewhere. Bessie Smith certainly showed how to get off the streets and succeed. Some of our students, a wide mix in every way, from the 1968 Project Straight Talk are Chattanooga leaders today, one the headmaster of the private and Christian McCallie School, R. Kirk Walker, son of the mayor who appointed me his speechwriter. It can be done with caring leadership and patience. Lincoln and FDR showed their love, hard and tough love; and each made a new America still perfecting itself with, unbelievably, today a "black" African-American president. Do such racial terms make sense any longer? I sense few notice any longer with so many more pressing issues? The times did, and will, change.

Those early ideas about difference and acceptance, about sameness and intolerance, persistently helped me make sense of historical as well as contemporary events. And they gave meaning to political and social conflicts in the news, such as the various social issue debates between "progressives" and "regressives," at times somewhat illuminated by my 1990 premise: "Difference embraces sameness; sameness rejects difference."
On this premise, I've made my stand through all these pages...and in real life, even from as long ago as 1961, especially against "racial" prejudice and later in 1968 in my "racial" relations Project Straight Talk in Chattanooga (see biographical notes below). As a Vanderbilt University college student, in 1961 at a Portland, OR Sigma Nu fraternity national convention as a chapter delegate, I spoke up against a proposed "waiver with honor" for chapters being forced by colleges to admit blacks and minorities. My critical remarks about this "dishonor" were printed in the fraternity magazine, my first such appearance in print. Sadly, as an instructed delegate, I voted in favor; the convention approved the disgraceful proposal. But no black student (only our black cook, cleaners or musicians) "darkened" our fraternity door, not to mention the campus at that time. Yet it soon was to change in the mid-1960's with Nashville sit-in's and national pressures. I visited the Sigma Nu fraternity there about 15 years ago. The gentleman said they had never had a black apply as far as he knew, that they continued to be an all-white house; he thought this was the case with other fraternities and sororities. Has change come at last?
I then saw the issue more as one of fairness than in its complex political, moral and historical dimensions, but I still, then, saw myself as a conservative politically and a person of faith. Now all religious and spiritual questions and matters represent the great unknown to me, but clearly they are a powerful social reality, can be a personal solace as I've seen in my family and merit close study if not blind adherence. That was during the times (which truly were "a changin'") when the Vanderbilt Divinity School refused to admit a black graduate

student, a position that soon changed under pressure but opened to question for many the nature of such exclusive doctrines based on color, gender, faith, beliefs. Yet it was not until the 1968 deaths of Martin Luther King and Robert Kennedy that I was energized to do my part in this struggle. After those tragedies, many of us became willing to get involved in the civil rights fight for equal opportunity, fairness and tolerance for all kinds of differences. I expect to also publish on Amazon, as Split Tree Press, my Boston University master's thesis on our Chattanooga "Project Straight Talk" soon. It is an example of one kind of civic response to a very complex and continuing global issue of official minority discrimination.

Has society changed? I see the May 2012 news that Vanderbilt University has announced a new "all-comers" policy prohibiting all official campus organizations from excluding persons of philosophical difference, meaning Christian gays in this case, or persons who do not share the group's "central beliefs," from being members or holding office, excepting gender in the case of same sex fraternities and sororities. Why gender exclusion would be acceptable is not clear except that it is the tradition at a private university; I would have been a far happier Sigma Nu with women members...and a far wiser one if women had been a regular and civilizing part of our daily lives.

Apparently sometime in the past year a Vanderbilt Christian fraternity expelled an office holder or member because the man was "gay." The administration objected to the grounds. Several national Christian associations, including the Southern Baptist Convention, announced their withdrawal of their Vanderbilt chapters, but reports said about 14 of 30 religious chapters would comply. The Republican Tennessee legislature voted to restrict the university policy but the Republican governor announced he would veto the bill. Many conservative Congressional representatives, 36 members of the Christian Prayer Caucus, wrote asking Vanderbilt to rescind its policy by exempting religious, faith-based groups.

I suppose this is a similar kind of Christian chapter "waiver with *honor*" like my Sigma Nu convention approved? How can one use the term "honor" with no sense of the irony? The sense of déjà vu and of the power of "sameness" was very real. In fact, one could research the same issue in reverse at the increasingly conservative Southern Baptist Convention's Shorter College in Rome, Georgia, which announced in 2011 such a strict list of alleged Biblical-based rules for faculty and staff that news reports were that dozens of teachers, staff and students, who would not sign the "Christian" declaration, left the college. Its president simply justified his decision by explaining he was only doing God's work; many of his faculty questioned his comprehension skills, if not his mental condition.

One thinks of suicidal bombers' identical explanations for their murders and ponders how to reach such minds. Someone shared a May 2012 Facebook poster, Freedom Explained, by Americans Against the Tea Party, which had some 4,000 likes and shares, and is apropos:

> You are FREE to have a gun.
> You are FREE to have a religion.
> You are NOT free to use your gun to take away the freedom of others.
> You are NOT free to use your religion to take away the freedom of others.

As one of many commenters noted, "The point is that our "rights" are not to be used to take away the rights of other people. It's ... well ... un-American." The critical importance of public education, or educating the public, speaks for itself, and not just in America. Yet, as the Facebook relationship status block offers, "It's complicated."

In 1988, when I had taught most of a semester at nearby Berry College and when the Dean handed me a form requiring me to report my church and Sunday school affiliation, and to sign my State of Georgia loyalty oath, I simply laughed at her and handed it back, saying I could not teach under such an illegal policy and that I would not return (though I needed the income badly). As campus newspaper advisor, I should have made that my own story at semester's end, and passed it since I was the administration's official censor. Critical inquiry was not stressed at Berry or Shorter. But at no time, while also teaching PR and writing that same semester at Shorter, was I asked for any similar declaration. Vanderbilt, Berry and Shorter are equally free up to a point but no one seems to be able to find the moral or spiritual consensus about where the elusive point of tolerance lies. I do think Emory University has found sound policies for the times.

It seems that the "times may be a changin' again" but now two or more separate cultural tracks of "reality" are diverging with little social cohesion or desire for understanding. This problem is largely what motivates me to include these stories and memories and to attempt to illustrate with fresher language some possible areas of overlapping interests. Separate cultures, like separate communities of color, seem an extremely dangerous prospect for modern society that depends more than ever on norms of tolerance and respect for difference. And no leader seems to have acceptable, workable solutions, though it appears President Obama has reached out much farther "across the aisle" than have the Republicans, though with much less success than he had expected due to unreasoned resistance.

For me, much stemmed from the ideas in this long hidden 1990 dissertation about Charleston, Chattanooga and Salzburg's powerful festive theaters and also about Chautauqua's inclusive summer celebration, another influential model of differences festivaling. Neither the Charleston nor the Chattanooga festival, each regarded as a grand success in its own way by its own fans, shows signs of evolving into the new, new participatory theater so successfully produced since the 1990s by the Burning Man Festival team in the Black Rock, Nevada desert. I was a "burner" there myself in my air-conditioned RV in 2003. For those who've never participated, Burning Man (it has no concert stages) is as hard to imagine as it was for those in 1981 who never participated in a Spoleto town festival or a Salzburg festival. You cannot buy anything except ice and coffee. You yourself, your art car, your ice cream, your beads, your edifice, your camp, your creation are the art. Check out their web page.

My gift was a waltz lesson advertised on a necklace calling card with a yin yang symbol (I regret not having images here; next book). The, at lesson times, degree of a lady partner's undress was disconcerting but one does his duty in a gift economy of radical self-expression and survival. I see no bridge between the active burners and the Spoleto type concert audiences but some morphing is likely of desirable elements, such as Spoleto fringe theater. Burning Man was no chaotic Woodstock '69, even though its hippie seeds were "blowin' in the wind" at that first pivotal celebration of "3 days of peace and music" at Max Yasgur's 600-acre farm at Bethel, NY.

I didn't make the 1994 Woodstock retrospective. But I did attend the angry, destructive one in 1999 at my old U.S. Air Force Griffiss Air Force Base at Rome, NY, where I was the senior information officer for three years after college. We fortunately left before the trash fires began. Something went very wrong with the Woodstock founder's 1999 effort to commercialize the counterculture, although that was in fact the original goal of the first Woodstock, where a celebration of "love and peace" was a happy accident it appears and largely due more to the half million laid-back participants than the organizers. But Woodstock was a performance, concert festival, not participatory. Today the forces of participatory arts are powerful and growing with the probable effect of changing traditional passive audience expectations and concert economics, removing the ancient idea of the fourth wall between actors and audiences and empowering individuals to wear the mask of an artist until it fits.

Now I've untied the black cloth of the present (Kundera quote, Preface and below) and taken that thoughtful, questioning glance at the past, first in sharing the ideas that started my, or more precisely our, dance community's experiences. Many hundreds built and sustained it, truly sustainable growth. Next follows extending this Afterword and publishing the Split Tree Participatory Arts Center narrative, which served, in retrospect, as my alternative classroom, and for informal "field" research. This book led to new meanings, for me and others too, about difference and sameness, active playing and motionless, silent concert listening, imagining and offering the new and accepting the old and familiar.

New York City frame drummer Randy Crafton, after the second fall 1994 Split Tree Festival, framed the question for an exhausted producer that Sunday night: "Sid, maybe you have to choose between producing concerts or creating participatory gatherings." With limited resources, and my mostly academic sense of differences and sameness, I chose participatory gatherings. The story then wrote itself. It seemed a niche that needed attention and invited some response into the beckoning, inviting "empty space" we had built in 1994 overlooking the NW Georgia mountains.

Sometimes all elements were blended in disruptive, creative, unexpected combinations, such as a few years of my silly Saturday Fool's School of Dance History, starting with various dancers teaching the "very first" one-step and ending with the "final" eight-step. It proved a very popular experiential learning experiment, a scene I somehow had improvised as a participant in one of Emory modern dance professor Lori Teague's weekend Split Tree workshops for her students. We taught one of several dances to the step levels, such as Ragtime and merengue for the "one-step." In the Fool's School, my friend Magdalena Z. once even taught beginning tango with partners standing in close contact rear to rear; one learned to lead, and follow, slowly, very slowly...and laugh. In our safe place to play, it worked. We all did laugh at ourselves; and proved it's easier to learn to dance if you're willing to make a fool of yourself. As the song from an ancient Japanese matsuri (festival) bon odori (ancestor) summer dance goes: "We're fools whether we dance or not, so we might as well dance." And, too, each year at Fool's Fest I celebrated the Hanani (small flowers) Festival of Shy Persons; no one came...or admitted if they did.

As intellectual history, this thesis was praised in a 1990 letter to me by University of Toronto Professor Paul Bouissac as groundbreaking and original. If so I am in debt to many, many people because this kind of intellectual ferment comes only at special times in our lives and rarely in the middle years. I was lucky to be highly motivated by an "ensemble" of positive, informed and caring energy.

Most who assisted are mentioned in the 1990 acknowledgements from that time.

Others from the Split Tree years will be noted in the forthcoming book, especially including Richard Powers, Angela Amarillas, Dan Bowles, Alan Dynin, Walter Parks, Stephanie Winter, Seth Tepfer, Steve and Vicki Herndon, Daniel Lee, Lynn Forrest, Lawrence and Mada Mathis, Don Walker, Alice Hunter, Heitzo, Anna Sue Courtney, Bart Ruark, Tom and Rebecca Zurn, Lonnie Lepore and Roxie Ray – all, and quite a few more, who contributed both to the physical building as well as artistic programming of the Split Tree Participatory Arts Center and dance floor from 1990 to 2007.

Dance friends, musicians, old friends, business associates, professors, family, and many local workers and volunteers built the space and made a dream come true...and they really did come year after year until the fire took the physical buildings away. Dreams don't burn down; they fire the imagination. The dream of participatory arts was not taken away. With some luck and some more dreamers, and a few more years beyond my current 71, the Split Tree participatory idea will continue.

Sidney N Hetzler, Jr. Ph. D.   May 2012
Split Tree Press
597 W Cove Road
Chickamauga, GA 30707

AFTERWORD, Part 2
--Sharing a Proprioceptive Write--
Essay on Difference and Sameness

These final informal, exploratory notes suggest how the difference~sameness idea could be extended beyond festivals to small matters. The following, somewhat planned and edited "proprioceptive write,"™ (Google these two words) shares my dancing stories that connect with this book. Most "writes" are free flowing and at times highly intimate, though as a social practice often read to the group; at times it seems you hear your own archetypal story coming from someone else's "read." My write likely is the beginning of a more personal draft, but closely edited, even censored in some cases, of the Split Tree book that will emerge. These word images illustrate how at some level the differences idea influenced my artistic decisions and imagination at Split Tree and the Atlanta Waltz Society. Note that the dance stories are not fully developed, and are vignettes to be enjoyed.

Does Sameness Reject/Destroy Difference?
    Hate, Love?
        Evil, Good?
Can Difference Embrace Sameness?
    Love, Hate?
        Good, Evil?
Question the questions.
    Change the answers.
        Waltz.

Dance "Write" #1

The dimly understood but sensed political and artistic ideas that slowly evolved from 1980, and from previous experiences, led me to imagine and produce my own small festivals and happenings. At my Split Tree Farm I was free to explore logodaedaly--combining a blend of place, idea and force through the 1990's up until the 2007 home fire.

The small world of social dancing taught its own lessons, especially under the open but well documented philosophy of Stanford

University's social dance guru and historian, Richard Powers, who led many dance weekends at Split Tree studio. He, starting out as a Stanford engineering and design major, had created the vintage dance movement in the 1980's in Cincinnati, Ohio. Powers deserves a MacArthur Foundation "genius" fellowship for creating, as a Menotti magician of small festivals of partner movement, as well as sustaining, a new, successful global philosophy of partner dancing (see web link below). At his Flying Cloud Academy of Vintage Dance, I first attended a very stressful, challenging vintage dance week in 1990. My first very tolerant, and very much taller than me, Monday morning class Argentine tango partner had to tell me to stop looking down at my feet since we could not dance the close embrace social style this way. (I confess I never did develop a feel for traditional tango and its rules and macho, ethnic culture). But European and American vintage dance, with its emphasis on 19th century waltzing and historical dances, always has been the foundation of much of my own fascination with the world of movement.

I had my own somewhat different emerging, evolving ideas beyond vintage, period dancing in its static, reconstructed forms. I wanted to share my love of social dancing, especially what I was learning of the largely unknown 1800's era waltzing in and around Vienna, Austria—a sort of dark side of the dance history moon. However, I had little interest in producing identical familiar, repetitive traditional programs and events if I could slightly bend them each time into some small new form, something like turning a musical evergreen into a blues variation with a flat or a sharp somewhere. Or, that is, like asking, as I had done at the last Split Tree 2007 Tivoli waltz weekend, for two favorite friends and original Split Tree musicians, pianist Alan Dynin and trumpeter Dan Bowles to bend and modulate the four-beat swing time of "Chattanooga Choo-Choo" into a bluesy waltz time "Chattanooga Choo-Choo" for the social dancers on the main stage. The pros can do that kind of improvisation and that video is on the You Tube page, "splittree," along with other STF and dance videos.

"Bend it" and "improvise" became my buzz words. Each dance weekend evolved from the previous one as mini-festivals, with some new element but also with repeating elements, "organized surprise," as Charles Wadsworth had remarked. Each Split Tree waltz weekend was unique in some way under Powers' artistic direction, from "Two Centuries of Waltzing" to the 1999 "Old Vienna Waltz Weekend" to my own favorite "Gypsy Waltz" weekends (with a dramatic gypsy dancing woman performing at the break) to the final more formal "Vintage Waltz Weekend."

Powers and I made a good team (he took his 1999 sabbatical semester in the farm's log cabin), but I always followed my 1990 festival thesis and played, in a miniscule way, Mayor Joe Riley to Gian Carlo Menotti, or political and financial power to artistic power, and did not interfere with Powers' imagination as long as I could afford it, having learned the Charleston mayor's lesson about "art power." Of course I could not escape the legal, financial and marketing responsibility that went with producing dance weekends on my property. But I completely delegated the program to him, and offered content responses if asked, based on my research about the value of an artistic director under any title, and ignored those who advised me to just tell him what we want when there was some disagreement on a class or music, which often included the classical waltzes I learned to love best. As a Menotti, I thought Powers' dream and vision well worth supporting with my energy and limited resources. This is somewhat like being a college dean providing maximum academic freedom—and resources-- to a talented faculty member, which I had done in effect for four years as first coordinator of the communications program at the University of Tennessee at Chattanooga. And this was done for me when teaching at Boston University, although not to the same degree at UTC or Berry and Shorter, where probably budget determines support more than intent.

It is rare to find a teacher who can share complex knowledge as well as Powers has done and enhance so many dancers via the "lively arts." And it was my own affirmation of the validity of highly valuing his talent, and protecting him from the business end of the dance weekends. This was no small thing to manage since about 80 people had to eat, sleep, rest, snack, have water, use bathrooms, etc. and my resources frequently were stretched to accommodate with such non-commercial facilities. Possibly it would have become a real business if the house had not burned and if I could have added more adequate facilities. Powers of course perfectly manages his own dance weekends and weeks at Stanford University and worldwide, alone or in partnership as with Split Tree. A new historic waltz week was planned July 2012 for Vienna, Austria in association with local waltz lovers, and is attracting dancers from many countries.

My continuing intent, particularly at my own annual Fool's Fest Dance Weekends, which had their own artistic directors as Head Fools teaming up with my own at times necessary foolish suggestions as producer and "banker," was to somehow introduce small variations and fusion within the traditional music and dance structures that had come to my attention. More and more it seemed the phrase "contra dancer fools" was an oxymoron, contra lines having too much structure to allow much bending—but we tried within the traditional patterns and music, at times achieving unexpected effects. I became more directly involved each year as we experimented with ways to dance and dramatize the "fool's way" and at some point I felt I too had become an artist in being willing to put my imagination to the test of paying participants.

[Publishing this book is similar, and not without its moments of anxiety about its reception...if anyone finds and reads it. But these "after words" written in 2012 are those more of an artist, as I understand the sense of a work being subjected to "aesthetic" criteria, than of those of the 1990 scholar. Yet I do not discard the requirement for documentable evidence in making my arguments and claims then and now. We can agree on language that represents that the sun does rise and set each day but disagree on the reasons why it appears to repeat this simple, "observable" motion; consensus took an incredibly long time. If the Pope rejected Galileo's philosophy and some of his logical interpretations, he did not reject his data for mariners. (Read Lucretius' lovely, philosophical circa 50 BC poem, "*On the Nature of Things*," for more about this interesting pattern of false casual connections in human behavior and history).

This continuous Split Tree variation strategy of course did not satisfy more than a minority of traditional dancers open to exploration, but I trusted in T. S. Eliot's wisdom in his "Four Quartets" poem that "We shall not cease from exploration / And the end of all our exploration / Will be to arrive where we started /And know the place for the first time." The trick was not to give up the first time if something did not work and to continue exploring possibilities. I suspected those passionate Vienna waltzers circa 1800 knew a secret we do not...yet. Historians today still do not agree on or know for sure what was danced in those huge ballrooms and also in the wine taverns, where early waltz, the German dance, seems to have originated along the Danube, as a BBC Strauss documentary suggests. Yet there is enough smoke in the old images and dairies to suggest much fire in the intimate waltzing embrace, even if Powers and other scholars are not certain whether the whirling bodies actually touched.

I suspect the younger they were the more they touched, just like today's twenty somethings are bringing back very close embrace slow blues dancing, always subject to the lady's acceptance. There is no one way, though most agree the woman should initiate the closeness, and each couple resolves the distance question. Only "sketchy guys" grab and drag, as in effect one of Powers' web pages observes (all look forward to his dance book). I've read that high schools today have had to make a rule requiring front-to-front dancing only at proms, rejecting the lady's rear tucked into her partner's front. Times really have changed...but not the behavior of the young.

One can see old images of dancers swirling around old Vienna ballrooms in the history books. I visited in 1996 the last Vienna ballroom, the 1826 Sofiensaal (originally a steam bath converted to a dance hall), before it burned in 2001, as had all the others in Vienna. Many of Strauss Father and Son's first waltzes premiered there, and Strauss I opened it. Possibly some ballrooms remain in other Austrian cities. They were architectural wonders, especially designed so the approximately 20-player ensembles could be heard by dancers, who at times make their own foot percussion music.

As the Fool's Festival weekends evolved, I learned that with an open "beginners mind" each "foolish" partner could do some slightly different move if they were flexible about who was leading and who was following, using a larger idea of just moving together with each other and the music, or without music as in completely free-style contact improvisation. At the last 2005 Fool's Fest we finished the afternoon with combined waltzing and contact improvisation in the fool's school of traditional dance to Alan Dynin's improvised piano sounds. A couple did not have to dance in a rigid frame to enjoy social dancing; it was ok to pause and connect, at any moving point, hand-to-hand, shoulder-to-shoulder, hip-to-hip—a lingering pause at times being very sensual...but respectful and proper without any other agenda, something new dancers often do not know or realize.

I found (from many teachers) that just about anyone could learn to "hand" dance together (getting the feet to work takes much longer) to simple music if they could laugh about mistakes and not waste a musical beat with fear but learn to enjoy "failure" as a creative move, even a new dance style, which maybe is how some new fads begin. Leaders usually did not signal very clearly nor did followers often understand the cue; all this one could overcome without fear of a "wrong" outcome. But, as in music improvisation, by just agreeing to move "together" we could think of a "wrong" step as merely a traveling "step" or "note," leading to the next unknown safe space to play. I learned from Powers that dancing couples could have fun improvising by using whole body moves, or even by just mirroring the instructors, rather than following precision prescribed steps.

I believed this mirrored, natural mode was the "lost art of waltzing" I read about in the histories of waltzing, when at a moment you felt, as young Werther did with his lady, a "lilt" as if rising off the floor. The old music, too, had its slightly emphasized, accelerated second beat, which helped create the "lilt," a profoundly real feeling if you and your partner share equal energy continuously turning and traveling around the hall, a near spiritual "transcendence" or slightly out of the body experience until the tension is released. This happened to me at one of the 1996 Vienna carnival balls with an extraordinary woman, and we danced without tiring on the stage for almost two hours until the music ended. She was married and I never even got her name; it's just as well (maybe she will read this book?). That kind of connection is rare but occasionally happens at dances where both partners share the sense of equal energy sharing, as I've come to believe, as opposed to lead/follow mode. Still, I would like to hear women's voices on this experience; it is gratifying to notice the expression of surprise and amazement when it happens, being so different from "catch and release" waltzing. It may be the "lost" art of the old romantic, risqué waltz that caught the attention of early writers visiting Vienna; one visitor claimed there were nearby birthing rooms for the energetic lady dancers. For me it was living the idea of embracing difference, man and woman blending into one pair yet made possible by the gender differences of the intimate close contact embrace while turning. (See "La Valse," as below).

If you could turn and travel like kids do, as Powers taught us, playing "Ring Around the Rosie," while holding hands and letting body weight keep you spinning, you soon could gradually come closer and closer into full embrace turning, traveling Viennese waltz—the old style that was so scandalous and that today is much more the norm for social continental European waltzing than American waltzing. And, too, that waltzing was condemned and outlawed by many cities and villages is well known; it could not have been as neutral as some would have us believe.

For example, at my first experience with this Vienna variation from the Powers' 19th century rotary waltz at the Hofsburg 1995 New Year's ball, as I begin to make the accustomed, proper "inches apart" frame, my very lovely, and taller, partner said: "No, ve don't do the British valse, ve do our valse," crushing me to her hip to hip as somehow we whirled down the huge hall to a Strauss waltz. This time I would not have looked down at my feet at all, or if I had tried the considerable décolletage would have pleasantly interfered; I understood by then a dance was just a dance, not eternal union. And I knew by then just enough to hang on with such a perfectly beautiful and powerful partner and go with the flow by adding my macho energy only if needed at a given moment.

The trick was to make a "V," staying connected and equally balanced with no break at all in the turning motion; it requires a delicate balance with hips joined and legs offset; such entwined turning is effortless. She was so stunningly beautiful with glowing youth and red hair that she must have been an actress, but surprisingly she was at the ball as a single woman (which was rare). That dance got the attention several other single and married ladies needing a partner, and I enjoyed dancing all styles in the several ballrooms of the enormous palace into the wee hours, just as Mozart did. One forgets how important social dancing was before movies and television. That Vienna trip was dance, sleep, eat; repeat each day.

Somehow the British, starting around 1815, and the Americans managed to "puritanize" waltz by insisting on no body contact, possibly I suspect due to Wilson's strict 1816 London dance manual for British public ballrooms, where at the time dancer contact was unthinkable, though a subject of poetic anger at the new dance. To grasp the close embrace idea, Google search for "La Valse [Claudel]," a circa 1890's golden sculpture by Rodin pupil, mistress and equal, as some feel, Camille Claudel. Imagine moving at moderate or slow tempo around the ballroom floor and that closely connected. She must have seen, or done, this kind of waltzing somewhere in Paris; it was made around the time of her affair with Rodin, who often used her as a model. The work was regarded as so erotic that French cultural ministers required her to drape the dancers below the waist. An undraped version was never found. If she had not titled it, "La Valse," the viewer might not know it was a waltz at all except for the swirling gown and the way the hands are lightly touching in the embrace of movement. There are several biographies of her fight against strong gender prejudice and the story is also told in the 1988 movie entitled with her name. It is a touching, heartbreaking tale of male sameness rejecting female difference, especially in her own unique style compared with Rodin; some then, and today, say she is a finer artist at capturing a wider range of detail and expression.

Other sculptures and images of the waltz from the 1800's to the 1900's have similar images of closeness; it seems the essence of the tradition of the spinning dance from its ancient origins as a solo trance whirling. [I omit all images in this book due to the difficulty of obtaining rights but all are easily found on the internet; the next book will include links and a possible web page and DVD/CD when images cannot be included]. At least one version of "La Valse" is at the Rodin Museum near Paris, France; one could hope Stanford University could add a replica to its Rodin garden. But today a replica can be purchased on Amazon for $85 and I have one in my waltz collection; in 2005 Sotheby's sold a second original casting for nearly one million dollars. One could dream of discovering one of these lost castings in some European village antique shop.

Due to the indirect effects of my basically unconscious, intuitive kinds of "embracing difference" ideas of partner dancing, I believe we always had sold out Fool's Fests of around 80-100 dancers in the 2,200 square foot Split Tree studio. And by 2005-6 Atlanta Waltz Society was enticing around 60-70 waltzers, over 100 with live music, each Sunday afternoon at Atlanta's Knights of Columbus hall. After I departed in 2006, the new team converted it into *Waltzplay* with a more standard ballroom teaching and dancing and music philosophy. My goal simply was to offer wide ranging alternatives to what I thought of as restrictive, inhibiting "sameness" of formal ballroom manner without in any way criticizing or excluding any of the many other popular styles. As a budding "artist" DJ, I never tried to please every dancer all the time—usually regularly offending at least one dancer with some tune radical to them, Strauss being what some called the hated "oom-pah" music. How could you host a three-hour energetic waltz without several Strauss melodies, if they were arranged for dancing and not just smaltzy pop versions as André Rieu plays, though only for seated audiences, not dancers? However, attendance remained high in the later years. Just as at Chautauqua, "all were welcome" on my floors. But clearly one creates a "context" with musical choices, floor, teachers, sound quality and ambience, just as at a festival or house party. And I always made it a point to introduce new dancers to old dancers who might not readily reach out.

I learned quickly in selecting guest teachers that, when a traditional ballroom dancer taught the lesson hour before our dances, a very different by the book style usually was offered as the "only" proper way to dance (i.e., women *never* led; this was "*the*" exact box waltz step; the woman's left hand *must* be placed on man's upper arm or possibly around his back with hand *straight out* horizontally; she *must look away* from the man's face into the distance, etc.). It was more about foot steps than the connection, more about arm angle than light fingertip touching, more about the scripted sequence than the unscripted improvisation and instant adjustment to each other with respect for the woman's right to offer her energy and motion. I faced the practical reality that if such a philosophy were allowed to be in charge of AWS that my openness idea would be discouraged or disallowed. Since our vintage waltzing was unique, and since there were plenty of ballroom studios in Atlanta, I saw no need to add this to our limited program, which was attracting more and more good dancers who loved variety in moves and music. But, six years was enough and the path was made open for their ideas.

Happily, Sunday afternoon waltz continued in some form and I did not have to rescue it; I've never discussed any of this, except with AWS colleague Jay Aland, until now. I only do so because of the connection to the book's main ideas, though there were strong feelings about some of the tactics used in rushing the transition. I always believed you should make room for new leadership after a volunteer project is underway, if, that is, they are informed and competent. I quickly became aware of the Sunday afternoon reality of sameness rejecting difference; AWS was in the hands of the new, politically conservative leadership who had disliked the non-ballroom, free alternative of social dancing, as well as the extreme musical diversity, such as Strauss and orchestral music. The new playlists, which I had passed on to them, excluded all "oom-pah" tunes in favor of virtually all folk and pop. My own favorite high energy waltz was the symphonic music from the movie, "The Gladiator," when the Roman general rides his white stallion along the troops with a sort of pre-battle pep talk to very unusual triple beat martial music. Few however would spin to this demanding fast tempo. I felt strongly music should be played for all tastes and levels even if there was only one couple on the floor, which was very rare. And all would be rested for the next slow contra waltz folk tune.

Waltzing has a long history as the first social dance fad, which started in Vienna, Austria as far back as Mozart's day; he once wrote he loved dancing more than music making. One memoir claimed as many as a quarter of the Viennese population danced each evening. Waltzing quickly spread worldwide after the Vienna political congress that "danced rather than marched" in 1814-15. A definitive waltz history is yet to be written; a number of these books are written by composers or conductors who bemoan the need to conform to dancer needs and tempos. I instead think it's the highest skill to be able to play well enough to have dancer energy with the musicians. My dance preference is to adjust to the music, to dance to different drummers, so to speak, or even without music.

The popular romantic waltz typically has included more musical variety and dance styles, such as the turning, traveling Viennese waltz, and the popular cross-step, as re-introduced by Richard Powers for his vintage and social dancers. One could see at our Atlanta Waltz Society on Sunday afternoons any of dozens of couples doing completely different moves from line of direction to center floor in-place East Coast swing moves or even slow blues dance, resembling the intertwined dancers of "La Valse," to ¾-music; this continues. Always my intuition as an "artist", influenced by my 1990 thesis, was to emphasize alternatives, diversity, difference, choices and individual dancer styles that pushed the edge a bit...without, as on the Fool Tarot card, going over the edge...a real balancing act with occasional hard landings.

For me the lesson was well learned (again after Riverbend) about the fragility of a "differences" vision in an ordinary social dancing context in both small and large ways. And, for me, dance had become a small environment of cultural reality with many lessons yet to be learned but with some of my concepts and terms affirmed at some personal emotional cost, both from Riverbend and from AWS. At least at Split Tree context, text, subtext; place, ideal, force; intent, function, effect was my theater of participation that would succeed or fail with no one else to blame. There were many signs of success, and most of the later weekends quickly sold out and were in the black without counting the original investment or my time…and without controlling patrons, advertisements or sponsors. One much appreciated California dancer, Phillip Garrison, volunteered, after an STF Powers weekend, a $5,000 matching grant in 1999. Powers donated his time for the 1999 Old Vienna weekend so that we could afford an air conditioning and heating system for the 2,200 square foot space. An insulated roof came soon after with much volunteer assistance, many of whom had helped build the original 1994 pavilion. This is a remarkable story to be told in the next work.

My Split Tree dance weekends in NW Georgia with mostly live music became known as a model of diversity for offering several types of partner dancing, not just one form such as contra, Cajun, or swing. Bart Ruark enjoyed the first 1996 Fool's fest at our new Split Tree studio so much that he created an autumn Dance Vortex there, except that he took out contra dancing and added Cajun and Zydeco to swing and waltz. This blend, in retrospect, would have worked better than contra dancing for a festival of fools but we had begun with contra dancing and stuck with the tradition. He would have continued at Split Tree but, after two years, it grew so fast to several hundred dancers that he moved it to a summer camp at Mentone, Alabama; he ended it in about 2007 or so for unknown reasons. He was a main builder of the new studio when he was artist-in-residence in the late 1990's for a year.

I never attempted "studio" ballroom or Western/country square dancing since these styles were readily available elsewhere; also Split Tree prohibited smoking and alcohol and that turned some people away. It is the customary practice now. Today, mixed or fusion dancing, such as blues and tango, is more popular and growing everywhere. But "sameness" of single styles still is the norm for North American forms of social dance, such as tango or contra or West Coast swing or Lindy Hop, which exclude most moves and music pieces that are outside its tradition. However, "new" or Nuevo Tango does offer very varied music and moves, displeasing the lovers of the traditional Golden Years of tango music and steps. And there is computer-generated techno contra dancing with its thumping regularity for the very young (but not for me, though I love live drumming and the small differences and imperfections of live music, not unlike "live" people). Fusion has its bright future, and various dance communities now are a regular part of Burning Man Festival.

Selected Biographical Notes and Background

These stories of festival origin and personal growth connect sequences of events that could have turned out differently at any crossroads. We who lived some of these stories know where the forks were in the road and some of the reasons why which paths were taken. Some may want to know how as career such as mine took shape due to various planned and accidental causes and how these some of the ideas in this book evolved.

My connection with Chattanooga as my hometown was strong. Our "organic" Chattanooga festival was started completely by local people with assistance from several national consultants funded by the visionary and generous Lyndhurst Foundation, created by the late Coca-Cola shareholder and Chattanoogan Jack Lupton. His and other foundations in 1968 had funded my proposal for a $30,000 racial relations project for 30 black and white youth leaders, called "Project Straight Talk," a summer program which I proposed and co-directed for the Chattanooga Chamber of Commerce. (Later this became the subject of my Boston University College of Communication master's thesis, "The Feedback Factor in the Communications Process").

Except for my Chattanooga Times brief newspaper reporting job in 1967, after returning from Air Force service, this was the first local recognition I had received. After that very educational and nationally chaotic summer ended with some concern expressed by conservative Chamber leaders about such a radical "social welfare" Chamber undertaking, I accepted a previously offered media spokesperson job with Exxon in Houston, where I was, due to my summer project, temporarily the corporate "black" issues advisor until an actual black person could be found. But Chattanooga had fascinated me since I had been a reporter for the Chattanooga Times newspaper in 1967, and I returned in 1971 to face the city's growing racial violence as Chattanooga Mayor Robert Kirk Walker's press aide and speechwriter for three years.

Then, my wife at the time needed to move to Boston for treatment, and I had a choice of the Boston Globe news room or Boston University. So, I chose communications/PR teaching and in 1974 happily joined Dr. Otto Lerbinger, my former public relations professor. I had benefited very much from Boston University's public relations and communications program, where I had been a graduate student 1967-68, especially from Al Sullivan's writing and values seminars. For several years I taught corporate PR, internships, newswriting and urban communications, a new course I developed that helped me build a useful and broad conceptual view of a city's information flow networks. I became a media speaker for the U.S. Conference of Mayors Newly Elected Mayor's workshops in various locations. The students, and faculty colleagues, were superb. I had thought to earn a doctoral degree and retire there.

But by 1976 my father had persuaded me he needed me to return home to learn and manage his declining food brokerage business. Then, in addition, I was asked in 1978 by Peter Consacro of the University of Tennessee at Chattanooga to create, teach and coordinate the new humanities communications degree program until we could find a permanent head; I thought each year would be my last one but continued to build the program. I loved teaching and helping students but I remained at the family business, which needed me due to various factors.

All these mixed experiences combined to make me receptive to the recognition of Chattanooga's empty downtown and open to effective responses. And I did respond in 1980-81-82. The chance, at a crossroads age of 40 and engaged in both teaching and our family business, to help Chattanooga in the early 1980's was a rare opportunity to continue my long interest in the city and again enter into the process of attempting to add to its cultural life. There were several examples of town "fathers" who took an active interest in the symphony, opera, ballet and museum, although this then was rare for a business executive. I even thought about leading the new festival but I could not have managed it without a qualified artistic professional, which had been prohibited, and dropped that alternative career idea. Also, it would have taken more diplomatic skills than I possessed with much higher career risk due to my inexperience in the arts world.

My stressful, double job period of food brokering and teaching ended in 1982, when the first Riverbend festival was held, and the university was able to recruit several teachers to take my place for the, by then, 100 majors. Some are Facebook friends today. I regretted leaving teaching, even with the stress of inadequate program staffing, but by then I had made the necessary choice to continue in the well-established family food brokerage business, which was founded in 1905 and purchased by my father in 1949. Yet business conditions were changing. Our suppliers, especially the heavy-handed Clorox Company, pushed our small firm to consolidate or sell to larger brokerages, although we were one of the top two in the city, and it was sold in late 1984, when my father retired after a year's continuity with a respectable income.

I departed but retained the small industrial ingredient portion, which the acquiring broker dropped, and continued to build it slowly with excellent customers such as McKee Foods (Little Debbie) and Chattanooga Baking Company (Moon Pie). (Both were early and continuing Riverbend sponsors). Now self-employed and working at home with a significant drop in income, my initial goal was to complete quickly my doctoral degree somewhere and return to college teaching somewhere. (As it turned out, I've been lucky enough to continue to this day as an independent businessman, an industrial food broker, working with fine, honest and honorable people, and to manage my arts projects as time permitted. I fortunately also had the resources to be able to continue my educational interests and the social dance community in creating an alternative "classroom" at Split Tree Farm and Studio, proving to me that seemingly conflicting interests can blend and support each other providing one keeps priorities in order and never neglects customer needs).

A friend recommended the Emory interdisciplinary studies program. It seemed perfect for my interests and background. With references and an identity as an "urban activist," as I was told, I was accepted at Emory University's Graduate of Institute of Liberal Arts in Atlanta, GA. It was the most important turning point in my life, next to the Times reporting job and teaching at BU. I began my Emory University doctoral studies in January 1985, initially in urban history but soon changed to semiotics after a seminar in 20th century intellectual trends. One professor suggested that with my festival experience that I might consider that as a dissertation topic. This new sign theory field I saw as advanced theoretical public communication studies similar to what I had learned and taught at Boston University's College of Communication, as it now is called. This semiotics discipline, unknown to me at BU, and festival subject carried me through five years of intense intellectual growth in Emory's well-known interdisciplinary studies program, although at times I barely could understand the theoretical books on the seminar reading lists.

There was no formal preparation for festival study, and two words, festivals and semiotics, generally were my tracks through all course work no matter the topic. I'll never forget the very first seminar, led by ILA director Robert Paul, with a close reading (or decoding as I later thought of it) of James Joyce's *Finnegan's Wake*...and my total lack of comprehension of any of it at first. It turned out to be very practical in making sense of complex festivals by searching for small repetitive clues, or meaningful signs in a more formal sense. I learned quickly not to fear ignorance early in the various seminars because the ideas and terms began to cross-connect with each succeeding semester. Later, the same approach applied to dance and other experimental workshops. As my confidence grew, I found I could relax enough to learn strange concepts and physical skills...what I later called the "fool's way," or, as some call it, "Zen beginner's mind."

More traditional education included the first 1985 summer studying Shakespeare and British social history at Oxford's University College and exploring British festivals. Emory at the time did not offer formal semiotic courses, and much of my semiotic (meaning making and sign production) background, in addition to one-on-one study with very supportive dissertation director Timothy J. Reiss at Emory, was obtained in the late 1980's during the International Semiotic Association summer institutes in Toronto and Chicago. These were directed by University of Toronto semiotician and anthropologist Paul Bouissac. His advice, and his study of the semiotics of circuses, was invaluable as a model of focus and method.

I had become a teacher and also businessman and learned once again to be a student, but I had much to learn about the arts. I enjoyed playing my Steinway grand piano, and enjoyed having it played by musicians at our parties. This is my earliest sense of a festival as a party, starting with the purchase of the Steinway in 1979, when I also had become single again. These musical gatherings at my farm, about a half hour south of Chattanooga, led directly from the energy of the Steinway to the festival organizing, then later to my Split Tree productions, where the fine piano was central to the music making and dancing, and thus connected directly to this book. The idea grew that there was much energy held within the Steinway if only one could learn how to release it, not unlike the notion of releasing artistic energies within a community with a nurturing context. When my 1979 5'7" Steinway burned in 2007, I was able to replace it with a rebuilt, rich sounding 1912 7' model B concert grand, more than adequate for my limited ability, though inadequately housed in my very small log cabin on the farm.

I reached well beyond my grasp toward humanistic, experiential modes of learning becoming popular in the late 1980's. From 1988 until the present, through workshop immersions at the Omega Institute for Holistic Studies, such as David Darling's music improvisation ensembles in his Music for People program, and Linda Metcalf and Tobin Simon's proprioceptive writing weeks, I added rich "right brain" overtones to my traditional Emory seminars and tutorials from 1985-1990. Omega, in Rhinebeck, NY was the perfect place to have what I began to see as a "break-up" experience, tossing yourself up into the air as little pieces and see how they re-connect in a safe place to play—wonderful for leading to new insights without fear of failure. In August 1988, I came back ready to write the dissertation after that first amazing proprioceptive writing week, and did my meditative writes (stories) early each morning before starting on this dissertation. Some of them may be published in the Split Tree book. The preceding dance section is an example, as if I were going to read this "write," or story, to you, of pulling a thread of personal meaning (by asking what certain words mean emotionally to "me") through the fabric and weaving connected patterns of ideas and signifiers. It is a simple but powerful method, though here I have had to continually edit out many interesting digressions (some left intact). The proprioceptive practice produces much material, which then has to be formed and sequenced suitable for a given format and reader. Toby, also a fine poet and Linda sell their PW book on Amazon, now conduct workshops near San Francisco, California and offer online coaching.

All of that energy was fresh and bubbling in my mind by the time I completed in April 1990 the program in theories of interpretation at Emory's interdisciplinary studies program, combining urban history, drama theory and semiotics. After three decades of focused hard work and career development—most planned, some not—I was ready to dance and play and reach beyond my grasp. This experiential learning mode, then, on top of the more "left" brain Emory education, led to a new kind of productive and interesting life and artistic practice at my Split Tree Farm. It opened new possibilities both challenging and enjoyable for me and led to many new dance and music friends in North America and some in Europe. One can speculate why Asia, Africa, India and the Middle East seem to have much less partner dance than Western societies.

Just after finishing this thesis, my first Fool's Fest Dawn Dance was produced Saturday, April 1, 1990, inspired by the idea from a Vermont all-night dawn dance, at nearby Hidden Hollow ballroom. I had noticed that April Fool's day fell on Saturday and the idea of celebrating "foolishness" as a dance festival popped in my mind. I had the naive idea contra dancers would not need a bed because all would dance all night; about a dozen of the 125 made it to the last waltz by the groggy live string band; tents and sleeping bags were everywhere outside the hall.

I had my fifteen minutes of fame, and, as Head Fool, I passed leadership on to other Atlanta Chattahoochee Country Dancer volunteers, such as Manuel Patillo, but no one else wanted the job by 1996. So I reclaimed it and moved it from Hidden Hollow as a one-night dawn dance to a more diverse, mostly dance weekend in our new open pavilion at my Split Tree Farm. It continued until the last one in 2005, when the show had run its course. All my ideas of diversity and difference were challenged by creating an annual program for this gathering, where I learned the dramatic value of the fool, as King Lear also discovered—if a bit late.

The need to return to this book's 1990 beginning is best expressed by a quote in the book's preface:

> "One sense of my subjective problem in studying this particular festival [Riverbend], its genesis, and its intended and unintended meanings was suggested by Milan Kundera in Laughable Loves:
> 'Man passes through the present with his eyes blindfolded. He is permitted merely to sense and guess at what he is actually experiencing. Only later when the cloth is untied can he glance at the past and find out what he has experienced and what meaning it had.' "

The present moment is about as important as the weather news in attempting to discover historical patterns and trends. I too was willingly blindfolded. As you now know, for about 20 years I created and produced a lively, living theater of my ideas at my 200-acre farm and in the 60' x 36' movement studio that many dancers and friends helped to build on the farm's hilltop in NW Georgia from 1994 through 2000. I waltzed there at 14 of Stanford University dance instructor Richard Powers' waltz weekends. I laughed with the Head Fool, often Atlanta contra caller Seth Tepfer, at my 15 Fool's Festival partner dance weekends. I drummed around the old split cherry tree that Stephanie Winters and Walter Parks suggested as the farm name and that became its symbol of differences (see www.splittree.org). I DJ'ed and taught diverse, eclectic waltzing most Sundays for my Atlanta Waltz Society 2000-2006. Other participatory programs, but rarely in performance mode, in the studio included dance and movement weekends, such as contact improvisation, yoga, NIA training and an old-time string music jam; also several weddings.

But I just danced my ideas and never wrote about any of the sign theories, never talked about any notion such as differences embracing sameness nor festivals as semiotic meaning making factories, never explained...only worked every day at taking small steps within my evolving dream of creating the Split Tree festive theater of participation. Its evolving web page from 1996 is found at the Split Tree web link.

Tragedy struck Split Tree August 3, 2007. A fire, likely from a bad electrical connection or bird's nest in a porch lamp, completely burned the house, our volunteer-built 60' x 36' studio and adjacent barn. All records and most photos were gone, except for digital archives and what little was stored in a guest cabin. The hilltop home for my participatory arts dream was lost, and it's been difficult to find an encore, although sharing this book of early, formative ideas for a few readers is very satisfying. After the fire we almost canceled the remaining fall waltz weekend. But with much help we were able to move it.

The planned and fully sold out November 2007 Richard Powers waltz weekend was moved from Split Tree studio to the main stage of Chattanooga's 1920's restored Tivoli Theater for 100 dancers. We even dined all weekend inside the ornate marble lobby, where one of the early Riverbend chamber ensembles performed with similar reverberations. And not a single ticket was sold for someone to just sit quietly, silently and watch us on the main stage; all danced and learned vintage steps and patterns and enjoyed the Grand Ball Saturday evening. The theater marquee showed the Tivoli as "sold out" for the unintended waltz weekend there; I'm proudly posed under that marquee in one of my Facebook albums.

The world's first full waltz weekends had been produced at Split Tree's new studio starting in 1997, after I had been much impressed by Richard Powers' artistic vision and skill at teaching all levels of social dancers, including a beginner like me. It was my first such national production. I had been inspired by his 1995 paper, "Zen and the Art of Waltzing," at Cincinnati's Vintage Dance Week. I had convinced him at the summer 1996 Paris/Prague Double Vintage Dance Weeks to lead a Zen of waltzing weekend at our new hilltop studio in the spring of 1997. This gave us time to complete the new studio's floor and enclose it with glass doors opening onto the decks.

That waltz weekend and even full weeks continues in various North American towns and Vienna, Austria. My belief by then was that if you erase the idea of passive audience, all on the stage or floor are artists as participants in a safe place to play—in the sense of the French term, audience "assisting" in the creating of meanings, or active witnesses, as Reiss points out in his Foreword.

The closest in concept to our Split Tree residential, experiential workshops and dancing weekends is Ken Crawford's Pocono Waltz Weekend at the historic 1906 Pocono Manor Inn, Pennsylvania. Each October since 2008 it has featured Richard Powers' charismatic teaching, with lovely dance partner Angela Amarillas [see author photo, back cover], of couples dance relationships...to three-quarter time live and recorded music. These weekends are the essence of participatory arts. I was proud to have joined with Powers and others in trying, with some success, since 1997 to bring back the romance of the 250 years of waltzing—really, really retro dance. In 1999, at our Old Vienna Waltz weekend, Powers DJ'ed and prompted what likely was the world's only all-Mozart contra dance on a Friday night. He taught some of the old energetic steps for a formal Saturday night Viennese Ball with music by Atlanta's Lenox Quartet.

Waltzing became a passion and remains so. But, by 2006 the Atlanta Waltz Society had transitioned to a new group, though it was difficult to let go of my child, and this made needed time for my writing and editing. Sadly, a torn heel tendon from the November 2007 waltz weekend, and then bad knees, prohibited much dancing until recently, after total knee replacements in mid-2011.

In August 2007 the house fire had ended the physical dream, and it takes time to work through the stages of grieving and loss. That was a hard act to follow. Still, there's new energy springing from the participatory gatherings that Burning Man has inspired globally. With funding and new energy something like it might spring up at my farm or elsewhere in the guise of another Fool's Festival Dance Weekend. This unusual event, which as noted above I started in 1990 with the help of Atlanta contra dancers and I ended in 2005, was noted in the New York Times in the early 2000s in an article about the very few fool's festivals and celebrations of that day. All it would take is resources for a new ballroom studio, bath and shower house, hot tub, kitchen, dorm rooms; maybe an angel will read this and find us.

My comic adventure in search of the lost art of waltzing (working title of a possible article or book) continues from blues taverns to Vienna's carnival balls to various waltz dances and waltz weekends as more and more flexible partners sense the old lead/follow, or control/passive dancer relationship, can be replaced by a collaborative, participatory partner dance in a turning, traveling playful connection. It does work, and it has to do with embracing differences...but just how is not yet clear except that it takes a smile and a willingness to make a fool of yourself.

I hope you enjoy your own adventure of imaginative, disruptive discovery and create your own new, new kind of festival...and let me know about it—especially if there's musical jamming and social partner dancing where none are leaders and all are foolish followers improvising the moves. Read more about this rich living tradition of innovative social dancing at www.richardpowers.com or at www.waltzetc.com. And our Split Tree story continues to unfold on our web page, where supplemental materials for this book can be found as a source of unending publication, or, as some would say, semiosis—the ongoing making and production of meanings. A printed book's fixed format is both an advantage and disadvantage in that new interpretations unfold to be shared (though with print on demand technology files can be updated as needed at little expense).

The terms and ideas offered here were meant only as a beginning of the effort to understand the elusive nature of loving difference and its limits when faced with the unyielding power of sameness in many open and disguised forms, such as traditional religious, ethnic and harvest festivals—or political or religious demagogues and tyrants—or rigid dance styles or partners.

The scholarly rewards of creating this work were high, as were the real costs; the social rewards were rich; the writing pleasures were real; the changes in the author were lasting; that you have read this is a great honor. Comments are welcome at splittreepress@splittree.org.

Sidney N Hetzler, Jr. Ph. D.   May 2012
Split Tree Press
www.splittree.org
597 W Cove Road
Chickamauga, GA 30707

LUZZATI MUSEUM AND THE COVER IMAGE

The cover image is from a painting by Emanuele Luzzati of the flutist Papageno in Mozart's Magic Flute opera. It was used as the 1993 poster for the Spoleto, Italy and the Charleston, SC Menotti festivals. It is used with permission of the Luzzati International Museum, Genoa, Italy in exchange for including this information about the museum.

Museo Internazionale Luzzati
Luzzati International Museum

Porta Siberia
Un edificio antico di Storia
per un nuovo polo culturale

Porta Siberia, concepita alla metà del '500 dal celebre architetto Galeazzo Alessi, è oggi un moderno polo culturale, parte attiva del tessuto urbanistico dell'Area, grazie all'intervento di recupero promosso da Porto Antico spa e realizzato da Renzo Piano.
Sede del Museo Luzzati, raccoglie i più diversi materiali dell'opera del Maestro (grafica, teatro, illustrazione, arte applicata, ecc.) ma anche mostre temporanee di altri artisti.

La struttura è gestita da Nugae srl progetti culturali mostre edizioni, Genova,
che cura e pubblica volumi illustrati e monografie, edita cartelle d'arte e multipli d'autore, progetta e coordina eventi culturali.

Porta Siberia
A new cultural pole
in a historical building

Porta Siberia, which was designed in the second half of the 16th century by the famous architect Galeazzo Alessi, is today a modern cultural pole and an active part of the urban fabric of the Area thanks to Porto Antico spa, that promoted its restoration and Renzo Piano who realized it.
It houses the Luzzati Museum, and gathers the most varied materials of the works by the Master (graphics, theatre, illustration, applied art, etc.), as well as temporary exhibitions of other artists.

The facility is managed by Nugae srl cultural projects exhibitions publishing, Genoa.
Editor and publisher of illustrated books and monographs, art portfolios and artist multiples. Nugae designs and coordinates cultural events.

www.ingramcontent.com/pod-product-compliance
Lightning Source LLC
Chambersburg PA
CBHW070547050426
42450CB00011B/2747